# DEFINING MOMENTS
# BROWN V. BOARD OF EDUCATION

DEFINING MOMENTS
# BROWN V. BOARD OF EDUCATION

**Diane Telgen**

615 Griswold, Detroit MI 48226

# Omnigraphics, Inc.

Kevin Hillstrom, *Series Editor*
Cherie D. Abbey, *Managing Editor*

Peter E. Ruffner, *Publisher*
Frederick G. Ruffner, Jr., *Chairman*
Matthew P. Barbour, *Senior Vice President*

Kay Gill, *Vice President – Directories*
Elizabeth Barbour, *Research and Permissions
Coordinator*
David P. Bianco, *Marketing Director*
Leif Gruenberg, *Development Manager*
Kevin Hayes, *Operations Manager*

Barry Puckett, *Librarian*
Cherry Stockdale, *Permissions Assistant*
Shirley Amore, Don Brown, John L. Chetcuti, Kevin
Glover, Martha Johns, Kirk Kauffman, *Adminis-
trative Staff*

Copyright © 2005 Omnigraphics, Inc.
ISBN 0-7808-0775-8

---

**Library of Congress Cataloging-in-Publication Data**

Telgen, Diane.
    Brown v. Board of Education / Diane Telgen.
        p. cm. — (Defining moments)
    Includes bibliographical references and index.
    ISBN 0-7808-0775-8 (hardcover : alk. paper)
    1. Segregation in education--Law and legislation--United States. 2.
Discrimination in education--Law and legislation--United States. 3. Brown, Oliver, 1918---Trials, litigation, etc. 4.
Topeka (Kan.). Board of Education--Trials, litigation, etc. 5. Segregation in education--United States--History--20th
century--Sources. 6. Discrimination in education--United States--History--20th century--Sources. I. Title. II. Series.
    KF4155.T45 2005
    344.73'0798--dc22

                                                    2005008887

---

The information in this publication was compiled from the sources cited and from other sources considered reliable.
Additional copyright information can be found on the photograph credits page of this book. While every possible effort
has been made to ensure reliability, the publisher will not assume liability for damages caused by inaccuracies in the data,
and makes no warranty, express or implied, on the accuracy of the information contained herein.

This book is printed on acid-free paper meeting the ANSI Z39.48 Standard. The infinity symbol that appears above indicates that the paper in this book meets that standard.

Printed in the United States

# TABLE OF CONTENTS

## NARRATIVE OVERVIEW

## BIOGRAPHIES

## PRIMARY SOURCES

# PREFACE

Throughout the course of America's existence, its people, culture, and institutions have been periodically challenged—and in many cases transformed—by profound historical events. Some of these momentous events, such as women's suffrage, the civil rights movement, and U.S. involvement in World War II, have invigorated the nation and strengthened American confidence and capabilities. Others, such as the McCarthy era, the Vietnam War, and Watergate, have prompted troubled assessments and heated debates about the country's core beliefs and character.

Some of these defining moments in American history were years or even decades in the making. The Harlem Renaissance and the New Deal, for example, unfurled over the span of several years, while the American labor movement and the Cold War evolved over the course of decades. Other defining moments, such as the Cuban missile crisis and the terrorist attacks of September 11, 2001, transpired over a matter of days or weeks.

But although significant differences exist among these events in terms of their duration and their place in the timeline of American history, all share the same basic characteristic: they transformed the United States' political, cultural, and social landscape for future generations of Americans.

Taking heed of this fundamental reality, American citizens, schools, and other institutions are increasingly emphasizing the importance of understanding our nation's history. Omnigraphics' *Defining Moments* series was created for the express purpose of meeting this growing appetite for authoritative, useful historical resources. This series, which focuses on the most pivotal events in U.S. history from the 20th century forward, will be of enduring value to anyone interested in learning more about America's past—and in understanding how those historical events continue to reverberate in the 21st century.

Each individual volume of *Defining Moments* provides a valuable resource for readers interested in learning more about the most profound events in our nation's history. Each volume is organized into three distinct sections—Narrative Overview, Biographies, and Primary Sources.

- The **Narrative Overview** provides readers with a detailed, factual account of the origins and progression of the "defining moment" being examined. It also explores the event's lasting impact on America's political and cultural landscape.

- The **Biographies** section provides valuable biographical background on leading figures associated with the event in question. Each biography concludes with a list of sources for further information on the profiled individual.

- The **Primary Sources** section collects a wide variety of pertinent primary source materials from the era under discussion, including official documents, papers and resolutions, letters, oral histories, memoirs, editorials, and other important works.

Individually, each of these sections is a rich resource for users. Together, they provide an authoritative, balanced, and absorbing examination of some of the most significant events in U.S. history.

Other notable features contained within each volume in the series include a glossary of important individuals, places, and terms; a detailed chronology featuring page references to relevant sections of the narrative; an annotated bibliography of sources for further study; an extensive general bibliography that reflects the wide range of historical sources consulted by the author; and a subject index.

## Acknowledgements

This series was developed in consultation with a distinguished Advisory Board comprised of public librarians, school librarians, and educators. They evaluated the series as it developed, and their comments and suggestions were invaluable throughout the production process. Any errors in this and other volumes in the series are ours alone. Following is a list of board members who contributed to the *Defining Moments* series:

Gail Beaver, M.A., M.A.L.S.
Adjunct Lecturer, University of Michigan
Ann Arbor, MI

Melissa C. Bergin, L.M.S., NBCT
Niskayuna High School
Niskayuna, NY

Rose Davenport, M.S.L.S., Ed. Specialist
Library Media Specialist
Pershing High School Library
Detroit, MI

Karen Imarisio, A.M.L.S.
Assistant Head of Adult Services
Bloomfield Twp. Public Library
Bloomfield Hills, MI

Nancy Larsen, M.L.S., M.S. Ed.
Library Media Specialist
Clarkston High School
Clarkston, MI

Marilyn Mast, M.I.L.S.
Kingswood Campus Librarian
Cranbrook Kingswood Upper School
Bloomfield Hills, MI

Rosemary Orlando, M.L.I.S.
Assistant Director
St. Clair Shores Public Library
St. Clair Shores, MI

## Comments and Suggestions

We welcome your comments on *Defining Moments:* Brown v. Board of Education and suggestions for other events in U.S. history that warrant treatment in the *Defining Moments* series. Correspondence should be addressed to:

Editor, *Defining Moments*
Omnigraphics, Inc.
615 Griswold
Detroit, MI 48226
E-mail: editorial@omnigraphics.com

# HOW TO USE THIS BOOK

Defining Moments: Brown v. Board of Education provides users with a detailed and authoritative overview of the era, as well as the principal figures involved in this pivotal event in U.S. history. The preparation and arrangement of this volume—and all other books in the *Defining Moments* series—reflect an emphasis on providing a thorough and objective account of events that shaped our nation, presented in an easy-to-use reference work.

*Defining Moments:* Brown v. Board of Education is divided into three primary sections. The first of these sections, the **Narrative Overview**, provides a detailed, factual account of the history of segregation in America and the landmark case that dissolved it. It explores the origins of Jim Crow laws in the South, the leading role of the National Association for the Advancement of Colored People (NAACP) in legal battles over school segregation, the struggle to enforce the *Brown* decision, and the long-term impact of the decision on American education and society.

The second section, **Biographies**, provides valuable biographical background on leading figures involved in the era, including civil rights lawyers Charles H. Houston and Thurgood Marshall, Supreme Court Justice Earl Warren, and Arkansas Governor Orval Faubus. Each biography concludes with a list of sources for further information on the profiled individual.

The third section, **Primary Sources**, collects essential and enlightening documents that provide perspective on the Brown decision. Featured sources include the Supreme Court's opinions in *Brown v. Board of Education* and *Brown II*, the Southern Manifesto statement of opposition to desegregation, and the harrowing recollections of Melba Beals Patillo, one of the "Little Rock Nine" who integrated Central High School in 1957. Other primary sources featured in *Defining Moments:* Brown v. Board of Education include excerpts from official documents, papers, memoirs, editorials, and other important works.

Other valuable features in *Defining Moments:* Brown v. Board of Education include the following:

• Attribution and referencing of primary sources and other quoted material to help guide users to other valuable historical research resources.

• Glossary of Important People, Places, and Terms.

• Detailed Chronology of events with a *see reference* feature. Under this arrangement, events listed in the chronology include a reference to page numbers within the Narrative Overview wherein users can find additional information on the event in question.

• Photographs of the leading figures and major events of the era.

• Sources for Further Study, an annotated list of noteworthy *Brown*-related works.

• Extensive bibliography of works consulted in the creation of this book, including books, periodicals, Internet sites, and videotape materials.

• A Subject Index.

**Editor's Note:** This volume includes quoted material containing racial epithets and offensive language. We regret any pain created by the inclusion of this language. We felt, however, that it was important to include this material because it reflects representative views and prejudices of the era.

# IMPORTANT PEOPLE, PLACES, AND TERMS

**14ᵗʰ Amendment**
Ratified in 1868, this Reconstruction-era amendment guaranteed "equal protection of the laws" to all citizens and formed the basis for many civil rights rulings of the twentieth century.

**15ᵗʰ Amendment**
Ratified in 1870, this amendment guaranteed the right of all citizens to vote.

**Affirmative action**
A broad term used to describe policies that attempt to increase minority involvement in government, employment, and educational programs. In education, it often refers to policies, especially at the university level, that seek to increase minority enrollment.

**Almond, Lindsay**
Virginia state attorney general who participated in the Supreme Court defense of *Davis v. County School Board of Prince Edward County.*

***Amicus curiae***
From the Latin for "friend of the court," a legal term referring to someone who is not a party to a lawsuit, but who files a brief in support of one side. In the *Brown* case, the U.S. government filed an *amicus curiae* brief in support of desegregation. The plural is *amici curiae.*

**Appellate Court**
See Circuit Court

**Bates, Daisy**
President of the Arkansas Conference of the NAACP and adviser to the Little Rock Nine.

*Belton v. Gebhart*
> See *Gebhart v. Belton*

**Bishop, Gardner**
> A barber and community leader who coordinated parent protests against overcrowded schools in Washington, D.C., leading to the *Bolling v. Sharpe* case.

**Black Codes**
> A series of laws passed in the South after slavery was banned in 1865, the "Black Codes" restricted the rights of African Americans to own property, work, marry, and travel.

**Black, Hugo L.**
> A Supreme Court Justice during the *Brown* cases known for his advocacy of civil rights and civil liberties.

**Blossom, Virgil**
> Superintendent of Little Rock Schools; his plan to desegregate the system over three years, beginning with the district's high schools, was called the "Blossom Plan."

**Bloody Sunday**
> See March on Selma

*Bolling v. Sharpe*
> Originating in Washington, D.C., one of the five cases heard as part of the Supreme Court's *Brown* decision.

**Border States**
> Those states that permitted slavery but did not secede from the Union during the Civil War: Delaware, Kentucky, Maryland, Missouri, and West Virginia, which was created in 1863 after splitting from Confederate Virginia. Most Border States had laws mandating segregation.

**Brief**
> A written summary of the facts and arguments in a case, drawn up by a lawyer and submitted to the trial judge.

*Briggs v. Elliott*
> Originating in Clarendon County, South Carolina, one of the five school segregation cases that made up the *Brown* decision.

**Brown, Oliver**

A plaintiff in the Topeka, Kansas, school desegregation case; since his name appeared first among the several parents suing the Topeka school board, the Supreme Court decision came to be known as *Brown v. Board of Education.*

**Brown v. Board of Education**

A segregation case originating in Topeka, Kansas, that became the collective name for five school segregation cases considered by the Supreme Court in its historic 1954 desegregation decision.

**Bulah v. Gebhart**

One of two school desegregation cases from Delaware—the only ones originally won by the LDF—that were combined into the Supreme Court's *Brown* decision.

**Burton, Harold H.**

A Supreme Court Justice during the *Brown* cases who was known for his moderate views.

**Carter, Robert L.**

LDF Associate Counsel who argued the *Sweatt* and *Sipuel* cases, as well as the original *Brown* case in Topeka. He later became NAACP Special Counsel and a judge on the U.S. District Court.

**Circuit Court**

Also called appellate court, a court authorized to hear appeals from district court cases. The United States has twelve Circuit Courts of Appeal.

**Clark, Kenneth B.**

The psychologist and professor who, with his wife Mamie, conducted groundbreaking research on the effects of segregation on African American children.

**Clark, Tom**

A Supreme Court Justice during the *Brown* cases, Clark also served as attorney general under Truman and filed one of the first government *amicus* briefs in support of civil rights in that capacity.

## Cold War

The ideological conflict between Communist Russia, also known as the Soviet Union, and the United States and its allies in Western Europe. Instead of a direct military conflict, the Cold War was waged through the buildup of military weapons and the acquisition of allies in Asia, Africa, and Latin America.

## Confederate South

Sometimes also called the "Deep South," the eleven states that seceded from the Union to form the Confederate States of America: Alabama, Arkansas, Florida, Georgia, Louisiana, Mississippi, North Carolina, South Carolina, Tennessee, Texas, and Virginia.

## Congress of Racial Equality (CORE)

A civil rights organization founded by interracial students in 1942, CORE was involved in the sit-in and freedom ride movements of the early 1960s.

## Contempt of Court

An act defying the authority of a U.S. court, either by ignoring the rules of the court or by deliberately disobeying a court order. Criminal contempt charges can result in fines and jail time.

## Court of Chancery

In the state of Delaware, the Court designated to hear cases involving equity, including civil rights.

## Davis, John W.

A former U.S. Congressman, U.S. solicitor general, and Democratic presidential candidate who served as lead counsel for South Carolina before the Supreme Court in the first two *Brown* arguments.

## *Davis v. County School Board of Prince Edward County*

Originating in Prince Edward County, Virginia, one of the five school segregation cases considered in the *Brown* decision.

## Deep South

See Confederate South.

## *De facto*

From the Latin for "by fact," a legal term meaning conditions that are established through actual fact, not by legal or official means. Northern cities often had *de facto* segregation, created by residential patterns or the drawing of school district lines.

## Defendant

The party sued in a civil lawsuit; defendants must defend themselves from charges they caused harm to the plaintiff.

## De jure

From the Latin for "by law," a legal term meaning conditions that are established through legal or official means. Southern states practiced *de jure* segregation because state laws required it.

## De Laine, Joseph

A teacher, minister, and community activist who organized parents to file suit in the South Carolina *Briggs* case.

## District Court

The lowest level of the court system, where most cases are initially heard. The United States has ninety-four district courts.

## Douglas, William O.

A Supreme Court Justice during the *Brown* cases who was known for his dedication to civil liberties.

## Du Bois, W. E. B.

One of the founders of the NAACP, educator and scholar Du Bois later left the group because of his belief that desegregation was not necessarily in the best interests of African Americans.

## Eastland, James O.

A Mississippi senator who was a vehement foe of desegregation, Eastland created the Federation for Constitutional Government, an interstate organization designed to coordinate segregationists' efforts.

## Eisenhower, Dwight D.

The 34th President of the United States (1953-1961), Eisenhower was forced to send federal troops to Little Rock, Arkansas, in 1957 to enforce a federal desegregation order.

**Faubus, Orval**

As governor of Arkansas, Faubus precipitated the Little Rock crisis by calling out the Arkansas National Guard to prevent the Little Rock Nine from entering Central High.

**Frankfurter, Felix**

A Supreme Court Justice during the *Brown* case who was noted for his legal scholarship and conservative judicial philosophy.

**Freedom Rides**

Organized efforts by white and black student activists to challenge segregation on interstate buses and bus terminals in the Deep South.

**Gaines, Lloyd**

The successful plaintiff in *Gaines v. Canada* (1938), the first Supreme Court case to rule that states must provide equal postgraduate programs for African Americans.

***Gebhart v. Belton***

One of two school desegregation cases from Delaware—the only ones originally won by the LDF—that were combined into the Supreme Court's *Brown* decision.

**Greenberg, Jack**

LDF Associate Counsel involved in the Delaware school desegregation cases, *Gebhart v. Belton* and *Bulah v. Belton*. He succeeded Thurgood Marshall as Director Counsel of the LDF in 1961.

**Harlan, John Marshall**

A Supreme Court Justice during the argument on relief in the *Brown* case, Harlan was a former federal appeals court judge and the grandson and namesake of the justice who made the famous dissent in *Plessy v. Ferguson.*

**Hawkins, Virgil**

An African American who was kept out of the University of Florida Law School despite several court orders mandating his admittance.

**Hayes, George E. C.**

A Howard Law School professor and Washington attorney who helped argue *Bolling v. Sharpe* before the Supreme Court.

**Hill, Oliver W.**

An NAACP attorney who helped litigate the *Davis v. County School Board of Prince Edward County* case that eventually became one of the five segregation cases that made up the *Brown* decision.

**Houston, Charles Hamilton**

The former dean of Howard University Law School and NAACP Legal Counsel who oversaw the NAACP's legal strategy against segregation from 1934 to 1940.

**Huxman, Walter**

Lead judge in the three-judge district court panel that originally ruled on the *Brown* case in Kansas, Huxman included a "finding of fact" in his decision upholding the Topeka law that nevertheless found segregation "detrimental" to African American children.

**Injunction**

A court order commanding or preventing an action.

**Jackson, Robert H.**

A Supreme Court Justice during the first two *Brown* arguments who was known both for his legal brilliance and conservative views. He died in 1954, prior to the argument on relief in the *Brown* case.

**Jim Crow**

Post-Reconstruction laws that codified segregation and discrimination against blacks in virtually all aspects of daily life across the South.

**Johnson, Lyndon B.**

The 36th president of the United States (1963-69), Johnson worked with Congress to pass the Civil Rights Act of 1964 and the Fair Housing Act of 1968. As a Senator from Texas, he was one of the few Southerners to refuse to sign the Southern Manifesto; he also sponsored the Civil Rights Act of 1957.

**Kennedy, John F.**

The 35th president of the United States (1961-63), Kennedy twice called up federal troops to enforce court desegregation orders. He also favored civil rights legislation but was assassinated in 1963 before it could be passed.

**King, Martin Luther, Jr.**
One of the cofounders of the Southern Christian Leadership Conference and a prominent activist in the civil rights movement of the 1960s.

**Korman, Milton**
Attorney representing the District of Columbia in the *Bolling v. Sharpe* case.

**Ku Klux Klan (KKK)**
A white supremacist organization first founded by former Confederate soldiers after the Civil War, then revived in the 1910s. The KKK used terrorist tactics, such as cross burning and lynching, to intimidate African Americans and advocates for civil rights.

**LDF**
The NAACP's Legal Defense and Education Fund, which litigates cases related to civil rights.

**Little Rock Nine**
The nine students who integrated Central High School in Little Rock, Arkansas, during the school year of 1957-58: Minnijean Brown, Elizabeth Eckford, Ernest Green, Thelma Mothershed, Melba Patillo, Gloria Ray, Terrence Roberts, Jefferson Thomas, and Carlotta Walls.

**Lucy, Autherine**
The first African American to register at the University of Alabama, Lucy was forced off campus by rioters and later expelled for suing for readmission.

**March on Selma**
Also called "Bloody Sunday," this 1965 voting rights march was interrupted by police who used tear gas, clubs, and whips to disperse a group of peaceful protesters. The images shocked the nation and galvanized public support for civil rights legislation.

**March on Washington**
A historic 1963 demonstration for civil rights in the nation's capital, highlighted by Martin Luther King, Jr.'s "I Have a Dream" speech.

**Marshall, Thurgood**
The first director-counsel of the NAACP's Legal Defense and Education Fund, Marshall oversaw strategy for the NAACP's desegregation cases,

including *Brown*. He later became the first African American to serve on the Supreme Court.

## McLaurin, George

The successful plaintiff in a 1950 Supreme Court ruling overturning the University of Oklahoma's practice of segregating students by race even within classroom facilities.

## Meredith, James

The first African American to be admitted to the University of Mississippi (Ole Miss), Meredith began attending classes in 1962 after federal troops were called out to enforce his attendance. He graduated from Ole Miss in 1963.

## Minton, Sherman

A Supreme Court Justice during the *Brown* cases who was one of the first on the Court to signal his support for ending segregation.

## Montgomery Bus Boycott

In one of the earliest actions in the civil rights movement, the African American community in Montgomery, Alabama, boycotted the local bus system between December 1955 and December 1956. The boycott forced the city to end segregation on buses.

## Moore, T. Justin

A Virginia attorney who represented the Prince Edward County school board in its desegregation case.

## Murray, Donald

The plaintiff in the first successful case to desegregate graduate school programs in the United States, Murray was admitted to the University of Maryland Law School in 1935.

## Nabrit, James, Jr.

A Howard University law professor who took over the *Bolling v. Sharpe* case from Charles Houston. He would later become dean of Howard Law School and associate counsel for the LDF.

## National Association for the Advancement of Colored People (NAACP)

A civil rights organization founded in 1909 by a multiracial group to lobby for political and social changes that would grant equal rights to all citizens.

**Plaintiff**

The party who brings a civil lawsuit, claiming harm was done to them by the defendant and asking for relief.

*Plessy v. Ferguson*

The landmark 1896 Supreme Court decision ruling that "separate but equal" facilities were constitutional.

**Rankin, J. Lee**

Attorney General under Eisenhower who represented the government before the Supreme Court in the *Brown* rearguments.

**Reconstruction**

The era from 1868 to 1877 during which the Confederate South was under Northern military control and rights for African Americans were enforced and expanded.

**Redding, Louis**

The first African American admitted to the bar and one of the attorneys who successfully litigated the Delaware school segregation cases, *Belton v. Gebhart* and *Bulah v. Gebhart.*

**Reed, Stanley**

A Southern conservative Supreme Court Justice, Reed was the last justice to agree to *Brown's* desegregation order.

**Robinson, Spottswood III**

Helped litigate the Virginia case *Davis v. County School Board of Prince Edward County* and later became dean of Howard Law School.

**Relief**

Compensation given to a plaintiff who has won a civil lawsuit. Relief can range from monetary damages to court injunctions against the defendant(s).

**Seitz, Collins**

High Chancellor (judge) of Delaware's Court of Chancery during the *Belton v. Gebhart* and *Bulah v. Gebhart* cases, Seitz ordered the immediate admission of African American students into white schools as relief for longstanding inequalities.

**Separate but equal**

A doctrine stating that government-mandated separation of the races is legal as long as the facilities for both races are equal. The phrase originated in the 1896 *Plessy v. Ferguson* Supreme Court case.

**Sit-Ins**

A movement in which black college students defied Southern segregation laws by sitting at white-only lunch counters and other public facilities.

**Solicitor General**

The lawyer responsible for representing the United States in court cases.

**Southern Christian Leadership Conference (SCLC)**

A nonviolent civil rights organization founded in 1957 by the Rev. Martin Luther King, Jr. and other ministers from around the South.

**Southern Manifesto**

A document signed by 96 Southern congressmen pledging resistance to the *Brown* decision.

**Student Nonviolent Coordinating Committee (SNCC)**

A civil rights group founded by college activists in 1960, the SNCC took a lead role in organizing sit-ins and freedom rides across the South.

**Supreme Court**

The highest court within the legal system, both in individual states and in the United States. State supreme court decisions can be appealed to the U.S. Supreme Court, which has final authority over legal decisions.

**Thurmond, Strom**

South Carolina Senator who drafted the Southern Manifesto, a declaration of Southern resistance to the *Brown* ruling.

**Truman, Harry S.**

The 33rd President of the United States (1945-1953), Truman pioneered desegregation in the federal government by establishing a presidential Committee on Civil Rights in 1946 and using executive orders in 1948 to desegregate the armed forces and federal agencies.

**Vinson, Fred M.**

Chief Justice of the Supreme Court during the first argument of the *Brown* case, Vinson died before the second *Brown* argument in 1953.

### Wallace, George

The governor of Alabama famous for his election pledge of "Segregation now! Segregation tomorrow! Segregation forever!" Wallace publicly opposed the integration of the University of Alabama in 1963.

### Waring, J. Waties

A federal court judge sympathetic to civil rights who gave an impassioned dissent condemning school segregation in South Carolina's *Briggs v. Elliott* case.

### Warren, Earl

The former governor of California who served as Chief Justice of the Supreme Court for the reargument of the *Brown* cases, Warren is widely credited as the chief architect of the Court's unanimous *Brown* ruling.

### White Citizens Council

An organization founded in response to the *Brown* decision, White Citizens Councils advocated segregationist policies and used economic pressure to stifle the African American fight for civil rights.

### White flight

A term used to denote large-scale migration of white families from urban areas into suburban areas.

### Wilson, Paul

Assistant Attorney General of Kansas who represented the state during the *Brown* argument before the Supreme Court.

### Young, H. Albert

Attorney General of Delaware who defended the state during the *Brown* argument before the Supreme Court.

# CHRONOLOGY

**1849**

In the earliest recorded school segregation case, *Roberts v. City of Boston,* the Massachusetts Supreme Court rules the city of Boston may maintain segregated schools. *See p. 13.*

**1865**

December 6, 1865 – The Thirteenth Amendment is ratified, ending slavery in the United States. *See p. 7.*

**1866**

The Civil Rights Act of 1866 is passed by Congress, ensuring the rights of all citizens to make contracts, own private property, and give witness in court. *See p. 7.*

**1867**

Congress passes the Reconstruction Act of 1867 *See p. 7.*

**1868**

July, 1868 – The Fourteenth Amendment is ratified, guaranteeing "equal protection under the law" to all citizens. *See p. 8.*

**1870**

February 3, 1870 – The Fifteenth Amendment is ratified, upholding the right of all citizens to vote. *See p. 8.*

May, 31, 1870 – The Civil Rights Act of 1870 is passed to ensure the provisions of the 1866 law under the Fourteenth Amendment. *See p. 8.*

**1873**

April 14, 1873 – In the *Slaughterhouse Cases,* the Supreme Court rules that it is the business of the states, not the federal government, to protect individual civil rights. *See p. 8.*

**1875**

March 1, 1875 – Congress passes the Civil Rights Act of 1875, extending "full and equal enjoyment" of public accommodations and transport to all citizens. *See p. 8.*

October, 1875 – In *United States v. Reese,* the Supreme Court undermines the Enforcement Act of 1870, saying prosecutors did not prove a man was denied the vote because of his race. *See p. 10.*

October, 1875 – In *United States v. Cruikshank,* the Supreme Court overturns the conspiracy convictions of a group of men charged with murdering several black militia members in a riot, stating that the Fourteenth and Fifteenth Amendments only apply to state, not private actions. *See p. 10.*

## 1877

Reconstruction ends with the withdrawal of federal troops from the Confederate South. *See p. 11.*

## 1883

October 15, 1883 – In their *Civil Rights Cases* decision, the Supreme Court rules that the Civil Rights Act of 1870 is unconstitutional because the Fourteenth Amendment only applies to the acts of states, not individuals. *See p. 11.*

## 1896

May 18, 1896 – In *Plessy v. Ferguson,* the Supreme Court rules that state laws requiring segregation are constitutional, establishing the "separate but equal" standard. *See p. 12.*

## 1898

April 25, 1898 – The Supreme Court rules in *Williams v. Mississippi* that poll taxes and literacy test requirements for voting are constitutional. *See p. 17.*

## 1899

December 18, 1899 – In *Cumming v. Board of Education of Richmond County,* the Supreme Court rules that federal officials do not have the authority to interfere with a Georgia school district that eliminated high schooling for black students. *See p. 14.*

## 1908

November 9, 1908 – The Supreme Court rules in *Berea v. Commonwealth of Kentucky* that a Kentucky statute forbidding integrated education applies to a private college incorporated by the state. *See p. 15.*

## 1909

February 12, 1909 – A coalition of concerned citizens meets to discuss bringing an end to racial discrimination; the organization born from this meeting is named the National Association for the Advancement of Colored People (NAACP). *See p. 21.*

## 1927

November 21, 1927 – Applying *Plessy* to education, the Supreme Court allows Mississippi to assign a Chinese student to a segregated "colored" school in *Gong Lum v. Rice.*

## 1930

The NAACP receives a Garland Fund grant to support legal action to eliminate segregated schools, and uses the money to hire lawyer Nathan Margold to research a legal strategy. *See p. 24.*

## 1936

January 15, 1936 – In *Pearson v. Murray*, the Maryland Court of Appeals upholds an order for the University of Maryland to admit African Americans to its law school because the state offers no law school for black students. *See p. 25.*

## 1938

December 12, 1938 – In *Missouri ex rel. Gaines v. Canada*, the U.S. Supreme Court holds that Missouri's program to offer out-of-state scholarships to black graduate students instead of admitting them to in-state universities does not afford "equal" education. *See p. 26.*

## 1939

The NAACP creates a separate Legal Defense and Education Fund, Inc. (LDF) to handle litigation. Thurgood Marshall becomes the first Director-Counsel of the LDF. *See p. 27.*

## 1940

June 18, 1940 – In *Alston v. School Board of City of Norfolk*, a federal appeals court rules that African American teachers should be paid the same as white teachers for equal work. *See p. 26.*

## 1942

In *Missouri ex rel. Bluford v. Canada*, the Missouri Supreme Court rules that the state of Missouri must create a graduate journalism program for black students or admit them to the University of Missouri; in response, the state creates a program at all-black Lincoln University. *See p. 28.*

## 1947

The Presidential Committee on Civil Rights publishes a report, *To Secure These Rights*, arguing for the ending of segregation in America. *See p. 30.*

## 1948

January 12, 1948 – In *Sipuel v. Oklahoma State Regents*, the U.S. Supreme Court directs the University of Oklahoma Law School to open its doors to an African American student. *See p. 30.*

July 26, 1948 – President Harry S. Truman signs Executive Orders 9980 and 9981, mandating equal opportunity in federal employment and ending segregation in the military. *See p. 30.*

## 1950

June 5, 1950 – The Supreme Court decides two key university desegregation cases. In *McLaurin v. Oklahoma State Regents*, the Court decides that after admitting an African American to its all-white graduate school, the University of Oklahoma cannot interfere with his education by segregating him within the classroom or other university facilities. In *Sweatt v. Painter*, the Court considers the "intangible qualities" of education when it orders a black student admitted to the University of Texas Law School. *See p. 32.*

## 1951

April, 1951 – A district court judge dismisses the argument in *Bolling v. Sharpe* that school segregation is unconstitutional in the District of Columbia. *See p. 49.*

June 23, 1951 – By a 2-1 vote, a three-judge district court panel upholds segregation in the North Carolina case *Briggs v. Elliott. See p. 36.*

August 3, 1951 – Another three-judge panel upholds segregation in *Brown v. Board of Education, Topeka* but in their finding of fact the judges denounce segregation as detrimental to the learning of African American children. *See p. 41.*

## 1952

March 7, 1952 – A three-judge panel in Virginia unanimously upholds segregation in *Davis v. County School Board of Prince Edward County. See p. 46.*

April 1, 1952 – In two Delaware cases, *Belton v. Gebhart* and *Bulah v. Gebhart,* the Chancellor of Delaware holds segregation constitutional but orders the immediate admission of African Americans into white schools as remedy for their unequal facilities. *See p. 42.*

December 9-11, 1952 – Oral arguments are heard before the Supreme Court in the five cases combined as *Brown v. Board of Education. See p. 54.*

## 1953

January 20, 1953 – Dwight D. Eisenhower is inaugurated 34th President of the United States. *See p. 58.*

June 8, 1953 – The Supreme Court announces its decision to reargue the *Brown* cases. *See p. 58.*

September 8, 1953 – Supreme Court Chief Justice Fred M. Vinson dies of a heart attack. *See p. 58.*

September 30, 1953 – Eisenhower nominates Governor Earl Warren of California as the new chief justice of the Supreme Court. *See p. 59.*

December 7-9, 1953 – The second oral argument in the *Brown* cases is heard before the Supreme Court. *See p. 59.*

## 1954

May 17, 1954 – The Supreme Court announces its decision in *Brown:* by a 9-0 count, the justices rule that "in the field of public education the doctrine of 'separate but equal' has no place." They call for a third argument on the issue of relief. *See p. 65.*

Summer, 1954 – In response to the *Brown* decision, the first White Citizens Council is founded in Mississippi. *See p. 81.*

October, 1954 – The death of Supreme Court Justice Robert H. Jackson delays the reargument in *Brown.* John Marshall Harlan is named to replace him. *See p. 67.*

## 1955

April 11-14, 1955 – The Supreme Court hears oral arguments on the issue of relief in the *Brown* case. *See p. 67.*

May 31, 1955 – In *Brown II*, the Supreme Court orders district courts to oversee relief "with all deliberate speed." *See p.70.*

December 1, 1955 – Rosa Parks is arrested after refusing to give her bus seat to a white man, sparking the Montgomery Bus Boycott. *See p. 115.*

## 1956

February 3, 1956 – Riots break out as Autherine Lucy attempts to integrate the University of Alabama. *See p. 84.*

March 12, 1956 – Southern members of Congress read a protest, the Southern Manifesto, into the Congressional Record against the Supreme Court's "clear abuse of judicial power" in the *Brown* case. *See p. 75.*

August 26, 1956 – Clinton High School in Tennessee becomes the first public high school in the South to desegregate; six days later, the National Guard is called out to deal with protesters. *See p. 84.*

August 30-31, 1956 – In Texas, Governor Allan Shivers calls out the Texas Rangers to prevent the enrollment of black students at Mansfield High School. *See p. 84.*

## 1957

September 2, 1957 – Arkansas Governor Orval Faubus calls out the Arkansas National Guard to prevent integration of Little Rock's Central High School. *See p. 86.*

September 4, 1957 – The Little Rock Nine fail in an attempt to enter Central High; Elizabeth Eckford becomes trapped within the mob while the National Guard looks on. *See p. 86.*

September 9, 1957 – Eisenhower signs into law the largely ineffective Civil Rights Act of 1957.

September 20, 1957 – After a court order, Faubus withdraws the National Guard from Little Rock's Central High. *See p. 86.*

September 23, 1957 – The Little Rock Nine begin classes at Central High, but are forced out before lunchtime by a gathering crowd. *See p. 86.*

September 25, 1957 – Eisenhower orders 1,100 federal troops to Little Rock, and the Little Rock Nine finally attend classes at Central High School. *See p. 88.*

## 1958

September 12, 1958 – In *Cooper v. Aaron*, the Supreme Court's overturns the Little Rock School Board's request to delay its desegregation plan. *See p. 93.*

## 1960

February 1, 1960 – The first sit-in of a segregated lunch counter is staged in Greensboro, North Carolina, by students from North Carolina A&T University. *See p. 115.*

November 10, 1960 – The Senate passes the Civil Rights Act of 1960.

## 1962

September 30, 1962 – President John F. Kennedy sends federal marshals to escort James Meredith as he enters the campus of the University of Mississippi; a riot breaks out and two people are killed. The following day Meredith registers for classes and becomes the first African American to attend Ole Miss. *See p. 96.*

## 1963

June 11, 1963 – Vivian Malone and James Hood are the first African Americans admitted to the University of Alabama after George Wallace makes his "stand at the schoolhouse door." That night President Kennedy makes a nationally televised address urging Congress to take action on a civil rights bill. *See p. 97.*

August 28, 1963 – In the March on Washington, 250,000 people gather in peaceful protest at the Lincoln Memorial; Martin Luther King, Jr. delivers his famous "I Have a Dream" speech. *See p. 116.*

November 22, 1963 – President Kennedy is assassinated in Dallas, Texas. Lyndon B. Johnson assumes the presidency. *See p. 98.*

## 1964

May 25, 1964 – In *Griffin v. County School Board of Prince Edward County,* a suit stemming from one of the original *Brown* cases, the U.S. Supreme Court rules that a Virginia county cannot close its public schools and refuse to levy taxes in order to avoid desegregation.

July 2, 1964 – President Johnson signs the Civil Rights Act of 1964 into law, making it illegal to discriminate in employment and illegal to segregate public facilities. *See p. 98.*

## 1965

March 7, 1965 – Voting rights marchers are beaten by state troopers while marching from Selma, Alabama. *See p. 117.*

August 6, 1965 – Johnson signs the Voting Rights Act of 1965 into law, making literacy tests and poll taxes illegal. *See p. 118.*

## 1968

April 4, 1968 – Martin Luther King, Jr., is assassinated in Memphis, Tennessee. *See p. 118.*

April 11, 1968 – Johnson signs the Fair Housing Act of 1968 into law. *See p. 118.*

May 26, 1968 – In *Green v. County School Board of New Kent County,* the Supreme Court rules that a Virginia county's "freedom-of-choice" plan fails to produce desegregation and orders its school board to devise a new plan that will create "a system without a 'white' school and a 'Negro' school, but just schools." *See p. 99.*

## 1969

September 5, 1969 – Ruling on a case from Mississippi, in *Alexander v. Holmes County Board of Education* the Supreme Court says "The obligation of every school district is to terminate dual school systems at once and operate now and hereafter only unitary schools." *See p. 100.*

## 1971

April 20, 1971 – In *Swann v. Charlotte-Mecklenberg Board of Education,* the Supreme Court upholds the use of busing as a means of desegregating schools. *See p. 101.*

## 1973

June 21, 1973 – In *Keyes v. School District No. 1, Denver,* the Supreme Court rules in its first desegregation case outside the South that districts where *de facto* segregation was created through administrative actions (such as drawing school boundaries) must enact desegregation plans. *See p. 102.*

In *Adams v. Richardson,* a federal appeals court upholds an order for federal education officials to enforce Title VI of the 1964 Civil Rights Acts, which prohibits discrimination by institutions that receive federal funding.

## 1974

July 25, 1974 – In a 5-4 vote, the U.S. Supreme Court rules in *Milliken v. Bradley* that interdistrict busing (e.g., between a city and its suburbs) cannot be used to integrate schools. *See p. 106.*

## 1978

June 28, 1978 – In *Bakke v. Regents of the University of California,* the Supreme Court holds unconstitutional a quota system used by the University of California at Davis Medical School to ensure minority enrollment, but rules that race can be taken into account in the admissions process. *See p. 108.*

## 1983

May 24, 1983 – The Supreme Court rules in *Bob Jones University v. United States* that the Internal Revenue Service may revoke the tax-exempt status of educational institutions that discriminate on the basis of race.

## 1991

January 15, 1991 – In *Board of Education of Oklahoma City v. Dowel,* the Supreme Court rules that once a school district has been found in compliance with a desegregation decree, the courts no longer need to supervise, even if changing conditions in the district result in *de facto* segregation. *See p. 107.*

## 1995

June 12, 1995 –In an eighteen-year-old litigation, the Supreme Court rules in *Missouri v. Jenkins* that some educational inequalities, such as student achievement, are beyond the authority of the federal courts to rectify. *See p. 108.*

## 1996

March 18, 1996 – In *Hopwood v. Texas,* a U.S. Court of Appeals finds the "dual-track" admissions system at the University of Texas Law School, with different standards for white and minority candidates, unconstitutional. The Supreme Court declines to hear the appeal. *See p. 109.*

## 2003

June 23, 2003 – In the cases *Gratz v. Bollinger* and *Grutter v. Bollinger,* the U.S. Supreme Court holds the University of Michigan's undergraduate admissions policy, which automatically assigned points for minority status, unconstitutional. The "narrowly tailored" policy of Michigan's Law School, which considers race as one of many factors contributing to diversity, is upheld; the Court rules that "student body diversity is a compelling state interest in the context of university admissions." *See p. 109.*

# NARRATIVE OVERVIEW

# PROLOGUE

T he forced segregation of people by race effectively became the law of the land in the United States during the first half of the twentieth century. Although the U.S. Constitution promised equal rights to all Americans, a series of Supreme Court rulings relentlessly eroded the civil rights and social standing of African Americans. When the Court ruled that "separate but equal" facilities and accommodations met the constitutional requirements, blacks and whites were segregated in virtually all areas of daily life. This system was enforced with particular ruthlessness in the American South. Blacks had limited or no access to public parks and swimming pools, theaters, restaurants, hotels, hospitals, and even government facilities such as courts and libraries enjoyed by white citizens. Segregation thus served to keep blacks trapped in an inferior position in American society.

This caste system was imposed on African Americans from birth, and there were few sanctuaries from this system during childhood. In fact, many of the nation's most egregious examples of racial bigotry and discrimination were codified in its public schools. In *Remembering Jim Crow: African Americans Tell about Life in the Segregated South,* Alabama native Ann Pointer recalled the galling injustice of attending a segregated black school:

> I tell you, I had to walk to school every day and back no matter if it was storming. We could not ride the buses although we were paying taxes. But we couldn't ride those buses. Nothing rode the bus but the whites. And they would ride and throw trash, throw rocks and everything at us on the road and hoop

and holler, "nigger, nigger, nigger," all up and down the road. We weren't allowed to say one word to them or throw back or nothing, because if you threw back at them you was going to jail. Now that's one of the things, that's the only bitter spot in my heart, and I shouldn't have it, but you know, you can't keep from thinking. We were paying tax, but yet we could not ride those buses; our school was the only [school for blacks]. We didn't have nothing at our school. They give the teachers some chalk and a couple of erasers for the board, but no kind of supplies. Not even heat. If your father didn't bring two loads of wood to that school, then they made you go to the woods and gather wood and you, you were not going to sit by the other children's fire. We were told, "All who ain't brought your wood, go to the woods." We had to go out there and walk up in water trying to find wood to help heat the school.

As Pointer's story illustrates, separate was never equal in the segregated South. With little political power to change segregation laws or compel equality of facilities, African Americans had but one avenue of recourse: the courts. The Constitution promised that all citizens were equal, and the American justice system had the duty of interpreting and enforcing that promise.

After a long series of legal battles led by the National Association for the Advancement of Colored People (NAACP), public school segregation was overturned with the Supreme Court's *Brown v. Board of Education* ruling in 1954. This judgment changed American education forever, and it ushered in a new era of increased civil liberties for all African Americans.

# Chapter One

# FROM SLAVERY TO SEGREGATION

◄━━◖◗━━►

We hold these truths to be self-evident, that all men are created equal, that they are endowed by their Creator with certain unalienable Rights, that among these are Life, Liberty and the pursuit of Happiness.

—The Declaration of Independence, 1776

No Person held to Service or Labour in one State, under the Laws thereof, escaping into another, shall, in Consequence of any Law or Regulation therein, be discharged from such Service or Labour, but shall be delivered up on Claim of the Party to whom such Service or Labour may be due.

—Article IV, Section 2 of the U.S. Constitution, 1787

The United States, although a bold experiment in democracy, was founded upon a profound contradiction. It recognized the equality of "all men," yet also permitted the enslavement of an entire race. Over time, this contradiction became the source of bitter anger and division in American society. Opposition to slavery and its spread into the newly settled territories of the West was strongest in the Northern states, a region of the country independent of slave labor for its economic well-being. The North-based abolitionist movement condemned the immorality of slavery with greater vigor with each passing year, and by the 1830s and 1840s it had become a powerful political force. White Southerners, though, recognized that their economic livelihood and way of life depended on the "peculiar institution" of slavery, and they saw any attempt to limit slavery as an attack on their rights and culture.

In 1857 regional tensions over slavery escalated further with the U.S. Supreme Court's *Scott v. Sandford* decision. This case was brought by a slave named Dred Scott who was seeking freedom after spending several years living in the "free" state of Illinois. But the Court ruled that no people of African ancestry—whether free or in bondage—could become citizens of the United States or sue in federal court (this latter judgment meant that Scott had no legal right to file his lawsuit in the first place).

The Supreme Court's Dred Scott decision also stated that the Missouri Compromise of 1820, which restricted slavery in the western territories of the United States, was unconstitutional because it deprived slaveholders of property. This part of the decision led many outraged Northerners to imagine not only swift expansion of slavery throughout the western frontier, but also nightmarish scenarios in which slaveholders who decided to settle in Northern states would be legally shielded from prosecution for practicing slavery— thus turning "free" states into slave states.

The sectional conflict over slavery came to a head four years later, when eleven Southern states seceded from the Union over fears that newly elected President Abraham Lincoln would act to limit slavery in American territories. These states promptly established a separate nation, the Confederated States of America.

Lincoln did not enter the Oval Office as an abolitionist. His main concern was to keep the Union together, not end slavery. But after Confederate forces attacked U.S. troops at Fort Sumter in South Carolina in April 1861, Lincoln approved the use of force to preserve the Union. After years of mounting anger and distrust, the war between North and South had finally been joined.

The first two years of the Civil War amounted to a bloody stalemate. Determined to restore the shattered country, Lincoln decided that freeing slaves would help win the war. He thought that this action would rally public support in the North by emphasizing the moral righteousness of the Union cause. He also believed that such a decree would make it more difficult for the South to control and direct its large slave labor force.

Lincoln was proven right on both counts. His presidential order, known as the Emancipation Proclamation, took effect on January 1, 1863. Over the ensuing months it brought thousands of freed and runaway slaves under the banners of the Union Army and Navy. By the war's end, over 200,000 African

Americans had fought "for Union and Liberty." And although some Northerners opposed Lincoln's decision, the proclamation has been credited with deepening Northern resolve at a critical time in the war.

## The End of Slavery

Although the Emancipation Proclamation only freed slaves in Confederate States—not those in the five slave states that had remained loyal to the Union—it marked a profound shift in the politics of the war. Abolition of slavery had become an acknowledged aim of Union leaders for the first time. In April 1865 the long and bloody conflict finally drew to a close, as the depleted Confederate army surrendered to Union forces. Eight months later, in December 1865, the United States outlawed slavery by ratifying the Thirteenth Amendment.

In 1857 Dred Scott petitioned the U.S. Supreme Court for his freedom after spending several years in the "free" state of Illinois.

White Southerners resisted the new amendment. Angling to keep freedmen as cheap agricultural labor, many Southern states passed laws known as "Black Codes." These laws restricted the rights of blacks to work, marry, own or lease property, and move from town to town: in other words, they returned blacks to a condition reminiscent of slavery in many ways.

The Civil Rights Act of 1866 (which was passed over President Andrew Johnson's veto) made the Black Codes illegal, but lawmakers recognized that stronger action was necessary to ensure the rights of black Americans. They proposed a fourteenth amendment to the U.S. Constitution, one that would grant the rights of citizenship to newly freed slaves in the South and extend "equal protection of the laws" to all citizens.

When Southern states balked at passing the amendment, the Republican-dominated Congress forced through the Reconstruction Act of 1867. This act authorized the use of federal troops to maintain order across the South, required each Southern state to rewrite its constitution, and allowed black men to vote and serve as delegates to the mandated constitutional conventions. It also required states of the former Confederacy to approve the Fourteenth Amendment as a condition of gaining readmittance to the Union.

## Reconstruction in the South

The Reconstruction Act enjoyed initial success. The presence of federal troops cautioned Southern communities against defying the U.S. government or lashing out at the former slaves that walked their streets. Meanwhile, black delegates helped the Southern states craft and pass new constitutions that called for more equal treatment of whites and blacks, and the flood of new black voters paved the way for ratification of the Fourteenth Amendment in state after state. In addition, African Americans gained election to a variety of state and local offices, and countless black entrepreneurs launched their own businesses. By July 1868 the Fourteenth Amendment was the law of the land and Southern black families dared to hope that a new era of social and economic equality was on the horizon.

These hopes were nurtured by a flurry of activity at the national level to protect the country's newest citizens. One of these milestones was the Civil Rights Act of 1870, also known as the Enforcement Act of 1870. This law established penalties for anyone guilty of conspiring to deprive people of their civil rights. It was essentially a duplicate of the Civil Rights Act of 1866, re-enacted to ensure its constitutionality under the new Fourteenth Amendment. In addition, the Fifteenth Amendment, which confirmed the right of all citizens to vote, was ratified in 1870. Finally, the Civil Rights Act of 1875 extended "full and equal enjoyment" of public accommodations and transport to all citizens, black or white. "Full and equal enjoyment" of schools was not included in the legislation, but the lack of such a provision did not seem important to Reconstructionists since public schools were rare at the time.

## Grim Tidings from the Supreme Court

Enforcement of these new civil rights laws was inconsistent, however, and in the mid-1870s the Supreme Court handed down a series of rulings that seriously undermined their effectiveness. The first of these rulings occurred in 1873, when a Court decision known as the *Slaughterhouse Cases* narrowed the definition of the Fourteenth Amendment by granting individual states greater

A montage of black and white members of South Carolina's first Reconstruction-era legislature, 1870.

responsibility for the enforcement of civil rights. The decision stemmed from a Louisiana law granting exclusive butchering rights in New Orleans and surrounding parishes to a small monopoly of businesses. This law was ostensibly intended to improve public health conditions by limiting slaughterhouse operations. Several independent butchers sued, claiming they were being denied their right to work and to hold business property without "due process" of the law. In a 5-4 decision, however, the Court ruled in favor of the monopolies, declaring that it was the business of the states—not the federal government—to protect individual civil rights.

In 1875 the Supreme Court further eroded the recently won civil rights of black Americans in two separate rulings. In the *United States v. Reese,* the justices considered the case of an African American, William Garner, who had tried to register to vote in Lexington, Kentucky, only to have his poll tax payment refused by local officials. When he tried to vote on election day, he was again denied. Angry over this clear flouting of the Fifteenth Amendment, Garner reported the incident to federal officials, who prosecuted the Kentucky election inspectors under the provisions of the Enforcement Act of 1870. The local court acquitted the officials, however, and when the case worked its way all the way up to the Supreme Court, the high court sided with the Kentucky officials. The Court held that since Garner had not proven his vote was denied because of his race, it would not overturn the ruling.

The Supreme Court ruling in *United States v. Cruikshank* had an even more chilling effect. In 1873 a political rally held in Colfax, Louisiana, for members of the state's black militia was interrupted by the White League, a paramilitary group similar to the Ku Klux Klan. During the ensuing riot, known as the Colfax Massacre, around seventy black men were murdered, many after they had surrendered. White League leaders were charged as conspirators under the Enforcement Act of 1870 and convicted of depriving their victims of their civil rights. The Supreme Court, however, overturned the convictions. The Court held that the Fourteenth and Fifteenth Amendments only applied to state, not private, actions—and it further claimed that prosecutors had failed to prove that the victims had been attacked because of their race.

Black Americans and white supporters of equal rights openly despaired about these rulings, for the implications were clear and frightening. According to the highest court in the country, it was the business of the states, not the federal government, to protect individual civil rights. And if the states failed to protect the civil rights of members of its citizenry, individuals had nowhere else to turn. This was a terrible realization for black families in Southern communities, many of which were simmering cauldrons of racial bigotry and resentment in the post-Civil War era.

## A New Era of Racism Begins

The Reconstruction Era in the South formally came to a close in 1877 with the withdrawal of federal troops from the former Confederacy. White politicians who held office before or during the Civil War promptly swooped in and regained control of state legislatures across the region. As they settled in, these lawmakers challenged or ignored the new federal civil rights laws. Their defiance triggered hundreds of lawsuits across the country from black citizens who believed that their rights—explicitly guaranteed under the Civil Rights Act of 1875—were being violated.

Five of these lawsuits were reviewed by the Supreme Court in 1883 in its pivotal *Civil Rights Cases* decision. Two cases dealt with hotels in Kansas and Missouri that refused to rent rooms to African Americans, while two others concerned theaters in New York and San Francisco that refused to seat black patrons. (These four cases came from non-Confederate states because local federal officials were more willing to prosecute offenders in these communities, not because such blatant discrimination was absent in the South.) The final case was brought by a black couple from Tennessee after the woman was denied entry to a ladies' railroad car.

All of these incidents of discrimination were prohibited by the Civil Rights Act of 1875, but the Supreme Court ruled in its *Civil Rights Cases* decision that the law was unconstitutional. The majority of justices held that the Fourteenth Amendment only applied to the acts of states, not individuals. Justice Joseph P. Bradley's majority opinion acknowledged that the "social rights" of the black plaintiffs had been violated, but not their civil rights. Bradley also declared that it was no longer necessary for black Americans to be "the special favorite of the laws." In a similar ruling that same year, the Court held in *United States v. Harris* that a federal law used to prosecute a man who led a lynch mob was unconstitutional because lynching was not a state-sponsored action.

Together, these 1883 high court rulings sent a clear message that the federal government did not have the authority to prevent discrimination by businesses or individuals acting independently of the state. This rebuke of Republican efforts to ensure civil rights for blacks gave white Southerners renewed confidence that they could roll back the civil rights gains African Americans had made over the previous few years.

Southern states subsequently enacted a wide range of laws requiring private businesses to maintain separate facilities for blacks and whites. Many of these laws not only imposed fines on operators who failed to maintain separate facilities, but also on any individual who challenged segregation by entering an area assigned to another race. These laws clearly constituted state actions against a racial group—a gross violation of the Fourteenth Amendment even according to the Supreme Court's extremely narrow interpretation of the amendment. With this in mind, civil rights advocates worked furiously to get the courts to overturn these discriminatory laws.

## Plessy v. Ferguson

In 1896, however, African Americans and their legal advocates suffered their most demoralizing defeat yet. That year, the Supreme Court issued its landmark *Plessy v. Ferguson* decision, holding that the existence of "separate but equal" facilities was permissible under the Fourteenth Amendment. This ruling was a crushing blow to black civil rights in the United States. It essentially made segregation legal, and over the next fifty years white politicians and communities enshrined the principle across all sectors of American society.

The *Plessy v. Ferguson* case originated in Louisiana, where in 1890 the state legislature had passed a law that required railroads to maintain separate railway cars for black and white passengers. Many Louisianans, particularly in racially tolerant New Orleans, were uncomfortable with the law, and a small group of black and white residents organized an association to challenge it. As part of this effort, the group persuaded a light-skinned, freeborn Creole (a French-speaking person of mixed race) named Homer Plessy to purchase a first-class ticket on the East Louisiana Railway in June 1892. He sat down in the car restricted to whites, and when he refused to move he was arrested. He was convicted under the two-year-old law and sentenced to pay a $25 fine by New Orleans Judge John Ferguson.

Plessy appealed his conviction, arguing that under the Thirteenth and Fourteenth Amendments he was a free man entitled to equal protection under the law. In 1896 the case came before the U.S. Supreme Court, which ruled 7-1 in favor of the Louisiana law (one justice abstained from the case). The Court majority ruled that the state could require separate accommodations for the races so long as the accommodations were "equal."

The Supreme Court resorted to some tortured arguments to justify this decision. As one of its supporting precedents, for example, the Court cited the 1849 *Roberts v. City of Boston* ruling by the Supreme Judicial Court of Massachusetts. While this decision did hold that segregated schools were constitutional, it was a case that *preceded* the passage of the Fourteenth Amendment. In addition, legal historians observe that the *Plessy v. Ferguson* ruling reflected a deliberate misreading of the intent of segregation laws, and that it constituted a total abdication of the Court's responsibility to enforce the "equal protection" clause of the Fourteenth Amendment. As Richard Kluger summarized in *Simple Justice,* the Court decision written by Justice Henry Billings Brown "would make no provision for the fact or purpose or result of the Civil War. He [Justice Brown] wrote as if the South had won."

*"In my opinion," wrote Justice John Marshall Harlan, "the judgment this day rendered [in Plessy v. Ferguson] will, in time, prove to be quite as pernicious as the decision made by this tribunal in the Dred Scott Case."*

Certainly, the Court resorted to some breathtakingly disingenuous reasoning. For example, Brown's opinion contended that U.S. segregation laws did not necessarily imply that one race was inferior to another:

> We consider the underlying fallacy of the plaintiff's argument to consist in the assumption that the enforced separation of the two races stamps the colored race with a badge of inferiority. If this be so, it is not by reason of anything found in the act, but solely because the colored race chooses to put that construction upon it.... If one race be inferior to the other socially, the constitution of the United States cannot put them upon the same plane.

Bolstered by the Supreme Court's decision, legislatures across the South passed another wave of laws instituting segregation in public places, from streetcars and theaters to parks and schools. Although people challenged these laws by arguing that *Plessy* only applied to transportation, later court decisions upheld the "separate but equal" doctrine. Finally, the *Plessy* ruling had a major impact on racial classifications in the United States. Since Homer

Justice John Marshall Harlan issued a blistering dissent in *Plessy v. Ferguson,* predicting "pernicious" consequences for the country.

Plessy was only one-eighth African—making him an "octoroon," according to the terminology of the day—he had challenged the government's classification of him as "black." By ruling that Plessy could indeed be segregated into the "colored" rail car, the Supreme Court affirmed the "one drop rule" of racial classification. This tenet, peculiar to the United States, meant that people with "one drop" of African blood, no matter how far back in their heritage, were considered black in the eyes of the law.

## A Prophetic Dissent

The sole justice to dissent from the majority opinion in *Plessy v. Ferguson* was Justice John Marshall Harlan, a former Kentucky slave owner who had come to support the postwar civil rights amendments after seeing the violence perpetrated on freedmen in his home state. Harlan issued a blistering condemnation of the majority opinion. He declared that the purpose of the Louisiana statute was, "under the guise of giving equal accommodation for whites and blacks, to compel the latter to keep to themselves while traveling in railroad passenger coaches. No one would be so wanting in candor as to assert the contrary." He also criticized the Court's decision as contrary to Constitutional principles: "In view of the Constitution, in the eye of the law, there is in this country no superior, dominant, ruling class of citizens. There is no caste here. Our Constitution is color blind and neither knows nor tolerates classes among citizens." In a prophetic moment, Harlan added that "in my opinion, the judgment this day rendered will, in time, prove to be quite as pernicious as the decision made by this tribunal in the Dred Scott Case."

The Supreme Court's string of rulings hostile to black equality continued three years later, with *Cumming v. Richmond Board of Education.* In this decision, the high court once again sided with the white establishment against black citizens desperate to protect their dwindling legal rights. The Supreme Court ruled that a Georgia county did not have to provide a high school to African American students, even though it operated a high school for white students (administrators had sacrificed the county's black high school facility to accommodate the county's growing number of black grade-school children).

The county's stance was a clear violation of the Supreme Court's own "separate but equal" doctrine outlined in *Plessy v. Ferguson*. Nevertheless, the Court insisted that "the education of the people in schools maintained by state taxation is a matter belonging to the respective states, and any interference on the part of Federal authority with the management of such schools cannot be justified except in the case of a clear and unmistakable disregard of rights secured by the supreme law of the land. We have here no such case to be determined."

## The Rise of Jim Crow

In the 1890s the steady erosion of the legal standing of African Americans, coupled with widespread Southern white anger at Republican-sponsored efforts to provide civil rights to blacks, provided fertile soil for a convulsive reversal of fortunes. All across the South, former Confederate states passed so-called "Jim Crow" laws that codified segregation and discrimination against blacks in virtually all aspects of daily life. These laws, implemented for the express purpose of returning blacks to a deeply subordinate position in American society, focused on preventing blacks from voting and on separating the races in parks, restaurants, theaters, railcars, hotels, and other public spaces.

Of the numerous public facilities and institutions targeted for segregation, schools were perhaps the most strategically important target to whites. Acting on the belief that black education posed a threat to their power (and to the way of life of their white constituents, who depended on uneducated blacks to provide cheap labor), white politicians passed a flurry of segregation laws designed to block black students from using the school facilities, textbooks, and other resources provided to white students. The Supreme Court upheld these laws in the 1908 decision known as *Berea College v. Commonwealth of Kentucky*. Berea College was a small, private college that had been committed to educating male and female students of all races since its founding as a one-room school in 1855. Berea had challenged Kentucky segregation laws on the grounds that it was a private college and thus free to use

15

its property as it saw fit. The Court ruled, however, that since the college had incorporated through the state, the state had an interest in regulating it. Berea was subsequently forced to segregate its student body through the creation of an alternate school for black students. This segregated system remained in place on Berea's campus until Kentucky amended its laws in 1950.

The concerted white effort to return all political, economic, and social power to white hands did not go wholly unchallenged. In the mid-1890s, for example, the Populist Party movement brought poor white farmers and black voters of the South together against the Democratic Party, which was dominated by wealthy white landowners. But two years after an alliance of Populists and black Republicans prevailed in North Carolina's 1896 state elections, white Democrats regained control of the state through a campaign of orchestrated violence and fraud. Their "victory" was capped off by a night of terror in the city of Wilmington. On November 10, 1898, marauding white mobs organized by white supremacist leaders in the community attacked the offices of black lawmakers and shot any African American they found on the streets. The official death toll from the riot was twenty-five, but some observers believe hundreds more were murdered and dumped in the nearby Cape Fear River.

> *"We have very dark days here. The colored people are in despair. The rebels boast that the Negroes shall not have as much liberty now as they had under slavery. If things go on thus, our doom is sealed. God knows it is worse than slavery."*

Similar acts of intimidation and violence against black citizens, albeit on a smaller scale, became commonplace across the South in the 1890s. Adult black males seeking to exercise their right to vote were particularly attractive targets to local bigots and white terrorist organizations such as the Ku Klux Klan, but any transgression of Jim Crow laws could bring pain and suffering down on black men and members of their households.

Lynching, in particular, became a favored method of disposing of black men and women who refused to bend to white authority. This act of terror not only eliminated perceived threats to the dominant white power structure, but also served as a grim warning to all black Americans against challenging the nation's white-dominated political, economic, and social spheres. In the twenty years after the Supreme Court's decision in the *Civil Rights Cases,* there were more than 3,000 reported lynchings in the South, most by terrorist groups such as the Ku Klux Klan. "We have very dark days here," wrote one black man in response to the surging Klan violence. "The colored people are in despair. The rebels boast that the Negroes shall not have as much liberty now as they had under slavery. If things go on thus, our doom is sealed. God knows it is worse than slavery."

Many of the victims of lynching were political activists and labor organizers, but others were simply black men and women found to be "insolent" or "disrespectful" to members of the white community. Lynching and other forms of violence had a dramatic impact on black voter registration across the South. In Louisiana, for example, the number of African Americans registered to vote dropped from over 130,000 in 1896 to only 1,342 eight years later.

Lynching, though, was just one tool used by white Southerners to suppress the black vote in the post-Reconstruction era. Southern white lawmakers also passed a multitude of laws and statutes specifically designed to disenfranchise African Americans of their voting rights. In 1890, for example, the state of Mississippi held a constitutional convention to establish a literacy test as a qualification for voting. "There is no use to equivocate or lie about the matter," acknowledged James Kimble Vardaman, who later represented the state as both governor and U.S. senator. "Mississippi's constitutional convention was held for no other purpose than to eliminate the nigger from politics; not the ignorant—but the nigger."

In 1898 the Supreme Court ruled in *Williams v. Mississippi* that such literacy tests were constitutional. "They do not on their face discriminate between the races, and it has not been shown that their actual administration was evil," declared the Court. "[It has been shown] only that evil was possible under them." Armed with this ruling, states across the South enacted similar laws to suppress black voting that was not already being nullified by violence or fraud. In addition, Southern states implemented "poll taxes," a tax levied on citizens as a requirement for voting. The high fees prevented impoverished blacks—and many poor whites—from exercising their right to vote, further consolidating political power in the hands of wealthy whites.

## Dispiriting Cultural Trends

The social status of blacks continued to deteriorate in the early twentieth century. Southern historians began characterizing Reconstruction as a tragic era, and it became an article of faith among white communities that segrega-

A movie poster for D.W. Griffith's *Birth of a Nation,* which glorified the Ku Klux Klan as guardians of Southern values.

During the administration of President Woodrow Wilson (shown here at opening ceremonies for the 1916 major league baseball season), most federal departments and agencies became segregated by race.

tion was the best way to restore a lost—and idealized—way of life to the victimized South. Popular novels and movies like D. W. Griffith's infamous *Birth of a Nation* (1915) portrayed Klansmen as heroes and African Americans as debased sexual predators. Anthropologists and other social scientists claimed that there were biological distinctions between the races. Social Darwinists, believing that life was a contest of "survival of the fittest," argued that African Americans' lower social status proved the inferiority of their race.

In this racially charged climate, Woodrow Wilson was elected president in 1912. Raised in Georgia, he was the first Southerner to occupy the Oval Office since Andrew Johnson, who succeeded Lincoln after his assassination in 1865. Although Wilson had promised African Americans a "fair deal" during his campaign, one of his first acts as president was to establish segregation throughout the federal government. Several black officials in the District of Columbia were dismissed from their posts and replaced with whites. He also appointed white ambassadors to Haiti and Santo Domingo (positions traditionally held by blacks), and his appointees in the Treasury and Post Office immediately segregated all aspects of departmental operation, including use of restroom and eating facilities. Many federal offices in the South also segregated their facilities, and the head of the Georgia office of the Internal Revenue Service fired all his black employees.

The U.S. Congress also proposed several federal segregation laws during Wilson's tenure, including one eliminating blacks from holding commissions in the armed forces. By the time the United States entered World War I in 1917, most black soldiers had been relegated to service or infantry positions, and black sailors could only serve as stewards. The rights and opportunities available to African Americans had reached a new post-Civil War low.

# Chapter Two

# THE NAACP'S PLAN TO DISMANTLE SEGREGATION

—◁◦◦◦◦∫◦◦◦▷—

Then should we speak but servile words,
Or shall we hang our heads in shame?
Stand back of new-come foreign hordes,
And fear our heritage to claim?
No! stand erect and without fear,
And for our foes let this suffice—
We've bought a rightful sonship here,
And we have more than paid the price....
That for which millions prayed and sighed
That for which tens of thousands fought,
For which so many freely died,
God cannot let it come to naught.

—James Weldon Johnson, "Fifty Years" [on the 50th anniversary of the Emancipation Proclamation], 1913

As African American community leaders of the early twentieth century surveyed the hostile, segregated society that surrounded them, they recognized that education was essential to any gains they hoped to make in improving black social and economic opportunities. Improving educational opportunities for African Americans thus became a primary focus of black activist groups such as the National Association for the Advancement of Colored People (NAACP).

The NAACP had been founded in 1909 by a multiracial group of Americans dedicated to advancing the cause of black civil and political liberties (see *The Founding of the NAACP* sidebar, p. 22). By the 1920s the NAACP had registered a number of important legal victories to emerge as the country's pre-

## The Founding of the NAACP

During the nineteenth century, America's small cadre of educated black professionals had recognized the need for an organization to fight for African American rights. This need remained acute at the onset of the twentieth century, when blacks in the South—and many in the growing northern populations—suffered under grim political and economic oppression.

Black leaders of the nineteenth century such as Booker T. Washington had promoted accommodation and education as a way for African Americans to survive. But in the early twentieth century, a new generation of black leaders arose for whom mere survival was not enough. Chief among these leaders was W. E. B. Du Bois, a Massachusetts native with degrees from Harvard and the University of Berlin who became the country's foremost black intellectual. He conducted pioneering sociological research into the African American condition and came to believe that the future of the race lay in the "Talented Tenth," those African Americans who "must be made leaders of thought and missionaries of culture among their people." By developing "the Best of this race," Du Bois explained in a 1903 collection of articles by African Americans titled *The Negro Problem,* the Talented Tenth would "guide the Mass away from the contamination and death of the Worst, in their own and other races…. The Negro race, like all other races, is going to be saved by its exceptional men."

In 1905 Du Bois and a group of thirty to forty similarly minded African American activists met in Canada near Niagara Falls. Their goals included an end to segregation, voting rights for all citizens, and increased opportunities for higher education. As Du Bois noted: "Education is the development of power and ideal. We want our children trained as intelligent human beings should be and we will fight for all time against any proposal

mier organization supporting black civil rights. In 1917, for example, the U.S. Supreme Court ruled in its favor in *Buchanan v. Warley,* declaring that state and municipal efforts to segregate African Americans into residential districts was unconstitutional. That same year, the NAACP won a pitched battle to to educate black boys and girls simply as servants and underlings, so simply for the use of other people. They have a right to know, to think, to aspire."

Du Bois's Niagara Group held annual meetings over the next few years, but failed to grow into a larger movement. After the 1908 meeting, however, a horrible lynching and race riot in Springfield, Illinois—the hometown of Abraham Lincoln—galvanized civil rights advocates of both races. They called a meeting on February 12, 1909, the 100th anniversary of Lincoln's birth, for concerned citizens to bring about an end to racial discrimination. The meeting included members of the National Negro Congress and Du Bois's Niagara Group, as well as prominent white activists such as social worker Mary White Ovington, wealthy Southern socialist William Walling, and Oswald Garrison Villard, the president of the *New York Post* and grandson of abolitionist William Lloyd Garrison. The meeting resulted in the founding of the National Negro Committee. The following year the group adopted another name: the National Association for the Advancement of Colored People (NAACP).

Early NAACP efforts included educating Americans about racial injustice; defending African Americans wrongfully charged or convicted of crimes; fighting segregation laws through lawsuits and protests; and lobbying the government to pass anti-lynching and other civil rights laws. By 1940 the NAACP had grown to more than 350 local branches with over 50,000 members, and it had created a separate Legal Defense and Education Fund (LDF) to handle the battle to end legal segregation. Although physical and economic threats led to a drop in membership during the late 1940s, the organization recovered in the 1950s and played a pivotal role in the civil rights gains of the 1960s. Since that time, the NAACP has remained the nation's best-known civil rights advocacy organization. Today, the organization has more than half a million members organized into some 2,200 adult and 1,700 youth or college branches across the country.

enable African Americans to be commissioned as officers in World War I. This triumph resulted in the commissioning of 600 black officers in the U.S. military. One year later, persistent pressure from the NAACP contributed to President Woodrow Wilson's decision to issue a public statement condemning the practice of lynching. And in 1923, the NAACP helped convince the U.S. Supreme Court to rule in *Moore v. Dempsey* that excluding African Americans from jury duty deprived black defendants of their right to a fair trial.

The NAACP also worked tirelessly to improve educational opportunities for African Americans. In the late 1920s, the organization received grants to study the state of segregated schools in the South. Not surprisingly, the organization found huge disparities in financial support for white and black schools. In some states, white schools received eight times the funding of black schools. In 1930 the NAACP used a grant from the American Fund for Public Service, also known as the Garland Fund, to hire lawyer Nathan Margold to craft a legal strategy to attack school segregation.

Margold spent a year investigating the NAACP's legal options. He ultimately determined that since legal precedents permitted segregated schools, the best course of action was to challenge Southern school districts to live up to the "equal" provision of "separate but equal." Margold believed that if U.S. courts ruled that spending on segregated schools must be truly equal, many districts would find it too expensive to maintain separate schools for black and white students. They would then be forced to abandon their segregationist educational systems and integrate their schools.

Margold left his position as NAACP Special Counsel in 1933 for a job in the Franklin D. Roosevelt administration. He was replaced by Charles Hamilton Houston, an honors graduate of Harvard Law School and the first African American to serve on the *Harvard Law Review* (see Houston biography, p. 150). Houston had also taken a lead role in transforming Howard University Law School, founded in 1869 for black Americans wishing to pursue careers in law, into a respected program with a focus on civil rights law.

Houston recognized that it would be easier to litigate suits dealing with higher education—particularly graduate school and professional programs—than those that concerned elementary and secondary education. He believed that since few black universities in the South even offered postgraduate programs, the task of proving inequality of facilities for black and white graduate and postgraduate students would be fairly easy. In addition, he sensed that white resistance to integration in postgraduate education would be less likely to spark widespread revolt within white communities because it involved a small number of adult students, rather than a whole generation of young children.

## Significant Legal Victories

Houston first pursued his strategy with a case brought to him by Thurgood Marshall, a talented young attorney who had been one of his star pupils at Howard (see Marshall biography, p. 156). The case concerned a black law student named Donald Murray. A Maryland native with impeccable qualifications—he had graduated in good standing from Amherst University—Murray had nonetheless been denied admission to the University of Maryland's law school because of his race. Instead, the university offered him only a small scholarship to attend Howard University.

Armed with support from Houston and the NAACP, Marshall argued Murray's case in a Baltimore courtroom. He pointed out that the scholarship offer was so small that it would not even cover Murray's travel expenses. More importantly, Marshall noted that by refusing to admit Murray, the University of Maryland denied the young law student valuable insights into the way law was practiced in Maryland. The court agreed, and ordered Murray admitted into the law school in fall 1935.

Murray attended class without incident while the university appealed the decision. In early 1936 the Maryland Court of Appeals upheld the initial ruling, declaring that the state "confuses the issue of segregation and exclusion.… Donald Murray was not sent to a separate school of the University of Maryland.… Donald Murray was excluded from the University of Maryland entirely." With this ruling, the NAACP had struck its first important blow against the walls of segregation in America's educational institutions.

In 1936 Houston hired Marshall as assistant counsel for the NAACP. The two men continued to work on behalf of black students, but before long they expanded their crusade for social justice to include black teachers. In school districts all over the South, black teachers received as little as one-quarter of the salary of their white counterparts, even though many of them were better educated (teaching being one of the few occupations readily open to African Americans with graduate degrees). Marshall began the campaign to raise black teacher salaries in his home state of Maryland, where the existence of a teacher tenure program assured plaintiffs that they could not be fired for participating in a lawsuit. Early successes in Maryland convinced Marshall and Houston to take the fight to districts around the country. Their efforts culminated in 1940, when the U.S. Circuit Court of Appeals ruled in their favor in *Alston v. School Board of City of Norfolk (VA)*. Segregationist opponents of this ruling tried to appeal it to the U.S. Supreme Court. But the high court declined to take the case, thus leaving intact an important legal precedent for equal teacher pay throughout the United States. Significantly, the *Alston* decision also resulted in equal pay for white female teachers. This development, which financially benefited numerous white households, significantly blunted organized white opposition to the ruling.

These legal victories dramatically raised the profile of the NAACP in the African American community. When the NAACP won equal pay for black teachers—who were often among the leaders in their communities—ordinary black citizens recognized that the organization's efforts had the potential to provide tangible financial benefits to their families and neighborhoods. This helped the NAACP make the gains in membership and fundraising it needed to continue litigation.

## The Missouri Decisions

*"The basic consideration is not as to what sort of opportunities other States provide, or whether they are as good as those in Missouri, but as to what opportunities Missouri itself furnishes to white students and denies to negroes solely on the ground of color."*

After their victory in the *Murray* case, Houston and Marshall hoped to get the Supreme Court to set a precedent that would force graduate schools all over the South to open their doors to African Americans. They took the case of Lloyd Gaines, who in 1935 had been refused a place in the University of Missouri Law School. The University of Missouri did not admit African Americans; instead, black students who wished a graduate education were offered a full scholarship to an integrated school out of state. This program was similar to the one the Maryland Supreme Court held unconstitutional. Unlike Maryland, however, Missouri had fully funded its scholarship program. Because of this, and the state's willingness to create a separate law school for black students, the state supreme court had upheld the university's position against all legal challenges.

In 1938, though, Houston and Marshall shepherded the case of *Missouri ex rel. Gaines v. Canada* (S. W. Canada was the name of the university registrar) to the halls of the U.S. Supreme Court. After the plaintiffs and the defendants presented their cases, the Supreme Court sided with Gaines by a 6-2 vote (see Open Racism on the Nation's Highest Court, p. 28). "The basic consideration is not as to what sort of opportunities other States provide, or whether they are as good as those in Missouri, but as to what opportunities Missouri itself furnishes to white students and denies to negroes solely on the ground of color," declared the Court. This was a momentous ruling, for although it did not address the constitutionality of educational segregation, it signaled that the Court was disposed to start enforcing the "equal" condition of the "separate but equal" doctrine.

The Supreme Court left it to Missouri's court to oversee a remedy in the case. The Missouri Supreme Court subsequently directed the state to create a separate state law school for African Americans. Missouri obeyed, creating a law school at its all-black Lincoln University. The facilities, however, were clearly inferior to those at the state university. Houston wanted Gaines to continue his lawsuit until the state provided a truly "equal" law school for blacks. But the plaintiff decided to get on with his life. Armed with a master's degree in economics from the University of Michigan, Gaines moved to Chicago while the case was being litigated. The NAACP lost contact with him after the Supreme Court decision.

## Marshall Takes the Reins of the LDF

Houston returned to private practice in 1938 and Marshall took over his position as NAACP Special Counsel. The following year, the NAACP spun off its legal department into a separate nonprofit entity, the Legal Defense and Education Fund (LDF), that was not subject to taxes. In the meantime, Marshall and the LDF continued looking for legal cases to advance their cause. This was a difficult quest, however, for they knew that prospective plaintiffs had to have impeccable academic credentials, high moral character, and the fortitude and determination to risk potential persecution (black plaintiffs and their families in this era often endured harassment, threats of violence, and job losses when their roles became public). In the years of the Great Depression, few were ready to risk so much.

In 1939, however, another Missouri case came to the attention of Marshall and the LDF. A black woman named Lucille Bluford, the managing editor of the *Kansas City Call,* had applied to the graduate program in journalism at the University of Missouri. Based on her excellent undergraduate career at the University of Kansas, the University had accepted her application. When she arrived on campus to register for classes, however, administrators saw that she was African American and told her to leave.

## Open Racism on the Nation's Highest Court

When NAACP lawyer Charles Houston rose to make his oral arguments before the U.S. Supreme Court in the historic *Missouri ex rel. Gaines v. Canada* case of 1938, an incident occurred which had "special resonance" to Robert Carter, who later became an LDF attorney himself. "I was a law student at Howard at the time," he recalled in *The Nation* in 2004,

> and it was the first Supreme Court argument I had heard. At the hearing, when Houston rose to begin his argument Justice James McReynolds turned in his chair and kept his back to Houston throughout his presentation. In retrospect, it seems remarkable that no one witnessing this petty discourtesy from an official supposedly representing all Americans, whatever their race, color, or ethnicity, reacted with disapproval. Nor do I myself recall feeling any outrage at the time. In 1938 the second-class status of blacks was accepted by both blacks and whites as a fact of life.

Houston filed a suit on her behalf, but again the state of Missouri argued that the journalism school they were planning to create at Lincoln University would satisfy the "separate but equal" standard. The court accepted this reasoning at the first hearing of *Bluford v. Canada.* Houston appealed the decision on the grounds that Missouri's "solution" did not give Bluford immediate admission into a program. But it took two years for the case to make its way to the state supreme court, as the university—like many other defendants in university segregation cases—resorted to a variety of delaying tactics. By the time the state supreme court heard the case, Lincoln's journalism program was ready. As a result, the court upheld Bluford's exclusion from the University of Missouri.

### Expanding Equality in Higher Education

The LDF suffered other setbacks as well during the 1930s, including unfavorable rulings in lawsuits filed in Tennessee and Louisiana. Nonetheless, by the end of the decade Marshall saw that measurable progress was being made in the NAACP's mission to improve educational opportunities for

President Harry Truman, seen here with wife Margaret, forcefully promoted new civil rights for African Americans.

African Americans. Before the *Murray* case of 1935, not a single graduate or professional school in the seventeen states of the South and the border region allowed black students. By the time of the *Gaines* ruling in 1938, seven of these states offered scholarships to programs out of state, and four allowed limited attendance of African Americans to all-white programs.

Other states, seeing the Supreme Court's rulings, also began creating graduate programs at some of their all-black colleges. Many of these, however, were poorly funded and markedly inferior to the programs at "white only" state universities. The end of World War II, meanwhile, brought home thousands of African American military veterans who were eligible to receive free college educations through the GI Bill, a federal program that provided college tuition aid and other benefits to returning soldiers.

Another pivotal factor in the growing determination of civil rights advocates was the sympathetic attitude taken by the administration of President Harry S. Truman, who took the oath of office in April 1945 after President Franklin D. Roosevelt's death. In the first years of his presidency, Truman emerged as a powerful promoter of civil rights. In 1946 he established the Presidential Committee on Civil Rights. One year later, this body issued a report, *To Secure These Rights,* that condemned segregation in blistering terms. The report declared that segregation was not only unjust, it gave America's enemies fodder for propaganda—a great concern in the opening years of the Cold War (see Cold War Politics, p. 60). "The separate but equal doctrine has failed in three important respects," concluded the committee:

> First, it is inconsistent with the fundamental equalitarianism of the American way of life in that it marks groups with the brand of inferior status. Secondly, where it has been followed, the results have been separate and unequal facilities for minority peoples. Finally, it has kept people apart despite incontrovertible evidence that an environment favorable to civil rights is fostered whenever groups are permitted to live and work together. There is no adequate defense of segregation.

In 1948 Truman signed executive orders ending segregation in the military and mandating equal opportunity in federal employment. He also called for Congress to enact legislation against lynching, poll taxes, and segregation in interstate transportation, and he pushed for the creation of a permanent Civil Rights Commission. Under Truman, the government also began filing *amicus curiae* ("friend of the court") briefs supporting desegregation in segregation cases before the U.S. Supreme Court.

Taken together, these various developments convinced the NAACP and the LDF that the time was ripe to attack segregation directly. They wanted the Supreme Court to rule that segregation was inherently unequal.

## Testing the New Strategy

Marshall and the LDF launched their new strategy with *Sipuel v. Board of Regents of the University of Oklahoma.* In 1946 Ida Sipuel had applied to the University of Oklahoma Law School, but had been turned down solely because of her race. When the case came before the state supreme court, the

Leading attorneys for the NAACP's Legal Defense and Educational Fund included (from left to right): Louis L. Redding, Robert L. Carter, Oliver W. Hill, Thurgood Marshall, and Spottswood W. Robinson III.

justices ruled that the new all-black school the state was planning would satisfy legal precedent—and they further ruled that since Sipuel had not applied to this school, she lacked the standing to bring a lawsuit. Marshall appealed the verdict to the U.S. Supreme Court, although he did not think it would consider the case. Much to his surprise, the Supreme Court agreed to hear it.

In presenting the *Sipuel* case before the Supreme Court, Marshall rolled out a new weapon: convincing sociological evidence that segregation was harmful to African Americans. Although the Supreme Court did not comment specifically on this evidence in its 1948 decision, which favored Sipuel, it cited the *Gaines* decision in ruling that Oklahoma should provide Sipuel a law school education, and "provide it as soon as it does for applicants of any other group." The Court delivered the decision *per curiam* ("by the court"), meaning it felt the point of law was so clear it did not require a signed opinion. Oklahoma tried to get around the decision by hastily assembling a new law school, but in 1949 it admitted defeat. That year, Sipuel became the first black American to attend the University of Oklahoma. She received her law degree in 1951.

After the *Sipuel* decision, the University of Oklahoma began admitting African Americans to its graduate programs under "special circumstances." One of these individuals was George McLaurin, a 68-year-old teacher who had entered the university's doctoral program in education after a federal court injunction ordered his admission in 1948. The university complied with the injunction, but placed McLaurin in a special alcove outside the lecture classroom and segregated him at a separate table at the university's libraries and cafeterias. Many of McLaurin's fellow students protested his treatment, and McLaurin asked the NAACP to continue litigation. The case eventually wound it way to the U.S. Supreme Court.

Again, Marshall and his team prepared briefs (transcripts and documents given to the court before the case is argued orally) that included sociological evidence that segregation was psychologically damaging to African Americans. The U.S. government also weighed in, filing its own brief in support of the NAACP's position. When the proceedings moved to the oral presentation phase, LDF associate counsel Robert Carter took the lead in arguing McLaurin's case. After it was all over, McLaurin and the leadership of the NAACP and LDF waited anxiously for the Court's decision.

In June 1950 the U.S. Supreme Court announced a unanimous 9-0 decision in *McLaurin v. Oklahoma State Regents* in favor of the plaintiff. The justices dismissed the school's defense of classroom segregation, noting that McLaurin "is handicapped in his pursuit of effective graduate instruction. Such restrictions impair and inhibit his ability to study, to engage in discussions and exchange views with other students, and, in general, to learn his profession." Removing the restrictions "will not necessarily abate individual and group predilections, prejudices and choices," the court concluded. "But at the very least, the state will not be depriving appellant of the opportunity to secure acceptance by his fellow students on his own merits."

## Triumph in Texas

On the same day the Supreme Court announced its judgment in the *McLaurin* case, it also issued an opinion in another graduate case litigated by the Marshall and LDF. In 1946, Heman Sweatt had applied to the University of

George McLaurin was relegated to segregated seating at the University of Oklahoma until the U.S. Supreme Court forced the university to end segregation in its graduate programs.

Texas Law School, only to be denied admission because he was black. A state court ruled that Texas could establish a separate facility instead of desegregating, but the state's first attempt—two rooms, two part-time instructors, and no library—was found lacking. The state legislature approved funds to improve the school. The upgraded facility, which featured professors from the university's existing law school and a library of 10,000 volumes, met the state court's approval. The new all-black school had no law review or moot (practice) court, however, and only one-sixth as many law books as the university library.

When Marshall argued *Sweatt v. Painter* before the U.S. Supreme Court, he again filed various sociological briefs, including one expert's testimony that there was no difference in intellect between the races, and thus no basis to separate them. He urged the Court to overturn *Plessy's* standard of "separate but equal" because the standard of equality was impossible to achieve. Although the Supreme Court once again refused to address the constitutionality of *Plessy*, it did rule 9-0 in favor of Sweatt's admission to the University of Texas. Significantly, the court's decision cited intangibles in its findings of inequality for the first time:

> What is more important [than superior physical facilities], the University of Texas Law School possesses to a far greater degree those qualities which are incapable of objective measurement but which make for greatness in a law school. Such qualities, to name but a few, include reputation of the faculty, experience of the administration, position and influence of the alumni, standing in the community, traditions and prestige. It is difficult to believe that one who had a free choice between these law schools would consider the question close.

These 1950 U.S. Supreme Court rulings gave great comfort to the African American attorneys and activists across the country who were battling to end segregation. Granted, the Court had not explicitly tackled the legitimacy of the "separate but equal" doctrine in its rulings. But in the wake of its verdicts, Marshall and others believed that they could see the first cracks in the walls of segregation that had trapped so many generations of black Americans.

# Chapter Three

# THE JOURNEY TO THE SUPREME COURT

⊸꧁꧂⊶

This case may mean nothing [today], but in A.D. 2000 somebody will look back on the record and wonder why the South spent so much money in keeping rights from Negroes rather than granting them.

—Charles Houston, NAACP Special Counsel,
after losing a case seeking to desegregate the
University of Tennessee School of Pharmacy

W hen the U.S. Supreme Court began issuing orders to desegregate graduate programs across the country, Thurgood Marshall and his staff at the NAACP's Legal Defense and Education Fund (LDF) felt the time was right to attack segregation in primary and secondary schools. They decided to only take cases that would enable them to target the "separate but equal" doctrine enshrined in American law since the Supreme Court's 1896 *Plessy v. Ferguson* ruling.

This strategy had significant risks, however. If segregation was upheld as constitutional, it would be a demoralizing setback for African Americans everywhere. In addition, Marshall and his allies had grave concerns about their ability to find willing plaintiffs for primary and secondary school cases. After all, black families that consented to join this fight would be putting their children squarely in the midst of an effort that would enrage large numbers of white citizens, who continued to control the nation's political, social, and financial institutions.

But the LDF's victories before the Supreme Court in 1950 had roused the African American community. Black Americans exhibited a new willingness

A Southern schoolhouse for black children during the era of segregation.

to pursue their legal rights, and by 1952 the NAACP had successfully litigated 34 of 38 civil rights cases across the country on issues ranging from housing to voting rights. Moreover, black communities showed a particular determination to defend their children's right to the same educational opportunities as white children. Lawsuits filed on behalf of black students, parents, and communities sprouted all across the land, many of them championed by Marshall and the LDF. Five of these lawsuits eventually coalesced into the landmark Supreme Court case known as *Brown v. Board of Education of Topeka.*

## South Carolina: *Briggs v. Elliott*

Clarendon County in South Carolina was typical of many rural school districts in the Deep South: the population was 70 percent African American, but most school funding went toward white schools. In 1949 Clarendon County spent only $43 per year on each black student. More than four times that amount, $179 per year, was spent on each white student. White schools had drinking fountains, indoor toilets, cafeterias, libraries, gymnasiums, and laboratories. Black schools had open buckets of water with a shared dipper, outdoor privies, and no extra facilities beyond the main classroom. Black students even had to provide their own supplies, because the district paid for nothing besides teacher salaries. This inequality extended to public transportation to and from school as well. White students were driven to their schools on buses, but some black students had to walk as far as nine miles to attend class.

In the late 1940s a group of black parents and activists led by teacher and minister Joseph DeLaine asked the local NAACP to represent them in legal action against the school district. DeLaine and his allies aimed to file a lawsuit to force the district to provide truly equal facilities and services in keeping with the "separate but equal" doctrine of the land. The branch brought the case to the attention of Marshall, who had conflicting feelings about the case. He had hoped to begin pursuing primary school litigation in a border state, where white racism was not as pervasive and poisonous as it was across much of the South. But the determination of the Clarendon County parents deeply impressed him—and ultimately convinced him to take the case.

Twenty families eventually joined the suit, even though many faced retaliation from whites who held the reins of power in their community. Several parents were fired from their jobs, and others were prevented from obtaining credit at area stores or leasing the farming equipment they needed to bring in their crops. DeLaine himself endured a particularly harsh stream of violence and malice from the white community (see The Price of Seeking Justice, p. 38). Still, the plaintiffs persevered, and in 1950 the case known as *Briggs v. Elliott*, after lead plaintiff Harry Briggs and school trustee chairman Roderick W. Elliott, was filed.

Marshall initially intended to file the lawsuit in district court because the federal judge who would hear it, J. Waties Waring, was sympathetic to the civil rights cause. Waring, however, advised Marshall to refile the case in federal court and challenge South Carolina's segregation laws as unconstitutional. This shift in venue would bring the case before a special three-judge panel, and would give Marshall the option of appealing directly to the U.S. Supreme Court in the event of an unfavorable verdict (see The American Civil Court System, p. 44).

# The Price of Seeking Justice

Joseph DeLaine Sr., led the charge that made Clarendon County, South Carolina, one of the flashpoints in the battle to end segregation in America's schools. But he paid a steep price for his valiant leadership in the battle to give the county's black children a brighter future, as Richard Kluger observed in *Simple Justice,* a critically acclaimed account of the *Brown v. Board of Education* case:

> Before it was over, they fired him from the little school-house at which he had taught devotedly for ten years. And they fired his wife and two of his sisters and a niece. And they threatened him with bodily harm. And they sued him on trumped-up charges and convicted him in a kangaroo court and left him with a judgment that denied him credit from any bank. And they burned his house to the ground while the fire department stood around watching the flames consume the night. And they stoned the church at which he pastored. And fired shotguns at him out of the dark. But he was not Job, and so he fired back, and called the police, who did not come and kept not coming. Then he fled, driving north at eighty-five miles an hour over country roads, until he was across the state line. Soon after, they burned his church to the ground and charged him, for having shot back that night, with felonious assault with a deadly weapon, and so he became an official fugitive from justice.

DeLaine eventually reached New York, where state officials declared that they would not honor extradition requests from South Carolina. He spent the next two decades leading various churches around the state before retiring in 1970 and moving to Charlotte, North Carolina. He died in 1974.

In 2000—forty-five years after DeLaine was forced to flee the state of South Carolina—state authorities officially dropped all charges against DeLaine and cleared his name. "We believe at last some justice has been done in this case," said Joseph DeLaine Jr., one of DeLaine's three children. "It is unfortunate it did not occur before his death, which would have allowed him to come back to his home state where his heart and soul was."

Marshall followed Waring's suggestion. He recognized that he had little hope of success with the three-judge panel, which consisted of Waring, Judge George Timmerman, and lead Judge John Parker. Waring would be receptive to his arguments, but Timmerman was a known white supremacist and Parker's reputation for fairness did not compensate for his track record of skepticism toward civil rights. Ultimately, though, Marshall knew that destroying segregation hinged on getting the U.S. Supreme Court to disavow the "separate but equal" doctrine. And if the panel ruled against him, as he anticipated, he would have the opportunity to petition the Court to hear his appeal.

*"I believe the 'separate but equal' doctrine in education should be rejected, but I also believe its rejection must come from that [Supreme] Court."*

As the trial unfolded, Marshall called several expert witnesses to testify about the harmful effects of segregation on African Americans. One of these witnesses was noted psychologist Kenneth Clark (see Clark biography, p. 131), whose studies showed segregated black children suffered greatly from segregation (see "The Effects of Segregation," p. 177). In a surprise tactic, however, South Carolina's lawyers conceded that their all-black schools were unequal. Their argument focused instead on the millions of dollars the state had recently appropriated to equalize facilities. They contended that there was no need to desegregate Clarendon County's schools because the state was poised to spend the necessary funds to make them equal.

In a decision announced on June 21, 1951, the three-judge panel upheld the "separate but equal" doctrine by a 2-1 vote, even though it acknowledged that the facilities were patently unequal. "The court should not use its power to abolish segregation in a state where it is required by law if the equality demanded by the Constitution can be attained otherwise," Judge John Parker wrote in his majority decision.

Waring, however, delivered a scathing dissent: "We should be unwilling to straddle or avoid this issue [of separate but equal] and if the suggestion made by these defendants is to be adopted as the type of justice to be meted out by this Court, then I want no part of it." He added that the standards used to label students as "white" or "Negro" were "unreasonable, unscientific and based on unadulterated prejudice." Referring to the expert testimony, Waring concluded:

> It was clearly apparent, as it should be to any thoughtful person, irrespective of having such expert testimony, that segrega-

tion in education can never produce equality and that it is an evil that must be eradicated. This case presents the matter clearly for adjudication [verdict or settlement] and I am of the opinion that all of the legal guideposts, expert testimony, common sense and reason point unerringly to the conclusion that the system of segregation in education adopted and practiced in the State of South Carolina must go and must go now. *Segregation is per se inequality.*

The South Carolina court gave the defendants six months to improve facilities and then report back to the court, at which time the panel would rule on the county's compliance. Marshall appealed the decision to the U.S. Supreme Court as expected, but in January 1952 the Supreme Court decided to delay a decision on whether to consider *Briggs v. Elliott* until South Carolina's three-judge panel rendered a judgment on whether the Clarendon County School District took the necessary steps to establish separate but equal school systems. As expected, the three-judge panel upheld South Carolina's improvement, and Marshall brought the case back to the Supreme Court. The Court agreed to hear arguments in fall 1952—the same time it had agreed to consider a segregation case from the state of Kansas.

> *"Let the Supreme Court take the blame if it dares say to the entire world, 'Yes, democracy rests on a legalized caste system. Segregation of races is legal.' Make the Court choose."*

## Kansas: *Brown v. Board of Education of Topeka*

The next school case filed by the NAACP's LDF was in Kansas, considered a Northern state because it had never permitted slavery. School segregation in Kansas was not mandatory. State law made segregation optional in elementary schools within districts that had populations larger than 15,000 (such as the state capital of Topeka, which had 100,000 residents). All junior high and high schools in Kansas were integrated, as were elementary schools in small districts. Segregation permeated other aspects of life in Kansas, however. Many hotels, theaters, and restaurants were off-limits to African Americans, Topeka's elementary schools were segregated, and Topeka's public pool was only open to black residents one day per year.

Initially, most middle-class blacks were afraid to endanger their financial security or their comparatively peaceful relations with white Kansans by seeking school desegregation. By 1950, however, many in Topeka's African

American community had become so frustrated by the inferior transportation resources given to their children, and the condescending treatment they received from Topeka's school superintendent, that they decided to challenge the city's segregated school system in court. The local NAACP branch recruited several parents, and local attorneys John and Charles Scott—sons of Elisha Scott, the state's most prominent black attorney—drew up a lawsuit. One of the parents recruited was Oliver Brown, a veteran with a secure job whose daughter had to cross a busy train yard in order to get to her all-black school. His name led the list of plaintiffs in the suit filed on February 28, 1951, in a Kansas federal district court: *Brown v. Board of Education of Topeka.*

The Scott brothers worked closely with the LDF's Robert Carter in preparing their arguments. In June 1951 they presented their case. Because the teachers, facilities, and curricula in Topeka's black schools were virtually equal to those in the white schools, the case focused mainly on the long distances many of the plaintiffs had to travel to get to their all-black school, and on the testimony given by experts on the psychological impact of segregation. Carter found several Midwestern experts who attested that black children were equally capable of learning as white children and that segregation harmed the self-esteem of black children.

As the arguments wrapped up, it was clear that the three-judge panel led by Judge Walter Huxman was sympathetic to the plaintiffs' line of reasoning. The judges felt, however, that as long as the Supreme Court upheld *Plessy,* they did not have the authority to declare the city's racial segregation as unconstitutional. As a result, their verdict favored the school board. Nevertheless, they did include the following statement within their August 1951 judgment as a "Finding of Fact":

> Segregation of white and colored children in public schools has a detrimental effect upon the colored children. The impact is greater when it has the sanction of the law; for the policy of separating the races is usually interpreted as denoting the inferiority of the negro group. A sense of inferiority affects the motivation of the child to learn. Segregation with the sanction of law, therefore, has a tendency to restrain the educational and mental development of negro children and to deprive them of some of the benefits they would receive in a racial [sic] integrated school system.

Carter and the NAACP immediately appealed the decision to the U.S. Supreme Court, which agreed to hear the case—a development that Huxman welcomed. In writing the panel's opinion on the *Brown v. Board* case, he had framed the paradox of "separate but equal" in such a way that the Supreme Court would be hard-pressed to dodge the case. "I tried to wrap it up in such a way that they could not duck it," Huxman later acknowledged in Jack Greenberg's *Crusaders in the Courts.* "They had whittled away at it long enough."

## Delaware: *Gebhart v. Belton*

Another case, meanwhile, was making its way through the courts of Delaware. A small slaveholding state that sided with the Union during the Civil War, Delaware had a long history of racial discrimination. After the war, poll taxes were implemented to keep African Americans from voting, and segregated schools for black students were funded solely by black taxes, virtually ensuring inequality with white schools that enjoyed a much more affluent tax base. Although philanthropic donations from the DuPont family helped upgrade black schools in the 1920s, only one four-year high school for black students existed in the entire state in 1950 (in the city of Wilmington).

In the years following World War II, though, the environment began to change. In 1950 LDF lawyer Jack Greenberg and local attorney Louis Redding—the first African American to be admitted to the Delaware Bar—successfully sued to desegregate the University of Delaware's undergraduate program. This verdict was a historic milestone, for it marked the first time in U.S. history that an undergraduate university program was ordered to end segregationist practices. The state did not appeal the decision, and many businesses and facilities, particularly in Wilmington, began desegregating voluntarily. As a result, black parents began to see equal educational opportunities as a real possibility for their children. They turned to Louis Redding for help.

In early 1951 Redding took on two related segregation cases on behalf of black families. His clients in the first case (*Belton v. Gebhart*) were a group of parents from the Wilmington suburb of Claymont who filed suit against the state board of education (of which Gebhart was a member). To attend high school, their children faced nearly an hour's bus ride into the industrial section of Wilmington, where the all-black school was located. Moreover, this school had fewer teachers and fewer subjects available to study than at their hometown high school, which was reserved for white students. In the second

An African American drinking from a "colored" water cooler outside a streetcar terminal.

case, Redding represented Hockessin resident Sarah Bulah, a white woman whose attempts to secure bus transportation for her adopted black daughter had been rejected. Redding consented to represent Bulah when she agreed to adjust the suit to demand her daughter's admission to a white school. As with the first suit, Redding filed *Bulah v. Gebhart* in federal district court.

Redding had asked for a special three-judge panel to hear the cases, for like Marshall (in *Briggs v. Elliott*) and Clark (in *Brown v. Board of Education of Topeka*), he wanted to be able to appeal directly to the U.S. Supreme Court if he lost. The state of Delaware, though, successfully petitioned to have the case heard in a state court first, since it dealt with a state law.

In Delaware's court system, cases involving equity—both in business and in civil rights—are heard by the Court of Chancery. There are no juries; instead, trials are heard by judges called chancellors. In 1951 the court had a new chancellor named Collins Seitz. As a vice-chancellor, Seitz had ruled in Redding's favor in the University of Delaware desegregation case, so Redding

## The American Civil Court System

When legal disputes arise between two or more parties—whether individuals, groups, businesses, or governments—a civil court is the place where these disputes are resolved. Civil trials can be conducted by state courts, which are particular to each individual state, or federal courts, which oversee trials involving the U.S. government, federal laws, or the U.S. Constitution. A civil trial begins when the *plaintiff,* or alleged injured party, files a complaint in court and also serves his complaint to the *defendant,* the party that allegedly caused the injury. In seeking relief for his injury, the plaintiff may ask for monetary damages from the defendant or for a court order instructing the defendant to stop the harmful action or take actions that will address the plaintiff's injuries. In most of the desegregation cases that led up to the Supreme Court's 1954 *Brown v. Board of Education* decision, the plaintiffs were students or parents of students; the defendants were school districts, school officials, or states; and the relief sought was an order admitting the plaintiffs to the segregated school in question.

Both state and federal courts have a similar structure: cases are first heard in a district court, the lowest court available. If either party is unhappy with the judgment, an appeal may then be heard by a court of appeals, provided the higher court agrees there is reason to continue the case. In the federal court system, these appeals courts are also called appellate courts or circuit courts, as each of the 94 U.S. district courts belongs to one of twelve regional circuit courts of appeals. If a state appeals court judgment is unsatisfactory, the parties have the option of petitioning their state supreme court to hear the case. The court can either agree or decline to hear the case.

and Greenberg entered the courtroom guardedly optimistic. As the trial unfolded, they called a variety of witnesses to testify to the inequalities between the white school in Claymont and the black school in Wilmington. They also called sociological, educational, and psychological experts to the witness stand. This parade of experts, which included Kenneth Clark, presented strong evidence that segregation harmed African American children in

The U.S. Supreme Court , which consists of nine justices appointed to lifelong terms by the president, can hear appeals from individual state supreme courts, as well as appeals from federal circuit courts of appeals. The U.S. Supreme Court usually only takes cases that address important questions about the Constitution or federal law. As the highest court in the country, a U.S. Supreme Court decision cannot be appealed—only another Supreme Court decision can change the justices' interpretation of the law.

Between the 1930s and 1950s, when the NAACP litigated many civil rights cases, it had a choice between filing cases in state courts or in federal courts. Many of the early desegregation cases were filed in state courts, including the NAACP's 1935 Maryland Supreme Court victory in *Pearson v. Murray.* If the NAACP filed a school case in federal court, there was always the chance a judge would refuse to hear the case and send it back to the state court. Because many state judges were popularly elected, however, there was little chance of getting favorable judgments when cases were tried in state courts of the Deep South.

After World War II, the NAACP began filing most of its cases challenging the constitutionality of segregation laws in federal court. The organization's lawyers viewed federal judges as more likely to find in their favor, and they knew that any federal lawsuit challenging a state statute as unconstitutional went before a special three-judge district court panel. The decisions handed down by those three-judge panels could be appealed directly to the U.S. Supreme Court, thereby skipping a stage in the usual appeals process. This wrinkle led to the Supreme Court agreeing to hear five separate cases—four of which were appeals of rulings by three-judge district court panels—in crafting its pivotal *Brown* decision.

a host of ways. For its part, the state of Delaware had little to say in its defense except that the state legislature had approved equal funding for schools earlier that year.

Five months after hearing closing arguments, Seitz released his opinion in April 1952. Seitz declared that all the evidence presented at trial led him to believe that segregation was inherently unequal. But he added that he could not ignore the Supreme Court precedent of *Plessy:* "I believe the 'separate but equal' doctrine in education should be rejected, but I also believe its rejection must come from that [Supreme] Court." He limited his findings to the fact that the black and white schools in question were unequal, but he offered a different remedy than the other courts:

> It seems to me that when a plaintiff shows to the satisfaction of a court that there is an existing and continuing violation of the "separate but equal" doctrine, he is entitled to have made available to him the State facilities which have been shown to be superior. To do otherwise is to say to such a plaintiff, "Yes, your Constitutional rights are being invaded, but be patient, we will see whether in time they are still being violated." If, as the Supreme Court has said [in *Sweatt*], this right is personal, such a plaintiff is entitled to relief immediately, in the only way it is available, namely, by admission to the school with the superior facilities. To postpone such relief is to deny relief, in whole or in part, and to say that the protective provisions of the Constitution offer no immediate protection.

Seitz ordered the immediate desegregation of the schools in question, adding that the state could revisit the issue once it felt it could provide separate but equal schools. After the Delaware Supreme Court upheld the decision (now known as *Gebhart v. Belton,* because the original defendants were appealing their loss), the state chose to appeal the case to the U.S. Supreme Court. The Supreme Court agreed to hear it, adding it to its growing pile of segregation-related cases.

## Virginia: *Davis v. County School Board of Prince Edward County*

The fourth school segregation case that the U.S. Supreme Court ultimately agreed to rule on came out of Virginia. This case was initiated by a group of African American students at all-black Moton High School in Prince Edward County. Like many rural districts in the South, Prince Edward County provided much less financial support to its black students than to its white students. The sole high school for African Americans in the Moton area had not been built until 1939, and it had no gymnasium, cafeteria, science equip-

Black schoolchildren received a mere fraction of the resources routinely provided to white children during the era of segregation.

ment, or locker rooms. By the late 1940s it was so overcrowded that many classes were held in leaky tarpaper outbuildings with only a stove for heat.

When the district kept delaying efforts to build a new black high school, a group of black Moton High School students led by sixteen-year-old Barbara Johns went on strike in April 1951. The students also wrote to the NAACP special counsels for their region, Oliver Hill and Spottswood Robinson III, asking for their assistance in pressing their case in the Virginia courts. Hill and Robinson knew litigating a desegregation case in rural Virginia would be extremely difficult, but the determination of the students impressed them so much they agreed to take the case—as long as the students demanded access to the white schools, not just a new segregated school.

The students agreed, and in May 1951 Robinson filed suit in federal court on behalf of 117 Moton High School students. The first plaintiff on the list was Dorothy Davis, so the case became known as *Davis v. County School Board of Prince Edward County.* The state of Virginia recognized that the legal action posed a major threat to its segregationist social structure, so it threw all its resources into defending the suit. State Attorney General Lindsay Almond, for example, worked closely with the school board's lawyer, T. Justin Moore, throughout the court proceedings. The state also "scouted" the *Briggs* trial in South Carolina and came away convinced that the state would need its own sociological experts to counter those put on the witness stand by the NAACP. Virginia's legal defense knew that it could not claim that the state's white and black schools were equal, but it hoped to show that a recent grant from the governor would soon enable it to upgrade black facilities to the point that they were equal to white schools.

When the special three-judge district court panel convened in February 1952, it heard dramatically different expert testimony from the two sides. Kenneth Clark and other sociological experts called by the plaintiffs described segregation as deeply harmful to African Americans' self-esteem. But the defense's star witness, psychologist Henry Garrett of Columbia University, argued that there was no clear evidence that segregation was psychologically harmful—and he further asserted that studies to the contrary had been framed to create those results. In closing arguments, meanwhile, Almond claimed that the people of Virginia would rather close down their public schools than desegregate them.

"There was never any doubt about the outcome of the trial," Oliver Hill said later. "We were trying to build a record for the Supreme Court." On March 7, 1952, the three-judge panel—all Virginia natives—returned a unanimous verdict in favor of the defendants. Citing statistics of black teacher employment and recent expenditures on facilities for African Americans, Judge Albert V. Bryan's opinion stated that "maintenance of the segregated systems in Virginia has not been social despotism." In fact, he declared that "whatever its demerits in theory, in practice [segregation] has begotten greater opportunities for the Negro." He added that segregation had "for generations been a part of the mores of [Virginia's] people ...[with] no hurt or harm to either race."

The panel did order the state to continue its equalization efforts "with diligence and dispatch," but added that a deadline for equalization was unnecessary because "an injunction could accomplish no more" than the state was already doing. The verdict was just what Robinson and the NAACP expected, so they immediately appealed the decision to the U.S. Supreme Court. The Court agreed to add the *Davis* case to the other school segregation cases crowding its docket.

### Washington, D.C.: *Bolling v. Sharpe*

The final case heard as part of the *Brown* argument came from Washington, D.C. In some respects, the nation's capital was one of the best cities in the country for African Americans. Thousands of black workers had secure jobs with the federal government, and the city supported a thriving black middle class made up of doctors, lawyers, teachers, and other highly educated professionals. The capital was also home to Howard University, the nation's largest black university. As elsewhere, though, daily life provided black residents with grim reminders of their inferior social and economic status. Housing was segregated and in short supply for African Amer-

NAACP icon Charles H. Houston led the legal battle against school segregation in Washington, D.C., in the late 1940s.

icans; public parks, restaurants, and theaters were segregated or even off-limits; and segregated black schools were overcrowded and underfunded, even as white public schools struggled to fill their classrooms (many wealthy white families in the region sent their children to private schools).

By the late 1940s, a steady influx of African Americans seeking work in the nation's capital forced administrators to stretch already meager resources for black students even further. The situation eventually became so bad that a group of parents organized a strike to protest the conditions in late 1947.

Their actions came to the attention of Charles Houston, who had been practicing privately in Washington after leaving his position at the NAACP. When the parents, led by barber Gardner Bishop, asked for his help, Houston agreed to file a series of lawsuits on their behalf asking for equalization of various segregated schools in the District of Columbia. Houston worked closely with Bishop to gather information to prove inequities, and through petitions, lawsuits, and public education they began making progress.

49

## "Young People Today Cannot Imagine What Segregation was Like"

Today, more than a half-century after the Supreme Court issued its historic *Brown v. Board of Education* judgment destroying the legal underpinnings of segregation, many African Americans who lived through that turbulent era assert that today's young people have no conception of what it was like to endure that level of bigotry on a daily basis. Civil rights leader Julian Bond, who has also served since 1998 as the chairman of the board of directors of the NAACP, commented in *The Unfinished Agenda of Brown v. Board of Education* that:

> Young people today cannot imagine what segregation was like. They have no idea. Parents don't talk to them about it because they want to protect children from it. Some young people say they would not sit at the back of the bus, that they would have demanded their seat. But they don't understand that they would have been killed, too. It's so hard to convince young people of what that life was like. I have yet to find an effective way to tell my students, black and white, what segregation was really like. I can give examples. I can talk about how silly it was that black and white people didn't even play checkers together. I can talk about the difference between public school expenditures for black and white kids, give the facts and figures, but I can't show them what it was really like. I can't make the white kids stand in the back, facing the back of the room, or tell every student who comes in that they have to walk in a particular door based on their race. I can't beat the ones who decide they won't walk through a particular door to show them that is what it really was like. It's hard to make them understand that experience now.

In late 1949, however, Houston fell gravely ill. On his deathbed he told Bishop to ask his colleague, Howard law professor James Nabrit, Jr., to take over the case. When Bishop contacted him, Nabrit refused to continue the equalization strategy pursued by Houston. He pointed out that since the District of Columbia was not a state, it was not bound by the Fourteenth Amendment's "equal protection of the laws" clause, which contained language explicitly requiring state compliance. But Nabrit stated that he would gladly take on a case challenging segregation itself. Bishop subsequently organized a group of parents as plaintiffs, and in 1951 Nabrit filed suit in U.S. District Court (the case was filed in federal rather than state court because it dealt with the District of Columbia, which is administered by the federal government). The case became known as *Bolling v. Sharpe,* named after one of the eleven young plaintiffs and the president of the District of Columbia's Board of Education.

A rundown theater in Leland, Mississippi—the only one available to the community's black residents.

As the trial got underway, Nabrit argued that the government had shown no reason to segregate students. He further contended that such segregation deprived black children of their rights to an equal education guaranteed under the Fifth Amendment's "due process" clause. The district court judge did not accept the argument, however, and ruled against Nabrit and the plaintiffs in April 1952.

While preparing his appeal, Nabrit spoke at an April 1952 Howard University conference on the ongoing efforts to end segregation through litigation. He noted that others had counseled caution, issuing warnings that legal success was unlikely because of strong opposition in the South and uncertainty about the Supreme Court's willingness to confront the issue. Nabrit, though, declared that the quest for equality would never be won if pro-integration forces never took the field of battle. "The Supreme Court will have to worry over community attitudes. Let us [black Americans] worry over the problem of pressing for our civil rights," he said. "Let the Supreme Court take the blame if it dares say to the entire world, '*Yes,* democracy rests on a legalized caste system. Segregation of races is legal.' Make the Court choose."

## On the Eve of Battle

By the end of that year, Nabrit's goal was in sight. After years of avoiding the issue, the Court seemed poised to face segregation squarely once again. In

addition to the four separate segregation cases that Court had already accepted from South Carolina, Kansas, Virginia, and Delaware, Chief Justice Frederick M. Vinson invited Nabrit to add *Bolling v. Sharpe* to the mix. Nabrit quickly accepted, bringing the number of segregation cases bundled together for
the Court's consideration up to five.

The Court scheduled opening arguments on the five segregation cases
for December 1952 in an effort to keep the issue from influencing the 1952
presidential election. These segregation cases came to be known collectively
as *Brown v. Board of Education,* after the Kansas case, because *Brown* was the
first school segregation case that the Supreme Court had agreed to hear
(South Carolina's *Briggs v. Elliott* case would have been first had it not been
remanded back to the South Carolina courts for several months). As a result,
*Brown v. Board of Education* became the shorthand term used by interested
parties of every race and political persuasion to refer to the five momentous
cases making their way to the storied halls of the Supreme Court.

# Chapter Four

# THE ARGUMENTS
# AND THE DECISION

You either have liberty or you do not. When liberty is interfered with by the state, it has to be justified, and you cannot
justify it by saying that we only took a little liberty. You justify it by the reasonableness of the taking. We submit that in
this case, in the heart of the nation's capital, in the capital of
democracy, in the capital of the free world, there is no place
for a segregated school system. This country cannot afford it,
and the Constitution does not permit it, and the statutes of
Congress do not authorize it.

—NAACP Attorney James Nabrit
to the U.S. Supreme Court, 1952

After accepting the five segregation cases collectively known as *Brown v.
Board of Education,* the U.S. Supreme Court announced that it would
open proceedings on the cases on December 9, 1952. Legal teams on
both sides of the issue feverishly prepared for the upcoming clash, preparing
voluminous written briefs and practicing their oral presentations. In the
meantime, Americans across the country—both ardent supporters of segregation and bitter critics of the practice—anxiously braced themselves for the
legal showdown.

The legal team assembled by the pro-segregation forces was spearheaded
by former U.S. Solicitor General and 1924 Democratic presidential candidate
John W. Davis (see Davis biography, p. 137). An eloquent, hard-working
lawyer, Davis had argued 67 cases for the government before the Supreme
Court during his tenure as U.S. Solicitor General from 1913 to 1918, winning

48 of them. Over his lifetime, the 79-year-old Davis had participated—either in preparing briefs or in conducting arguments—in more than 250 cases before the nation's highest court. Although Davis was practicing corporate law in New York City in 1952, he took a leave of absence to donate his services to the case. He was joined by a legion of high-priced attorneys hired by the Southern states and school boards to defend their segregationist practices.

The NAACP's Legal Defense and Education Fund (LDF) team was not as experienced or well-known as Davis and his allies. But the LDF lawyers had focused their entire careers on civil rights law, and they had developed an impressive stable of social scientists and legal experts to bolster their case. In addition, the lame-duck Truman administration had contributed a brief in *Brown v. Board of Education* urging the Court to overturn segregation (see The U.S. Government's *Amicus Curiae* Brief, p. 187). These factors—combined with deep convictions about the moral rightness of its cause—made the LDF team a formidable force in its own right.

## The Arguments of 1952

Oral arguments before the Supreme Court are unlike those in a regular trial. Since the Supreme Court justices have already familiarized themselves with the legal details via trial transcripts and written briefs submitted by the defendants and the plaintiffs, each side receives only a limited amount of time—less than an hour—to emphasize the main points of their position. During their oral presentations, attorneys frequently are forced to respond to pointed questions from the bench. The justices use this power to explore legal issues that trouble them—or sometimes to signal their feelings to their colleagues on the Court.

> *Pro-segregation forces were led by John W. Davis, a former U.S. Solicitor General and 1924 Democratic presidential candidate.*

The Supreme Court began the proceedings by hearing arguments regarding the *Brown v. Board of Education* case from Kansas. The LDF's Robert Carter opened by stating that segregation was inherently unequal and that the Court's early decisions in *Sweatt* and *McLaurin*—that equality of education could not be judged merely on equality of physical facilities—should apply to public schools as well as universities. In response, Kansas Assistant Attorney General Paul Wilson insisted that the Kansas statutes in question were not unconstitutional because *Plessy v.*

John W. Davis (left) and Thurgood Marshall (right) represented opposing sides in a South Carolina case that was included in the *Brown v. Board* decision.

*Ferguson* remained the law of the land. In his rebuttal, Carter reiterated his belief that segregation was an arbitrary government classification, and thus unconstitutional.

The Court then moved on to hear oral arguments in the *Briggs v. Elliott* case from South Carolina. This phase had been highly anticipated by legal scholars and Court watchers for it featured the most prominent attorneys from each side, Thurgood Marshall and John W. Davis. Marshall opened by emphasizing that the state of South Carolina had not challenged any of the sociological evidence alleging segregation's psychological damage to black children. He went on to claim that earlier Court decisions, or precedents, striking down racial restrictions on voting and property rights were just as important as the precedent of *Plessy*. He concluded by noting that he was not asking the Court to force the plaintiffs to be admitted into a particular school, but rather to declare segregation unconstitutional and give local districts time to comply in good faith.

Davis countered by listing the numerous precedents—including *Plessy*—which supported the segregationist position, and he insisted that South Carolina was in the process of equalizing funding and other resources for its black and white schools. Finally, he argued that even if the LDF's sociological evidence was valid, it had no bearing on constitutional matters. In his rebuttal, however, Marshall highlighted a fact Davis had left unchallenged: "For some reason, which is still unexplained, Negroes are taken out of the mainstream of American life in these states. There is nothing involved in this case other than race and color."

> *"For some reason, which is still unexplained, Negroes are taken out of the mainstream of American life in these [Southern] states,"* observed LDF attorney Thurgood Marshall. *"There is nothing involved in this case other than race and color."*

Virginia's *Davis v. County School Board of Prince Edward County* case followed next. During his oral presentation, LDF attorney Spottswood Robinson noted the severe inequality between the segregated schools in question and emphasized the plaintiffs' right to a "personal and present" remedy. He also cited the ruling of Delaware Judge Collins Seitz, who had ordered immediate desegregation of the state's schools, as a model for the Court to consider in its deliberations. When his turn came, school board attorney T. Justin Moore insisted that segregation in Virginia was based on tradition, not racism. He also reminded the Court that social scientists consulted by his legal staff believed that segregation was not harmful to black children or communities. Finally, he suggested that the Fourteenth Amendment was not intended to apply to local matters such as schools—a position Robinson ably challenged in his rebuttal.

The final two cases mostly underscored issues and arguments already presented to the court in the first three cases. The *Bolling v. Sharpe* case, argued by George E. C. Hayes and James Nabrit for the LDF, focused primarily on Congress's historical intent in establishing segregated schools in the District of Columbia and the LDF's contention that the Fifth Amendment's due process clause made segregation unconstitutional. (Because the case came from the District of Columbia, Hayes and Nabrit could not use the "equal protection" argument of the Fourteenth Amendment, which applies only to states.)

Opposing attorney Milton Korman, the District of Columbia corporate counsel, also explored the issue of historical intent but undermined his arguments—and raised more than a few eyebrows—when he quoted the infamous *Dred Scott* case of 1857, in which the Supreme Court held that slaves were property with no rights. In the Delaware *Gebhart* cases, Delaware Attorney General H. Albert Young argued that Seitz's 1952 order requiring immediate integration had been rendered before the state was given reasonable time to "equalize" schools. Arguing for the plaintiffs, Jack Greenberg and Louis Redding countered that the black students in question deserved immediate relief from the patently "unequal" resources and facilities they had been given.

## The Supreme Court Gets a New Chief Justice

The oral arguments in the *Brown* case left the Supreme Court little choice but to confront the constitutionality of the "separate but equal" principle. In their initial private discussions, the nine justices of the Supreme Court were divided on the issue. Four of them—Hugo L. Black, William O. Douglas, Harold H. Burton, and Sherman Minton—indicated they were inclined to overturn *Plessy*, while Justice Stanley F. Reed was likely to uphold it. Chief Justice Fred M. Vinson and Justice Tom Clark were so concerned about how the Court could enforce a ruling overturning segregation that they were leaning toward upholding *Plessy* rather than taking action. Justice Robert H. Jackson thought there was no reason of precedent to overturn *Plessy* but indicated a willingness to go along if the Court held that it had been wrongly decided.

The ninth justice, Felix Frankfurter, was troubled by many of these issues. Paramount in his mind, however, was his certainty that if the Court was going to hold segregation unconstitutional, it needed to do so unanimously if the country was to accept the ruling. Recognizing that there was no consensus among the justices, he suggested that the case be reargued in the fall 1953 term with a focus on five specific issues: 1) Was there any evidence the creators of the Fourteenth Amendment considered its effect on segregated education? 2) If not, did they consider whether segregation could be abolished by future courts or Congresses under the Amendment? 3) Is it within the power of the Fourteenth Amendment to abolish segregation in public schools? 4) Assuming it is abolished, must desegregation happen immediate-

In 1953 Earl Warren was chosen by Eisenhower to lead the U.S. Supreme Court.

ly or can the Court permit gradual adjustment? 5) If the court does approve desegregation, should it issue decrees, appoint a supervisory power, or remand the matter to lower courts? His colleagues agreed to Frankfurter's proposal, and on June 8, 1953, the Court announced its decision to reargue the case in six months.

The delay came as an unwelcome development to President Dwight Eisenhower (see Eisenhower biography, p. 142), the Republican war hero who had succeeded Truman in January 1953. Because the Eisenhower administration would have the job of enforcing the *Brown* decision, the Supreme Court invited it to submit a new brief (Eisenhower was only president-elect when *Brown v. Board* was first heard in December 1952) and allotted time for the administration to participate in the upcoming oral arguments.

Eisenhower, however, was not enthused about stepping into such a controversial issue. Although the Republicans had made civil rights part of their platform in the 1952 campaign, they had just won the White House and both houses of Congress for the first time in over twenty years. Eisenhower did not want to expend political capital on an issue he felt should be addressed by Congress, not the Supreme Court. Nevertheless, the administration felt compelled to comply with the Court's request for participation. Attorney General Herbert Brownell stepped in to supervise the brief's preparation by members of the Solicitor General's office. While the brief was exhaustive—more than 600 pages—it was not nearly as forthright as the Truman administration's brief had been in saying segregation should be overturned.

Still, Eisenhower had a decisive impact on the ultimate outcome of *Brown v. Board of Education.* On September 8, 1953, Chief Justice Vinson died of a heart attack at the age of 63. This was a momentous event for a couple of different reasons. First, in the weeks prior to his death Vinson had indicated that he was leaning toward upholding segregation as constitutional. His demise, then, deprived of the segregationists of an all-important vote for their side. In addition, the Court had become intensely fractious and divisive during his tenure as chief justice, with relations between several justices deteriorating badly. Vinson's death gave the president an opportunity to reverse the Court's slide into internal acrimony.

After careful consideration, Eisenhower chose Earl Warren, the popular Republican governor of California, to take Vinson's place (see Warren biography, p. 164). A former district attorney and state attorney general, Warren was known as a fair and steady politician. Although he had never served as a judge, he proved to be an inspired choice. His political skills and capacity for consensus building proved invaluable in the months to come.

## The Reargument of 1953

The two sides came before the Court again in December 1953 after six months of exhaustive research and preparation. The crucial issue in the reargument was the history of the Fourteenth Amendment and the intent of its creators. The LDF team acknowledged that the same Congress that had drafted the Fourteenth Amendment had also created the segregated school system in Washington, D.C. This fact had been repeatedly cited by segregationists as evidence that Congress felt that separate but equal school systems could be achieved. But the LDF emphasized that there was little evidence that the amendment's framers had even considered its effect on education, since public education was not widespread at the time. Instead, the LDF attorneys insisted that the framers of the Fourteenth Amendment intended it as a vehicle to ensure equal rights in myriad aspects of American life—including public education. The lawyers for the pro-segregation forces responded by contending that the Fourteenth Amendment had a narrow focus that covered only those rights articulated in the Civil Rights Act of 1866. This act, they pointed out, did not mention attendance at public schools.

In the reargument, the *Briggs* and *Davis* cases from South Carolina and Virginia were combined because of their similarities. As proceedings began, they were argued first, with Spottswood Robinson leading things off for the LDF. He forcefully argued that the purpose of the Fourteenth Amendment was to prevent states from using the law to create "castes," and he characterized segregated education statutes as deplorable examples of such caste systems. Thurgood Marshall spoke next, sparring with the justices on the meaning of previous Court decisions and the extent of the Court's power to strike down segregation.

## Cold War Politics

In 1952, when *Brown v. Board of Education* first came before the Supreme Court, the United States was embroiled in an ideological conflict with the Soviet Union known as the Cold War. The two nations had been allies in World War II, when both fought against Nazi Germany and the Axis Powers. But in the years following World War II, when the two nations became universally recognized as the planet's "superpowers," diplomatic relations deteriorated quickly.

Many people in the United States feared that the Soviet Union and its allies were determined to force their Communist ideology on the rest of the world. Leaders of the Soviet Union, meanwhile, were deeply suspicious of the United States and dismissive of its governing principles and ideology. The ensuing Cold War—defined not by open warfare, but by escalating hostilities between the two nations and the division of the major world governments into pro-U.S. and pro-Soviet blocs—led the U.S. government to place an increased emphasis on national defense. U.S. leaders promoted the development of weapons and technology in hopes that the country would achieve a decisive military advantage over its Communist rival.

In the 1950s newly independent countries of Asia and Africa became the focus of American efforts to promote Western-style democratic governments. The Soviets made similar efforts to convert countries to Communist-style rule, and propaganda and financial assistance came from both sides. The Communists ruled with an iron hand, but they promised equal access to jobs, health care, and material goods to everyone in the system. The United States, meanwhile, promised freedom and equality to potential allies. These promises, however, were questioned by skeptics who could not help but notice that the United States treated an entire race within its borders as second-class citizens. As the Cold War deepened and intensified, addressing that paradox became a matter of growing international importance for the United States.

John W. Davis then spoke on behalf of the defendants. He argued that the framers of the Fourteenth Amendment had no objection to segregated schools. He further asserted that states capable of providing equal education within a segregated school system were in full compliance with the "equal protection" clause. The state "is convinced that the happiness, the progress, and the welfare of these children is best promoted in segregated schools," Davis said. "Here is equal protection, not promised, not prophesied, but present. Shall it be thrown away on some fancied question of racial prestige?" After Davis concluded his presentation, T. Justin Moore and Virginia Attorney General J. Lindsay Almond offered additional defenses of segregation. They insisted that there was no prejudice driving the imposition of segregation, and that segregated schools worked to the benefit of both races. Finally, they flatly warned that court-ordered desegregation would cause considerable social unrest in the South.

Marshall responded with a clear and concise rebuttal. "As Mr. Davis said yesterday, the only thing the Negroes are trying to get is prestige," he observed. "Exactly correct. Ever since the Emancipation Proclamation, the Negro has been trying to get what was recognized in *Strauder v. West Virginia* [an 1880 decision against exclusion of blacks from juries], which is the same status as anybody else regardless of race." Marshall went on to decry school segregation laws as Black Codes with no justification behind them besides feelings of white supremacy. He noted that children of both races often play together without trouble; why, then, should educating them together be more problematic? He finished with an impassioned plea:

> The only way that this Court can decide this case in opposition to our position … is to find that for some reason Negroes are inferior to all other human beings…. Now is the time, we submit, that this Court should make it clear that that is not what our Constitution stands for.

After Marshall finished, Assistant Attorney General J. Lee Rankin presented the Eisenhower administration's stance on the case. Since the Eisenhower administration's 1953 brief was less forthright in declaring segregation unacceptable than the 1952 brief submitted by the outgoing Truman administration, the Court pointedly asked him for a clear statement about the government's position. "It is the position of the Department of Justice that segregation in public schools cannot be maintained," he responded. The justices also questioned him about how the Court should enforce desegregation, if that was its ultimate decision. Rankin outlined a gradual procedure in which desegregation would be supervised by district courts "according to criteria presented and set out by this Court." According to Rankin's outline, school districts would have a year to create desegregation plans that would be executed "with all deliberate speed."

The Court then moved on to the three remaining cases included under the *Brown v. Board of Education* banner. Arguments in these cases covered by now familiar territory, but they were punctuated by a number of powerful statements about the corrosive impact of segregation and the need for the United States to begin living up to its stated ideals of equality. LDF attorney James Nabrit, for example, made effective reference to a famous 1945 novel that had satirized Communist Russia:

> America is a great country in which we can come before the Court and express to the Court the great concern which we have, where our great government is dealing with us, and we are not in the position that the animals were in George Orwell's satirical novel *Animal Farm,* where after the revolution the dictatorship was set up and the sign set up there that all animals were equal, was changed to read "but some are more equal than others."
>
> Our Constitution has no provision across it that all men are equal but that white men are more equal than others.
>
> Under this statute and under this country, under this Constitution, and under the protection of this Court, we believe that we, too, are equal.

## The Decision

When the Court met to discuss the *Brown* case in December 1953, it was led by a man who had no doubt what the court's decision should be: "On the merits, the natural, the logical, and practically the only way the case could be decided was clear," recalled Warren in Richard Kluger's *Simple Justice.* "The question was *how* the decision was to be reached."

In early discussions, most of the justices seemed willing to hold segregation unconstitutional provided the Court permitted a gradual transition to desegregated schools. Douglas, Black, Burton, and Minton had not changed their minds, and Warren made a majority of five. Frankfurter had overcome

The members of the U.S. Supreme Court that ultimately delivered the momentous *Brown v. Board* decision. Seated from left to right: Felix Frankfurter, Hugo Black, Earl Warren, Stanley Reed, William O. Douglas. Standing from left to right: Tom C. Clark, Robert H. Jackson, Harold Burton, and Sherman Minton.

his reservations about the court "making policy" and was ready to overturn *Plessy* as well. And Clark was willing to join the majority as long as the South was given some flexibility in implementing desegregation.

Two of the justices, however, were reluctant to strike down *Plessy v. Ferguson* and its segregationist doctrine. Jackson did not believe that the intent of the framers of the Fourteenth Amendment was to "require full and equal racial partnership in all matters within the reach of the law." He expressed doubts about how the Court could interpret the Constitution to justify declaring segregation unconstitutional. But he was finally convinced that evolving public opinion regarding African Americans, as well as the changing role of public education, made it necessary for the Court to change the constitutional doctrine of *Plessy*. He then consented to sign on to Warren's straightforward opinion and forgo writing a concurrent opinion that might well have included statements of doubt about the constitutionality of overturning *Plessy*.

Jackson's change of heart left Justice Stanley Reed as the sole justice who remained convinced that "separate but equal" was theoretically achievable, and thus constitutional. His position was vexing to Warren, who wanted a unanimous decision ending school segregation. In addition, Warren faced the difficult task of reconciling widely different proposals from the various justices for implementing desegregation.

Again, it was Frankfurter who pointed out a potential compromise. In January 1954 he circulated a memo among his colleagues suggesting that the Court separate the statement of rights—that segregation took away the rights of African Americans—from a statement of remedy—how segregation should be dismantled. Warren began crafting a straightforward opinion dealing solely with the statement of rights, bringing Jackson on board.

During this period, Warren also convinced Reed that it would be in the best interests of the country if there was a unanimous decision, since a dissent from a Southern judge could encourage resistance in the South. Reed put aside his misgivings and agreed. Frankfurter was so relieved by Reed's decision that he later wrote to him: "As a citizen of the Republic, even more than as a colleague, I feel deep gratitude for your share in what I believe to be a great good for our nation."

On May 17, 1954, the Court announced its decision (see The U.S. Supreme Court's *Brown v. Board* Decision, p. 193). By a 9-0 count, the justices declared that "in the field of public education the doctrine of 'separate but equal' has no place." Regarding the historical intent of the Fourteenth Amendment, Warren's accompanying opinion was brief and to the point:

> In approaching this problem, we cannot turn the clock back to 1868 when the Amendment was adopted, or even to 1896 when *Plessy v. Ferguson* was written. We must consider public

education in the light of its full development and its present place in American life throughout the Nation. Only in this way can it be determined if segregation in public schools deprives these plaintiffs of the equal protection of the laws.

In exploring this issue, Warren cited the Court's previous opinions in *Sweatt* and *McLaurin,* that education included "intangible considerations"; he then quoted sociological testimony from the first *Brown* trial that "segregation of white and colored children in public schools has a detrimental effect upon the colored children." As a result, he wrote, students in segregated schools are "deprived of the equal protection of the laws guaranteed by the Fourteenth Amendment." (In his companion opinion in *Bolling v. Sharpe,* Warren also cited "violation of the Due Process Clause" of the Fifth Amendment as a factor in ordering desegregation of the nation's schools.)

NAACP attorneys George E. C. Hayes (left), Thurgood Marshall (center), and James M. Nabrit (right) celebrate after hearing the Supreme Court issued its historic ruling that segregation is unconstitutional.

The Court's announcement that "segregation is a denial of the equal protection of the laws," however, did not include a remedy for the plaintiffs. Instead, Warren and his cohorts called for the defendants and plaintiffs to prepare another round of legal arguments to help the Court decide how to dismantle the segregated system that had held sway across the American South for the previous half-century.

# Chapter Five

# IMPLEMENTATION "WITH ALL DELIBERATE SPEED"

⟞⟝

I think that nothing would be worse than for this Court ...to make an abstract declaration that segregation is bad and then have it evaded by tricks.

—Supreme Court Justice Felix T. Frankfurter, during the 1952 argument of *Brown v. Board of Education*

The Supreme Court scheduled arguments about how desegregation should be implemented in the fall of 1954. As the two sides prepared for their third bout before the Court, the legal landscape was once again altered by the death of a Supreme Court justice. Justice Robert H. Jackson died in October of that year, creating a vacancy on the Court bench and pushing the resumption of the legal struggle over segregation back to the spring of 1955. Eisenhower nominated John Marshall Harlan, whose grandfather and namesake had written the powerful dissent against segregation in *Plessy v. Ferguson,* to take Jackson's place. Southern senators delayed his confirmation for a time, but Harlan was approved to sit on the Court by the time arguments on the issue of remedy began in April 1955.

As the proceedings began, the NAACP staunchly maintained that districts should be permitted no more than one year to arrange for desegregation; any further delay, they claimed, would constitute an unacceptable abridgement of the rights of the plaintiffs. In addition, Marshall and his allies asserted that delays of more than one year would be attributable to racism—not administrative challenges associated with desegregation.

Speaking on behalf of the federal government, Solicitor General Simon Sobeloff suggested that school boards be given ninety days to come up with a

## Segregationist Attacks on the NAACP

During the 1950s the NAACP and its Legal Defense and Education Fund (LDF) won a series of major legal battles to gain greater civil rights for African Americans. These successes, however, exposed the NAACP to attacks from white individuals and organizations who viewed the group as "agitators" upsetting the natural order of life in the South. After *Brown v. Board* made it clear the South could no longer rely on the Supreme Court to uphold segregation, attacks against the NAACP and its lawyers intensified.

One tactic employed by opponents was to accuse NAACP lawyers of violating legal ethics by soliciting clients (barratry), paying clients to participate in a lawsuit (maintenance), or prosecuting lawsuits for material gain (champerty). The NAACP took steps to reduce its risk of being attacked for violations of legal ethics. In taking on cases, for example, LDF director Thurgood Marshall had been scrupulous in choosing plaintiffs who approached the NAACP, rather than the other way around. Nevertheless, many NAACP lawyers were charged with ethics violations. None of the charges were ever upheld, but they forced the LDF to spend time and money on its own defense rather than other cases.

In the mid-1950s seven states changed their barratry laws to include attorneys who were paid by an organization instead of by their clients. This change was a clear effort to target the NAACP. Again, many of these statutes were eventually found to be unconstitutional obstacles to political expression and equal protection of the laws, but they forced LDF lawyers into expensive, time-consuming litigation in order to protect their rights.

At the same time the Southern establishment attacked NAACP lawyers, it sought to undermine the organization itself. Southern states

desegregation plan. But instead of advocating a firm timetable for implementation of those plans, he suggested to the Court that the states merely proceed with "deliberate speed." To ensure compliance, he suggested that district judges be given the power to impose implementation time tables on schools that failed to act in good faith.

challenged the tax-exempt status of the NAACP and the LDF, accusing both groups of political agitation rather than advocacy. They passed laws requiring the NAACP to register with the government and turn over its financial and membership records—which could then be used to identify and intimidate local members. When local chapters refused to reveal their membership lists, their leaders faced huge fines and even arrest.

These laws—which sprouted in Alabama, Florida, Louisiana, Arkansas, and Virginia—were overturned in court, but defeating them was a costly and time-consuming process. In Alabama, sympathetic local courts kept the NAACP from operating in the state for almost ten years. In Louisiana, where several NAACP chapters reluctantly provided membership lists to the state, membership dropped from more than 12,000 to only 1,700.

The South also took aim against individual members of the NAACP. South Carolina banned NAACP members from teaching and other jobs in the public sector. Before the Supreme Court could overrule the law as blatantly unconstitutional, the state changed it to require teachers and other public employees to notify the state of all their organizational affiliations. Laws such as these were more difficult to fight because they did not specifically target the NAACP. In a close 5-4 vote, though, the Supreme Court ruled in *Shelton v. Tucker* (1960) that such legislation was too broad and too restrictive.

Finally, harassment and violence were used to discourage individual involvement in the NAACP. The most notorious instance was the 1963 murder of Medgar Evers, the NAACP's field secretary for Mississippi. In two separate trials, an all-white jury could not agree on whether white supremacist Byron De La Beckwith had shot Evers in the back, despite strong evidence of his guilt. It was only in 1994 that Beckwith was finally convicted of murder and sentenced to life in prison.

Attorneys representing Kansas, Delaware, and the District of Columbia contributed little to the discussion, as their districts had already begun desegregating voluntarily. Attorneys for the Southern states, however, insisted that gradual "relief"—with no set deadline—was the only practical way to desegregate the schools in their communities. Moreover, they warned that even a gradual approach to desegregation would ignite fiery protests from Southern whites. "So far as I know now, I would say that the chance that North Carolina in the near future will mingle white and Negro children in her public schools throughout the state is exceedingly remote," observed Assistant Attorney General I. Beverly Lake of North Carolina. "That is the reason that I have the gravest fear that [an immediate desegregation] decree would result in the abolition of our public school system."

Virginia Attorney General J. Lindsay Almond, meanwhile, noted to the Court that Virginia's legislature had already voted to pull state funding from any integrated school. He predicted that if states were not given "reasonable time" to devise integration plans acceptable to Prince Edward County and other communities, there "will not in my judgment in the lifetime of those of us hale and hearty here, be enforced integration of the races in the public schools of that county."

In his rebuttal remarks, Marshall dismissed these pleas for time as a transparent delaying tactic. Instead he urged the Court not only to avoid the gradualist approach, but to make its ruling a class action—that is, applicable to all African Americans in segregated schools, not just the plaintiffs listed in *Brown v. Board of Education.* As for white opposition, he concluded that "the history of our Government shows that it is the inherent faith in our democratic process that gets us through, the faith that the people in the South are no different from anybody else as to being law-abiding."

After the oral presentations concluded, the Court retired to begin its deliberations. The justices knew there would resistance to any desegregation decree. Justices Black and Douglas, who were from the South, were sure the resistance would be violent. The justices believed that publicly acknowledging their concern about public opposition would only encourage it, however, so there was no mention of resistance in their ruling, which was released on May 31, 1955.

The decision the Court crafted plainly reflected concern about reaction in the South. Rejecting the NAACP's request that they render a class-action judgment, the justices limited relief to the plaintiffs in the cases collectively known as *Brown v. Board of Education.* The decision—which came to be commonly known as *Brown II*—also provided significant latitude to the states to devise their own integration procedures and timetables. Acknowledging that local conditions varied all over the South, the justices had decided against setting a particular date for full desegregation. Instead, they directed the defendants to "make a prompt and reasonable start toward full compliance," and admit the plaintiffs "to public schools on a racially nondiscriminatory basis with all deliberate speed." The Court decision handed responsibility for supervision and enforcement of the decree to federal district courts (see The U.S. Supreme Court's *Brown II* Decision, p. 204).

## Early Desegregation Successes and Failures

Even before the Supreme Court announced its decision in *Brown II*, several school districts around the country began desegregating their schools voluntarily in order to avoid the expense of an inevitable court battle. Baltimore, Maryland, for instance, adapted its "freedom-of-choice" plan for the 1954-55 school year to allow nearly 3,000 black students to attend formerly all-white schools. Although this was only 3 percent of the black student population, it was a start. By October of 1954, according to the *Southern School News,* the states of Kansas, Missouri, West Virginia, Maryland, Delaware, Texas, Oklahoma, Arkansas, and Kentucky were all taking the first steps toward desegregation.

*The Southern Manifesto promised "to use all lawful means to bring about a reversal of this decision which is contrary to the Constitution and to prevent the use of force in its implementation."*

After the *Brown II* decision was handed down, desegregation accelerated in many regions of the country. The city of Louisville, Kentucky, desegregated over 12,000 black students in all twelve grades during a single semester in 1956, and the city of St. Louis, Missouri, completed desegregation over the course of two semesters. Twenty-five counties in West Virginia and one community in Arkansas initiated desegregation programs without incident, and eleven junior colleges in Texas opened their doors to African Americans.

Not all early attempts proceeded without trouble, however. In 1956 nine African American students registered at previously all-white Sturgis High School in Union County, Kentucky. After their admittance, a mob of white townspeople blocked streets and burned crosses in an attempt to prevent the new students from attending classes. Kentucky Governor A. B. "Happy" Chandler, who had been the commissioner of Major League Baseball when Jackie Robinson integrated the majors in 1947, quickly called out the National Guard to protect the students. Shielded by soldiers and tanks, the students returned to school. At that point, however, state Attorney General Jo M. Fer-

After the Supreme Court issued *Brown II,* some communities were able to integrate their schools without incident.

guson ruled that the black students were attending Sturgis illegally because they were not part of an official school board desegregation plan. The students were expelled from the campus until the following year, when a court order enabled their return. The black students were greeted by crowds of white protestors, but this time the protests were orderly and the students were able to attend school without a military escort.

As the months passed by, it proved difficult to predict where desegregation efforts might trigger community unrest. In New Castle, Delaware, for instance, 106 black children were integrated with 2,190 white students without significant community disruption in 1956. Two years earlier, however, integration efforts in Milford, located only fifty miles south of New Castle, had roiled the community. The initial integration of eleven black students into previously all-white Milford High School had not sparked protests. But after rumors spread that a black boy was going to take a white girl to a school dance, parental outrage led the school board to close the school and send the black students home for a "cooling off period." Before the board could reopen the school, a mob of some 1,500 white protesters gathered.

Frightened that events were spinning out of its control, the school board turned to the state for assistance. Attorney General Albert Young was willing to enforce the state's newly minted integration laws—he offered to personally escort the students into school—but neither the state Board of Education nor Governor J. Caleb Boggs defended the integration effort in Milford. A short time later, the State Supreme Court ruled that the Milford school board had failed to follow proper procedure in creating an integration plan.

Beleaguered by widespread public opposition, the threat of violence, and the absence of support from state institutions, the members of the Milford school board resigned and a new board dominated by segregationists was elected in their place. "The Milford outcome presaged how many state courts would treat school segregation issues in the following years: uphold *Brown* rhetorically, but frustrate it by allowing the imposition of justice-mocking procedural obstacles," LDF lawyer Jack Greenberg later recalled in his memoir *Crusaders in the Courts*.

The troubles in Milford underscored the importance of institutional support to successful integration efforts. If local and state authorities supported a community's decision to integrate, the process generally proceeded without significant incident, and flare-ups that did occur tended to be short-lived. On the other hand, if segregationists were allowed to organize—and particularly if outside individuals or groups became involved—opposition often developed to the point that it interfered with, or even prevented, integration efforts.

## Defiance from the Bench

Integration also depended greatly on the willingness of federal district judges to comply with the *Brown* rulings. Although these judges were appointed by the federal government, in most cases they were natives of the region over which they presided, and in the South their personal feelings about integration often reflected the local community's sentiments.

Moreover, judges who supported integration efforts were often reluctant to risk condemnation from the community in which they lived. Charleston native J. Waties Waring, for example, was so thoroughly ostracized from the

## The Case of Virgil Hawkins

The most egregious case of court delay in implementing desegregation occurred in the state of Florida. Virgil Hawkins had first applied to the University of Florida Law School in 1949. When he was turned down because of his race, he turned to the courts. But even with the *Gaines* precedent the Florida Supreme Court refused to admit him. Instead, the Court unveiled a compromise, offering to send him out of state or create a facility for African Americans at Florida A&M University.

Shortly after the 1954 *Brown* decision, the U.S. Supreme Court ordered Florida to reconsider Hawkins's case in light of its ruling. The Florida Supreme Court held that since Hawkins had not claimed "psychological damage" similar to the plaintiffs in *Brown,* it did not need to admit him. After the Supreme Court directly ordered his admittance in the 1956 decision *Hawkins v. Board of Control,* Florida's courts upheld the state's claim that admitting a black student to the University of Florida posed an unacceptable risk of inciting violence on campus—despite student surveys showing 72 percent approval for integration. By the time a district court ruled Florida had to integrate all of its universities in 1958, the university had made so many ugly attacks on Hawkins's character that he had given up his suit at his wife's request. He earned his law degree in Massachusetts in 1976, 27 years after first applying to the University of Florida.

city's white community after his anti-segregation dissent in South Carolina's *Briggs v. Elliott* case that he reluctantly relocated to New York. His seat on the bench was taken by Judge John Parker, whose 1955 pronouncement that the Supreme Court's *Brown* decision "does not require integration…. It merely forbids the use of governmental power to enforce segregation" was met with widespread approval by the white folk of Charleston.

Although judges were not willing to risk open defiance of the Supreme Court, they often used delaying tactics to postpone desegregation efforts. In Tennessee, for example, when Memphis State University defied an appeals court order admitting African American students, the court did not schedule a hearing on the matter until the end of the school year. In Louisiana, by contrast, a district court judge took only ten days to overturn a ruling that kept African Americans from enrolling at the New Orleans campus of Louisiana State University.

## "Massive Resistance" to Integration

Although a number of Southern judges obstructed the *Brown* ruling, the most serious resistance came from Southern politicians—from local school board members to state governors and U.S. Senators. These lawmakers signaled their defiance almost as soon as the *Brown* ruling was handed down. After the first decision was announced in 1954, Mississippi Senator James O. Eastland told his constituents that "you are not obliged to obey the decisions of any court which are plainly fraudulent." Georgia Governor Herman Talmadge fumed that "no force whatever could compel" desegregation. In Virginia, Senator (and former governor) Harry F. Byrd spoke out against the *Brown* decision and urged fellow Southerners to mount "massive resistance" to integration. The legislative program that Virginia and other states subsequently adopted was soon known by that name.

Fury over the Supreme Court's desegregation decree did not wane with the passage of time, either. In 1956 Southern members of Congress read a protest into the Congressional Record against the Supreme Court's "clear abuse of judicial power." The Southern Manifesto, as this protest was called, promised "to use all lawful means to bring about a reversal of this decision which is contrary to the Constitution and to prevent the use of force in its implementation." Ninety-six Southern congressmen signed the declaration, including every Senator from the South except for three: Al Gore Sr. and Estes Kefauver of Tennessee, and Lyndon B. Johnson of Texas (see The Southern Manifesto, p. 209).

State legislatures were equally opposed to desegregation, and they crafted numerous laws designed to avoid complying with *Brown*. Alabama, Georgia, Louisiana, Mississippi, the Carolinas, and Virginia all passed laws that required schools to close rather than integrate. Many of these same states passed laws permitting the sale of public schools to private groups, since privately owned and operated schools were not legally bound by the *Brown* ruling. Some Southern states further authorized the distribution of state tax dollars to fund private white schools. The Georgia legislature even passed a law that criminalized desegregation efforts and a resolution "impeaching" the nine members of the U.S. Supreme Court. Finally, several Southern states passed

Georgia Governor Herman Talmadge angrily denounced the Supreme Court's integration directives.

laws clearly designed to punish or intimidate the NAACP's lawyers and membership (see Segregationist Attacks on the NAACP, p. 68).

These laws enjoyed broad public support from white residents. In the years after *Brown,* voters in these states approved constitutional amendments supporting segregation by margins as large as four to one. Several of these states also passed resolutions of interposition, a method by which individual states could "interpose" their governments between their citizens and what they saw as an unconstitutional action by the federal government. While the concept of interposition had never been accepted nationwide—Union victory in the Civil War had essentially invalidated it—it was very popular in the South, where the doctrine of "States' Rights" remained a potent political rallying cry.

U.S. courts eventually overturned the majority of these massive resistance laws, but even temporary laws gave segregation supporters additional political power and enabled them to delay desegregation. "The massive resistance statutes were obviously unconstitutional, and the federal courts routinely agreed," observed Mark Tushnet in *Making Civil Rights Law.* "Yet combating massive resistance was time consuming, rather like swatting off a swarm of flies, and the political forces behind massive resistance meant that no desegregation would occur until the last possible moment."

Even when districts were forced to proceed with desegregation, local school boards came up with new assignment plans that resulted in token desegregation—or none at all. For example, when school boards devised "freedom of choice" enrollment plans, white families withdrew their children from integrated schools in huge numbers. In Greensboro, North Carolina, for instance, a formerly all-white school became a segregated black school after the district granted transfer requests to all white students and teachers. Pupil placement plans, meanwhile, gave authorities the ability to use "local conditions" as criteria for denying black students places in white schools. If an

African American family wished to protest a placement, it had to exhaust a series of time-consuming administrative appeals before it could file a lawsuit.

These procedures were blatantly discriminatory. But they did not include direct references to race, so they were harder to fight in court because the burden was on the plaintiffs to prove discrimination. Although the NAACP won such a case in Virginia, the organization lost similar ones in North Carolina and Texas. Armed with these plans—and the array of other roadblocks raised by state legislators—the states of Alabama, Florida, Georgia, Louisiana, Mississippi, Virginia, North Carolina, and South Carolina each managed to keep their segregated school systems intact for more than three years after the *Brown* ruling.

## Black Concerns about Integration

Not all opponents of desegregation were white, either. Some members of the African American community questioned the wisdom of challenging segregation—in large part because of concerns about the emotional and physical toll that such efforts might have on their children. Back in 1935, when blacks had begun to make minor gains in their bid to improve their educational opportunities, prominent African American educator W. E. B. Du Bois had openly promoted the idea of keeping schools segregated. Writing in an essay entitled "Does the Negro Need Separate Schools?" he declared that as long as white society looked down on African Americans, segregated schools would provide black students with a more supportive learning environment:

> A separate Negro school, where children are treated like human beings, trained by teachers of their own race, who know what it means to be black ...is infinitely better than making our boys and girls doormats to be spit and trampled upon and lied to by ignorant social climbers, whose sole claim to superiority is the ability to kick "niggers" when they are down.

Black educators were also concerned about the effects of desegregation on their own jobs. If black and white students were to mix, they recognized that many white parents would object to the idea of black teachers and

*American have long believed "that there is no greater delight to Negroes than physical association with whites," declared Zora Neale Hurston. "I can see no tragedy in being too dark to be invited to a white school social affair."*

administrators directing their children's education. Since educated black teachers were usually leaders in the communities in which they lived, their expressions of apprehension—or outright silence—on integration served to dampen enthusiasm for the effort in many black areas.

Finally, a small number of African Americans argued that the *Brown* decision insulted them by casting doubts on their abilities as educators and insinuating that blacks benefit just from being in the presence of white people. "Since the days of the never-to-be-sufficiently-deplored Reconstruction, there has been current the belief that there is no greater delight to Negroes than physical association with whites," wrote black author Zora Neale Hurston in an August 11, 1955, letter to the *Orlando Sentinel.* "I can see no tragedy in being too dark to be invited to a white school social affair. The Supreme Court would have pleased me more if they had concerned themselves about enforcing the compulsory education provisions for Negroes in the South as is done for white children.... It is a contradiction in terms to scream race pride and equality while at the same time spurning Negro teachers and self-association."

## Lonely Voices

In this heated political climate, it was difficult for those Southerners who accepted the *Brown* decision to make themselves heard. Some officials initially responded with acceptance. The day after the 1954 decision, for example, the school board of Greensboro, North Carolina, voted 6-1 to comply with desegregation. Several Southern governors, while expressing unhappiness with *Brown,* also said they would obey the law. However, upon seeing the lack of public support for desegregation—two of three Congressmen from North Carolina who refused to sign the Southern Manifesto lost their re-election bids—many of these moderates backed away from their positions.

The White House, in the meantime, maintained a stony silence on the desegregation issue. President Dwight Eisenhower's failure to publicly affirm his support for the Supreme Court's *Brown v. Board* ruling proved devastating, as did his refusal to criticize Southern states that flouted the ruling. Instead, he merely stated that "it makes no difference whether or not I endorse [*Brown*]. The Constitution is as the Supreme Court interprets it; and I must conform to that and do my very best to see that it is carried out in this country."

When national leaders failed to speak out against the segregationists, local Southern politicians who might have willingly carried out the Court's

Three high school students show off picket signs created to protest the integration of Clinton High School in Tennessee in 1956.

wishes followed suit. "Moderates had been telling their communities that the federal government was going to force them to integrate so that the only wise course was to accept the fact that integration must come and try to contain it," J. W. Peltason observed in his study *Fifty-Eight Lonely Men.* "When Eisenhower let defiance go unchallenged, segregationists' pressures mounted."

# Chapter Six
# CRISIS IN LITTLE ROCK

We in America face today within our country a crisis which can lead to our destruction. For if we cannot, as Americans, regardless of race or color, live in peace and harmony as a united people, our disunity may well destroy us. How can we be trusted with the peace of the world if we cannot keep peace among ourselves?

—Tennessee Governor Frank Clement, after calling out the National Guard against a segregationist mob, 1956

Stone this time. Dynamite next.

—Note attached to a brick thrown through the window of Daisy Bates, president of the Arkansas NAACP and advisor to the Little Rock Nine, summer 1957

When U.S. courts began to strike down newly minted Southern laws meant to block desegregation, many Southerners organized to find other ways to prevent "race mixing." Among the most notorious of these were the "White Citizens Councils" that sprouted across the South in the mid-1950s. The first White Citizens Council was founded in Mississippi in 1954, and others quickly followed. By 1957, White Citizens Councils had some 250,000 members across the Deep South, including numerous congressmen, judges, and state legislators. Their efforts were coordinated by an interstate organization called the Federation for Constitutional Government, founded in 1955 by Mississippi Senator James O. Eastland.

The goals of White Citizens Councils were similar to those of the Ku Klux Klan, but their methods were more sophisticated. Instead of cross burnings and lynchings, they used economic threats—loss of employment and bank loans, among other things—to pressure black parents not to enroll their children in newly desegregated white schools. White moderates who spoke out in favor of desegregation received the same treatment. Anti-desegregation forces also spread propaganda that falsely framed school integration efforts as anti-Christian schemes driven by Communists, Jews, and other groups perceived negatively by many white Southerners.

## Emmett Till and Other Victims of White Rage

The threat of physical violence also hovered over African American communities. Nothing made that clearer than the brutal slaying of fourteen-year-old Emmett Till in 1955. A Chicago native, Till was spending the summer visiting relatives in Mississippi. After he allegedly whistled at a white woman in front of a store, two of her relatives kidnapped him from his great-uncle's home. His body was found three days later in the Tallahatchie River, shot in the head. An all-white jury took only one hour to acquit the men charged with Till's murder, and a grand jury refused to indict them for kidnapping even though they had confessed to abducting Till during sworn testimony.

Although Till's murder galvanized many in the coalescing civil rights movement, it also served as a reminder to Southern blacks of the rage many whites felt over the integration issue. In fact, between 1954 and 1959, there were over two hundred officially recorded acts of white violence against African Americans across the South, including six murders, twenty-nine firearms assaults, forty-four beatings, and sixty bombings. The *New York Herald Tribune* reported the number was over five hundred.

This poisonous environment undoubtedly contributed to the dearth of legal challenges to school segregation across much of the South. By the end of the 1950s, not a single desegregation lawsuit had been filed in Mississippi, and only two challenges to segregation had been registered in South Carolina. The numbers were similarly low across all states of the Deep South.

Public officials and politicians were reluctant to speak out against these violent acts. Some even dared to call them "peaceful protests" comparable to the Boston Tea Party, the famous 1773 political protest by American colonists against the tax policies of the British Parliament. In fact, some historians believe that Southern officials worsened these conflicts with their warnings that desegregation would incite violence; when they did nothing to discourage the mobs, their warnings became self-fulfilling prophecies.

## Fear-Based Protests

Most of the anti-integration violence stemmed from lower-class, rural whites. The typical "hard-core" resisters, according to J. W. Peltason in *Fifty-Eight Lonely Men,* were "blue-collar workers, with little or no education, and little or no exposure to newspapers, radio, television, and national magazines. It [was] these people who [were] most directly in competition with Negroes for jobs, homes, and social prestige. Living in residential zones closest to Negro neighborhoods, they [were] most immediately affected by the abolition of segregation."

The lies propagated by White Citizens Councils and other leading segregationist voices thus found fertile soil in the hearts and minds of poor and working-class whites. Bombarded by warnings that their already

The murder of Emmett Till (shown here in an undated photograph) in Mississippi in 1955 was a major factor in the growth of the civil rights movement.

modest social stations were at risk from integration, they rushed to defend their livelihoods and families from the perceived threat. But many observers attributed their resistance to baser emotions as well. "For them, separate-and-unequal was more than a racial policy, it was a self-defeating narcotic under the influence of which even the lowliest white person could feel superior," former LDF lawyer Derrick Bell charged in *Silent Covenants.*

This cauldron of emotions came to a boil in Little Rock, Arkansas, in 1957. That year, a plan to desegregate a single white high school populated primarily by kids from surrounding blue-collar neighborhoods triggered a historic clash between segregationist and integrationist forces. This battle, which swirled around nine vulnerable but enormously brave black teenagers, is recognized today as a major milestone in the American civil rights movement.

## Flames of Hatred across the South

When African Americans were willing to stand up for their rights, they often faced violent resistance. In Tennessee, John Kasper organized a crowd in 1956 to threaten black students attempting to desegregate Clinton High School. Although Kasper was eventually arrested on federal contempt charges, he returned to the state in 1957 to organize demonstrations against Nashville's desegregation plan. On the first night after first-graders attended desegregated classes, a school was firebombed and destroyed.

White mobs similarly thwarted a 1956 attempt to desegregate a high school in Mansfield, Texas. When a court ordered that three black students be admitted, a crowd gathered to surround the school. The mayor and police chief left town while the throng stopped any car that passed and held up signs scrawled with slogans like "A Dead Nigger Is the Best Nigger." Texas Governor Allan Shivers, meanwhile, called out the Texas Rangers to protect the mob and arrest any "threats to peace"—meaning black students. After the students withdrew their request to attend the school, the governor claimed that his actions showed racial disputes could be settled "without violence."

Similar riots prevented Autherine Lucy from entering the University of Alabama in 1956. After a 1955 Supreme Court decision ordered her admission, a crowd showed up when Lucy came to register on campus. Administrators suspended her "for her safety," and after she sued for reinstatement the university expelled her for bringing legal action against it.

## Desegregation Comes to Little Rock

After the initial *Brown* decision in 1954, several communities in Arkansas began planning for voluntary segregation, including Little Rock. The Little Rock school board unanimously approved a plan to integrate in three stages, beginning with the city's high schools. In 1955, however, the local NAACP chapter, led by local resident and Arkansas NAACP President Daisy Bates (see Bates biography, p. 125), filed suit against the school board, alleging that the integration plan was being implemented too slowly.

In 1956 a federal district judge upheld the school board's plan—but also ruled that it had to begin immediately. As a result, the district prepared to admit African Americans to Central High School, one of Little Rock's three high schools, in the fall of 1957. Little Rock's other two high schools—all-black Horace Mann High School and all-white Hall High School—were to be left untouched until administrators could assess the integration effort at Central High.

Some sixty black students applied to enter Central High. Seventeen were eventually approved by the school administration, but only nine chose to actually register for classes. These students—Minnijean Brown, Elizabeth Eckford, Ernest Green, Thelma Mothershed, Melba Patillo, Gloria Ray, Terrence Roberts, Jefferson Thomas, and Carlotta Walls—would come to be known as the "Little Rock Nine."

Initially, there was little community objection to this arrangement, called the "Blossom Plan" after Superintendent Virgil Blossom. Although Arkansas voters had

Arkansas Governor Orval Faubus warned that "blood will run in the streets" if authorities tried to integrate the state's schools.

approved segregationist measures in the 1956 state election, Little Rock had a fairly tolerant reputation. The city had already desegregated several public facilities, including its bus system, and in early 1957 city voters had elected two moderates to the school board over segregationist candidates.

As the school term drew near, however, Arkansas Governor Orval Faubus (see Faubus biograph, p. 146) publicly warned that Little Rock's desegregation plans were bound to stir up trouble. Georgia Governor Marvin Griffin then gave a rousing speech advocating resistance to integration during a tour through Arkansas. These incendiary remarks from high-profile officials sparked a rumble of unease throughout Little Rock, and by midsummer white opposition to the integration plan was clearly on the rise.

Blossom still believed that integration of Central High School could proceed without major community unrest. But Faubus asked for and received a state court injunction against the plan. After a federal court overturned the injunction, the governor called up the Arkansas National Guard, warning that "white supremacist caravans" were on their way to Little Rock and that "blood will run in the streets" if black students tried to enter Central High.

Faubus's actions angered Little Rock Mayor Woodrow Mann, who said that "I am sure a great majority of the people in Little Rock share my deep resentment at the manner in which the governor has chosen to use this city as a pawn in what clearly is a political design of his own." But in reality, the governor's heated rhetoric and his decision to use National Guard troops to prevent integration energized segregationists in Little Rock and surrounding communities.

## Showdown at Central High

By the time classes opened on September 2, 1957, Central High School was surrounded not only by Arkansas National Guard troops, but also by a crowd of angry segregationists. The Little Rock Nine stayed home that day and the next, while the school board petitioned for delay. On September 3 a federal district judge ordered the school to proceed with its integration plan—and ordered Governor Faubus to stop interfering in Little Rock.

Armed with the judge's ruling, Daisy Bates made plans to meet the Nine early the next morning (September 4) at a location two blocks away from school. From there, they would be escorted by police into the school. But student Elizabeth Eckford never received the message, and she became trapped by the white mob when she approached the school. Members of the Arkansas National Guard looked on impassively as the horde hurled insults and spat upon the small, fifteen-year-old girl. Eckford was eventually rescued by a sympathetic onlooker, but the ugly incident convinced Bates to abandon her plans for the day.

It took another court order before the Nine could finally enter Central High. Backed by the Department of Justice, the NAACP asked a federal court for an injunction against the governor and the National Guard. The injunction was granted, and on September 20 the National Guard was withdrawn from Central High. The Nine made plans to attend school the following Monday, September 23. Escorted by police, they slipped into the school unnoticed that morning. As the news of their attendance escaped the school, however,

Elizabeth Eckford, one of the Little Rock Nine, endures a nightmarish walk to school, trailed by a threatening mob of angry whites.

an angry mob formed outside. The black students were forced to leave shortly after lunchtime before the mob—which attacked several visiting reporters and photographers—could storm the school. That evening, local police stopped a caravan of cars on their way to Bates's house. A search of the caravan revealed an assortment of dynamite and guns. Over the course of the school year, Bates was also the target of drive-by shootings and bombings (although her home sustained no damage). Bombings also targeted the mayor's office, the school board offices, and the fire chief's house.

## Federal Troops Move In

After the Nine were driven out of Central High on September 23, Mayor Mann appealed for federal help. He cabled President Eisenhower on September 24:

On September 24, 1957, President Dwight Eisenhower finally ordered federal troops into Little Rock to enforce federal integration directives.

People are converging on scene from all directions. Mob is armed and engaging in fisticuffs and other acts of violence. Situation is out of control and police cannot disperse the mob. I am pleading to you as President of the United States in the interest of humanity, law and order and because of democracy worldwide to provide the necessary federal troops within several hours. Action by you will restore peace and order and compliance with your proclamation.

Eisenhower recognized the seriousness of the situation. Although he was wary of desegregation by court order, he could not ignore the lawlessness in Little Rock, especially when the FBI informed him that Governor Faubus had deliberately obstructed a court order by telling the Arkansas National Guard to prevent the Nine from entering Central High School. By making his obstruction explicit, Faubus forced the federal government to deal with his rebellion. Eisenhower ordered 1,100 troops from the U.S. Army's 101st Airborne Division to Little Rock to enforce the city's desegregation plan.

On September 25, the Little Rock Nine finally began classes at Central High School under the protection of federal troops. The protests gradually lost strength, and by November 27 the crowds had subsided enough for Eisenhower to withdraw the 101st Airborne. He then placed the Arkansas National Guard under federal control, and they remained at the school throughout the year to act as bodyguards for the Nine.

Meanwhile, the Little Rock Nine bravely endured an enormously painful school year. Initially, many of the white students at Central had been open to the new students, but pressure from parents, segregationists, and schoolmates took its toll. Once the Nine were able to begin school, few white students proved willing to risk social ostracism by acting friendly toward them.

Members of the Little Rock Nine arrive at Central High School on September 25, 1957, the day that they finally were able to begin attending classes.

Instead, the Nine were subjected to a barrage of verbal and physical harassment throughout the year.

The school administration was not oblivious to these incidents, but they did not act on harassment complaints unless an adult had witnessed it. This seems a callous policy at first glance, but school officials felt besieged. After all, the Department of Justice decided not to prosecute the riot's leaders because it did not believe that a local grand jury would vote to indict them, and state and local officials also refused to prosecute troublemakers. Without support from federal, state, and local officials, administrators knew they had to pick their battles carefully. As Central High Vice-Principal of Girls Elizabeth Huckaby recalled in her memoir *Crisis at Central High:*

> The "moderate" leadership of the city was paralyzed. Federal
> officials were evidently not going to prosecute and punish

# What Became of the Little Rock Nine?

The nine students who integrated Little Rock's Central High School during the 1957-58 school year soon went their separate ways, but they remain heroes in the eyes of many Americans. The group received the NAACP's Spingarn Medal in 1958, and in 1999 each member was awarded the Congressional Gold Medal, the nation's highest civilian honor. Here is an update on the Little Rock Nine, as of 2004:

**Minnijean Brown-Trickey** was expelled from Central High in 1958 after a series of conflicts with white students. She finished high school in New York City, and then earned a degree from Southern Illinois University. During the Vietnam War, she moved with her husband to Canada, where she earned a master's degree in social work and began a career in Ottawa as a social worker, filmmaker, and writer. In 1999 she joined the Clinton administration as Deputy Assistant Secretary for workforce diversity in the Department of the Interior. She later returned to live in Little Rock, where she gives lectures and is working on an autobiography tentatively titled *Mixed Blessing: Living Black in North America.*

**Elizabeth Eckford** is the only one of the Nine to live most of her adult life in Little Rock. After her year at Central she moved to St. Louis, Missouri. She earned her GED and served in the U.S. Army, working as a journalist for a time. She earned a B.A. in history from a university in Illinois and became the first African American to work in a St. Louis bank in a clerical position. In the 1960s she returned to Little Rock to be closer to her parents. She worked for a time as a social studies teacher, then became a probation officer. She is employed in that capacity by the Pulaski County District Court.

**Ernest G. Green** spent his senior year integrating Central High and in 1958 became the first African American to graduate from the school. He attended Michigan State University, where he received both bachelor's and master's degrees. He served in the Carter Administration as Assistant Secretary of Housing and Urban Affairs from 1977 to 1981. Since then he has worked in the financial and securities industries, including periods as a consultant in his own investment banking firm. He is a managing director of public finance for Lehman Brothers in Washington, D.C.

**Thelma Mothershed Wair** did not return to Central High after the 1957-58 school year, but she earned enough credits through correspondence courses to receive her Central High diploma. She graduated from Southern Illinois University with a master's degree in guidance and counseling and worked in the East St. Louis school system for 28 years. After her retirement in 1994, Wair volunteered as a counselor for abused women in Illinois, and then returned to live in Little Rock.

**Melba Patillo Beals** left Central High for Montgomery, California, where she graduated from high school. She received her bachelor's degree in journalism from San Francisco State University, and her master's degree from Columbia University. She has worked as a television news reporter in San Francisco and has published articles in national magazines, including *People* and *Essence*. Beals has written two memoirs, the award-winning *Warriors Don't Cry* (1994) and *White Is a State of Mind* (1999). Beals has also run her own public relations business, and she gives diversity seminars and lectures around the country.

**Gloria Ray Karlmark** graduated from Illinois Technical College and married a Swedish citizen. She moved to Stockholm, where she earned a graduate degree and began a career as a successful computer science writer. She published a European computer magazine and served as an executive officer for a Dutch company. Since retiring, she splits her time between Amsterdam and Stockholm.

**Terrence Roberts** moved with his family to Los Angeles, California, after Central High closed for the 1958-59 school year. He finished high school there, then earned his bachelor's degree at California State University-Los Angeles. He received a master's degree in social work from University of California at Los Angeles (UCLA) and a Ph.D. in psychology from Southern Illinois University. A registered social worker and clinical psychologist, Dr. Roberts founded his own management consulting firm in 1975 and lectures around the country on diversity, education, and management issues. He taught and served as assistant dean at UCLA's School of Social Welfare. Since 1993 he has been chairman of the master's in psychology program at Antioch University, Los Angeles.

**Jefferson Thomas** returned to Central High after it closed for the 1958-59 school year and graduated in 1960. He worked for Mobil Oil in California, then passed the civil service exam and began working for the federal government. In 1988 he relocated to Columbus, Ohio, where he worked as an accountant for the U.S. Department of Defense until his retirement in 2004. He has expressed interest in writing a book about the events that led the Little Rock Nine to enroll at Central High.

**Carlotta Walls LaNier,** the youngest of the Little Rock Nine, also returned to Central High to graduate in 1960. She attended Michigan State University for two years, then moved with her family to Denver, Colorado. She graduated from Colorado State College (now the University of Northern Colorado) in 1968 and worked for several years for the Denver YWCA. She founded her own real estate company in 1977 and has worked as a broker in the Denver area since 1987.

those who were obstructing and opposing federal court orders. And there [were] constant indications that the state government was actually assisting in, if not directing, the harassment. We could only try to outlast them: to run school for our 1,800 boys and girls, black and white, meanwhile trying to protect the Nine from physical injury.

Over the school year at Central High, none of the Nine suffered serious physical injury. But they endured a steady stream of racial epithets, shoves and kicks from classmates, vandalism to their lockers and schoolbooks, and a wide range of other insults. One of the Little Rock Nine, Minnijean Brown, was unable to endure these assaults for the full year. She was expelled from Central in February 1958 after exchanging insults with a white girl. The remaining eight finished the school year, and senior Ernest Green graduated on schedule in 1958, becoming the first African American to graduate from Central High.

## The Supreme Court Weighs In

After the school year was over, the Little Rock school board went to court once again, asking for a stay in their desegregation plan until they could build the necessary community support to enact it peacefully. "If the complete burden of desegregation was placed on the school, without the cooperation—no, with the active opposition of the community and the state, and with only a sort of scolding and half-hearted federal backing such as we had had the past year— we could not run the school with safety for children of either race," wrote Huckaby. District Judge Harry J. Lemley heard the case and approved the delay. A federal court of appeals overturned the decision, however, noting that "the time has not yet come in these United States when an order of a federal court must be whittled away, watered down, or shamefully withdrawn in the face of violent and unlawful acts of individual citizens in opposition thereto."

Unwilling to accept the ruling, the Little Rock board appealed to the U.S. Supreme Court. The Court called a special session to hear the case (*Cooper v. Aaron*) on September 11, 1958, and issued a decree upholding continued integration a day later. In an unprecedented move, all nine justices signed the opinion, which held that "the constitutional rights of [students] are not to be sacrificed or yielded to the violence and disorder which have followed upon the actions of the Governor and Legislature." The opinion concluded by noting that the three new justices to join the Court since the historic 1954 *Brown v. Board of Education* ruling

> are at one with the Justices still on the Court who participated in that basic decision as to its correctness, and that decision is now unanimously reaffirmed. The principles announced in that decision and the obedience of the States to them, according to the command of the Constitution, are indispensable for the protection of the freedoms guaranteed by our fundamental charter for all of us. Our constitutional ideal of equal justice under law is thus made a living truth.

Although the federal government and the Supreme Court had weighed in on the side of Little Rock's desegregation efforts, segregationist forces still did not admit defeat. Governor Faubus arranged a special election in Little Rock in which residents were asked to vote on a segregationist plan to close the high schools and lease them to private companies, which could then maintain segregation. The issue passed by a vote of 19,000 to 7,500, and Little Rock's high schools closed for the entire 1958-59 school year—despite a court judgment that leasing public schools to private companies was invalid.

During this period, however, the Little Rock community underwent a shift in attitude. Moderate businessmen in the city were weary of the conflict's negative impact on their companies' financial fortunes, and ordinary citizens increasingly expressed a desire to accept the reality of integration and move on with their lives. In 1957 the city's voters defeated a segregationist slate in city council elections, and two years later they elected a majority of desegregationists to the school board. When Little Rock's high schools reopened in 1959, a small number of black students were enrolled at both Hall High and Central High. Black students at Central High that year included seniors Jefferson Thomas and Carlotta Ray, the only two of the original Little Rock Nine to return.

## The Impact Beyond Little Rock

Both the nation and the world had watched as events unfolded in Little Rock. The new medium of television brought the images of racial conflict into living rooms across the country. Many of the Americans watching felt shame at the stark images of racial hatred beamed from the city's streets—and admiration for the stoic bravery of the Nine. The Little Rock conflict thus gave further impetus to the growing civil rights movement, broadening its political support and bringing new activists to the cause of racial equality.

Significantly, the events in Little Rock—specifically President Eisenhower's decision to use federal troops to integrate Central High—"made clear once and for all that the federal government would not tolerate rebellion against the *Brown* decision," LDF lawyer Jack Greenberg noted in his memoir *Crusaders in the Courts*. Opponents of desegregation had hoped that violent resistance would convince federal authorities that the Supreme Court's *Brown v. Board of Education* ruling could not be enforced, paving the way for a return to the segregationist days of old. But even though further confrontations involving desegregation continued to flare across the country in the 1960s and 1970s, the events in Little Rock signaled that the days of Jim Crow were at an end.

# Chapter Seven

# BROWN'S LEGACY IN EDUCATION

───◄◖◗►───

You do not take a person who, for years, has been hobbled by chains and liberate him, bring him up to the starting line of a race and then say, "You are free to compete with all the others," and still justly believe that you have been completely fair. Thus it is not enough just to open the gates of opportunity. All our citizens must have the ability to walk through those gates.

—President Lyndon B. Johnson, in a commencement speech at Howard University, June 1965

The fierce battle over desegregation in Little Rock, Arkansas, had ended in victory for integration proponents and civil rights advocates. But even in that struggle's aftermath, it would take the combined efforts of America's legislative, executive, and judicial branches to bring about nationwide compliance with the *Brown* ruling.

In the first decade after *Brown*, these efforts resulted mainly in token integration. In 1960 not a single African American student was attending a desegregated school in South Carolina, Alabama, or Mississippi. In Arkansas, North Carolina, Florida, Tennessee, and Virginia the total number of black students attending school with whites statewide ranged from 34 to 169. The picture was marginally better in the District of Columbia and the border states of Delaware, Kentucky, Maryland, Missouri, Oklahoma, and West Virginia. All of these states had enrolled thousands of African Americans in formerly all-white schools. But observers noted that no white students had integrated the many all-black schools that still remained in these states.

Frustrated by the lack of progress, the NAACP devised a strategy for black families wishing to see desegregation in their communities. The first step in this strategy was for parents to formally petition their local school board to create a desegregation plan, making it clear that they were willing to negotiate with officials on the details. The NAACP and black parents hoped that by indicating a willingness to work together, they would receive cooperation in return. Only if discussions broke down would the NAACP consider bringing legal action.

> *In 1960 a Houston judge condemned the city's desegregation plan as "a palpable sham."*

This strategy, coupled with the limited money and resources of the NAACP's Legal Defense Fund, kept the number of litigated cases relatively low for several years. In 1960, for instance, there were only 46 cases pending in Southern states. The outcome of those legal actions often depended on the personal convictions of the judges assigned to hear the cases. In Houston, for example, Judge Ben C. Connally overturned the city's "voluntary preference" plan in 1960, calling it a "palpable sham and subterfuge designed only to accomplish further evasion and delay." The following year, however, Judge T. Whitfield Davidson overturned Dallas's plan to integrate one grade per year in favor of voluntary preferences, calling the twelve-year plan "hasty."

### Increased Federal Support for Integration

Under the John F. Kennedy administration in the early 1960s, the federal government proved more willing to get involved in desegregation efforts. The Department of Justice began filing suits, and Kennedy himself called out federal troops on two notable occasions. The first instance was in 1962, after a U.S. Court of Appeals ordered the admission of James Meredith to the University of Mississippi, commonly known as Ole Miss.

Mississippi was perhaps the most obstructionist state in the union. Previous African American applicants to Ole Miss had been institutionalized as mentally incompetent, and Meredith himself had been arrested on trumped-up voter registration charges after he filed suit against the university. Mississippi Governor Ross Barnett defied the court ruling and several injunctions by refusing to let Meredith register. This defiance of U.S. law angered Kennedy, who issued an executive order mandating Meredith's admittance. To ensure that his order was obeyed, he also sent 500 U.S. Marshals to accompa-

James Meredith makes his way through a jeering crowd on the University of Mississippi campus, accompanied by two U.S. Marshals.

ny Meredith to registration. When it became clear that Ole Miss would not be able to stop integration, white protestors erupted into a riot that resulted in the death of French photojournalist. But even this violence failed to derail Meredith's quest. Accompanied by bodyguards on a campus occupied by tanks and as many as 23,000 troops, he graduated on schedule in 1963.

A similar clash took place in 1963 in Alabama, where efforts to secure greater civil rights for blacks were met with violent protests and police actions that garnered nationwide attention. Alabama Governor George Wallace, who only months before had delivered an inaugural address vowing "Segregation now! Segregation tomorrow! Segregation forever!", was determined to block desegregation at all levels of education in the state. But when Wallace obstructed a federal order to admit two black students, Vivian Malone and James Hood, to the University of Alabama, Kennedy mobilized the might of the federal government. The president federalized the Alabama National Guard and ordered federal marshals to accompany the students to campus. After making a symbolic "stand in the schoolroom door," Wallace stepped aside and allowed the students to register on June 11, 1963.

That same evening, Kennedy delivered a nationally televised address to the nation on the integration issue. During his address, he framed the battle to integrate the nation's schools as a worthy and laudable one—but also one that might never come to fruition without the willing support of the American people:

> We face, therefore, a moral crisis as a country and as a people. It cannot be met by repressive police action. It cannot be left to increased demonstrations in the streets. It cannot be quieted by token moves or talk. It is a time to act in the Congress, in your state and local legislative bodies and, above all, in all of our daily lives.

Kennedy's speech signaled a new determination to advance the cause of civil rights. "A great change is at hand, and our task, our obligation, is to make that revolution, that change, peaceful and constructive for all," he declared. But his proposal to pass a sweeping new civil rights act languished in Congress. In November 1963 Kennedy was assassinated in Dallas. As the stunned nation mourned his death, civil rights advocates anxiously speculated about whether his successor, Texan Lyndon B. Johnson, would continue Kennedy's support for civil rights.

As it turned out, Johnson proved a willing ally. A Southerner with a history of supporting civil rights—he helped author the Civil Rights Act of 1957 and refused to sign the Southern Manifesto—Johnson threw his considerable congressional experience behind Kennedy's civil rights bill. His support was pivotal to the bill's passage in the summer of 1964.

A key provision of the Civil Rights Act of 1964 was Title VI, which prohibited racial discrimination in federal programs and gave the federal government the power to oversee compliance and withhold federal funds from schools that practiced segregation. Combined with the Elementary and Secondary Education Act of 1965, which multiplied the amount of federal funds apportioned to education by almost seven times, Title VI began affecting real change in Southern school districts. Title VI also forced local communities to reconsider their opposition to desegregation. "Many citizens remained silent until faced with the loss of their schools," observed J. W. Peltason in *Fifty-Eight Lonely Men*. "But when the alternative clearly became token integration or no schools, leaders discovered it was no longer politically dangerous to champion token integration."

The efficacy of Title VI was evident in enrollment patterns across the American South. In the ten years after *Brown II,* the number of African Americans attending school with whites had increased by only 1 percent each year; and in the 1963-64 school year, only 1.17 percent of black students in the eleven states of the former Confederacy attended school with whites. That percentage rose to 2.25 percent the following year, but after Title VI had time to take effect it nearly tripled, to 6.01 percent in the 1965-66 school year.

As president, Lyndon B. Johnson pressed for a wide range of new civil rights for African Americans.

## The Supreme Court Affirms and Expands *Brown*

Because many of the methods Southern school districts created to obstruct desegregation did not employ explicitly race-based language, it took several years for cases challenging them to make their way to the U.S. Supreme Court. These cases demonstrated how *Brown II*'s vague decree of "all deliberate speed," chosen in the hope of inspiring Southern cooperation, had utterly failed. In the late 1960s, however, these cases finally began to settle at the doorstep of the Supreme Court.

In 1968 the Supreme Court heard *Green v. County School Board of New Kent County,* a case from Virginia. The litigation hinged on Virginia's use of "freedom of choice" plans after its first desegregation strategy—pupil placement plans—had been ruled unacceptable. In New Kent County, Virginia, administrators allowed students to choose their school each year, keeping them in their same school if they did not express any other preference. Over the course of three years, 115 African Americans chose to attend a formerly all-white school, but no white student chose to switch enrollment to the county's all-black school. As a result, 85 percent of the district's black students still attended completely segregated schools.

After weighing legal arguments from both sides, the Court unanimously overturned the plan, noting that it placed the burden of desegregation on parents instead of the school board. The court ordered New Kent County to create "a system without a 'white' school and a 'Negro' school, but just schools," adding that "a plan that at this late date fails to provide meaningful assurance of prompt and effective disestablishment of a dual system is intolerable."

> *In 1969 the U.S. Supreme Court unanimously ruled that the "standard of allowing 'all deliberate speed' for desegregation is no longer constitutionally permissable."*

The following year the Court heard a case from Mississippi (*Alexander v. Holmes County Board of Education*), where 33 school districts had challenged a Circuit Court of Appeals ruling—handed down in July—that they had to present desegregation plans by the beginning of the upcoming fall term. The districts claimed that the ruling did not provide them nearly enough time to develop workable desegregation plans. Their position was supported by the administration of President Richard Nixon, which pressured the Department of Health, Education, and Welfare (HEW) to join the districts in requesting a delay in the court order. When the delay was granted by another appeals judge, the U.S. Supreme Court agreed to hear the case.

One month later, the full Court unanimously overturned the delay and declared that the "standard of allowing 'all deliberate speed' for desegregation is no longer constitutionally permissible. Under explicit holdings of this Court the obligation of every school district is to terminate dual school systems at once and to operate now and hereafter only unitary schools." Nixon was disappointed in the decision, but he encouraged the South to cooperate, promising conservative judicial appointments that would avoid such "activist" decisions in the future. In the meantime, the Supreme Court's judgment had an immediate impact on the pace of integration. The number of black students attending previously all-white schools in the South jumped from 23.4 percent in the 1968-69 school year to 33.1 percent in the 1970-71 year.

## Court-Ordered Busing

Even as these gains were being made, however, a Supreme Court decision further expanding *Brown* became mired in controversy. In 1971 the Court heard arguments in *Swann v. Charlotte-Mecklenburg Board of Education.* The case pitted a federal district judge who had overseen desegregation of a North Carolina district during the late 1960s against the district's board of education. By 1969 two-thirds of the district's 21,000 black students were attending schools with white students. The judge had called for "true desegregation" by 1970, however, and he mandated the use of cross-district busing in order to achieve this goal. Board members responded with a series of legal moves to block the implementation of the busing order.

Justice Hugo Black voted to use busing schemes to integrate the nation's schools, despite serious misgivings.

Justice Black and recently appointed Chief Justice Warren Burger were hesitant to approve "forced" busing. But they also did not want to give the appearance that the Court was reining in *Brown*. This concern eventually led them to set aside their misgivings and join the rest of the Court in ruling that the lower court did indeed have the power to use busing, ratios, and other tools to achieve desegregation. In addition, the Court noted that the use of a "racially neutral" assignment plan, if it failed to bring about desegregation, was "not acceptable simply because it appears to be neutral." Opponents of continuing desegregation measures did find some cause for optimism in the ruling, however. The opinion acknowledged that "neither school authorities nor district courts are constitutionally required to make year-by-year adjustments of the racial composition of student bodies once the affirmative duty to desegregate has been accomplished and racial discrimination through official action is eliminated from the system."

The final Supreme Court case to expand *Brown* had widespread implications, for it was the first case to involve a school district in the northern part of the country. Although northern states did not have laws requiring school segregation—known as *de jure* (by law) segregation—there existed a long tradition of racial separation that often resulted in *de facto* segregated schools (segregated in fact but not by law). For years the NAACP had battled against *de facto* segregation in the North. During the 1961-62 school year alone it had engaged in legal action against 55 Northern school districts. But no case against a Northern school reached the Supreme Court until 1973, when the Court heard arguments in *Keyes v. School District No. 1, Denver.*

The plaintiffs in this case claimed that the school district had deliberately drawn attendance zones to create segregated schools in one section of the city. In a 7-1 decision, the Supreme Court agreed with the lower court's ruling that the school district's actions constituted state-created segregation, and it approved the use of busing as a remedy. Although the ruling did not state that *de facto* segregation was automatically unconstitutional, it did place the burden of proving intent on the school district. If deliberate segregation is found in one area, the Court stated, "the burden is on the school authorities (regardless of claims that their 'neighborhood school policy' is racially neutral) to prove that their actions as to other segregated schools in the system were not likewise motivated by a segregative intent."

By the mid-1970s, several other Northern cities were under court desegregation orders, including Stamford, Connecticut; Fort Wayne, Indiana; Omaha, Nebraska; Milwaukee, Wisconsin; Buffalo, New York; and the Ohio cities of Dayton, Columbus, and Cleveland. The Northern city that saw the most conflict over desegregation was Boston, Massachusetts. In June 1974 a federal judge ordered the busing of over 20,000 students in order to achieve proportional racial representation throughout the district. Many parents objected to busing their children away from familiar neighborhood schools, and class issues further clouded the matter. Critics of the court-ordered busing plan fumed that it mainly affected working-class white families, while children who lived in the wealthy white suburbs avoided busing entirely.

When forced busing began in the fall of 1974, only ten of the 525 white students assigned to the former majority-black Roxbury High School showed up. Meanwhile, buses carrying 56 African Americans to their new school, South Boston High, were greeted by angry, stone-throwing protestors. Mobs also surrounded black students inside South Boston High, and there were widespread protests around the city. These protests sometimes turned violent. For example, gunshots were fired into the offices of the *Boston Globe,* which had expressed support for the busing plan, and the local NAACP branch was

Anger over Boston's 1974 busing plan was so great that school buses received police escorts.

firebombed. During the worst of the violence, more than 1,600 state and city police maintained a visible presence in Boston, joined by 100 riot-trained U.S. Marshals. The 82$^{nd}$ Airborne Division of the Army was even kept on stand-by in case it was needed to keep order. The protests over busing continued for some time, but many white families ultimately evaded the busing scheme by sending their children to private schools or moving to the suburbs. This "white flight," which took place in city after city in the 1960s and 1970s, led many observers to debate the effectiveness of busing and other desegregation measures.

## The Supreme Court Retreats from *Brown*

During President Richard Nixon's first term (1969-1973), he appointed four new members to the Supreme Court. These justices, who were generally

# Desegregation and the Hispanic American Community

Hispanic Americans—American citizens descended from Spanish-speaking families—have been an important minority within the United States since 1848, when the Treaty of Guadalupe Hidalgo ceded Mexican territory in the Southwest to the United States. Although they never endured enslavement like African Americans, Latinos historically have faced considerable discrimination in America, including school segregation. States with large Hispanic American populations, such as Texas and California, often maintained separate classrooms and schools for Latino students—although there were no specific laws mandating segregation, since Latinos were usually classified as "white" by the government.

At the same time that the NAACP fought against *de jure* segregation in the South, various Hispanic American parent and advocacy groups worked tirelessly to dismantle *de facto* segregation in the Southwest. The first school segregation case involving Latinos, *Del Rio Independent School District v. Salvatierra,* took place in Texas in 1930. When the district planned to expand a segregated "Mexican" school where children were taught in Spanish, Jesús Salvatierra and other parents sued, claiming that their children were being denied the resources given to "other white races." The League of United Latin American Citizens (LULAC) helped litigate the case, and a state judge issued an injunction against the school district. The parents lost their case on appeal, however. The higher court acknowledged that "school authorities have no power to arbitrarily segregate Mexican children … solely because they are Mexicans," but it ruled that it was permissible for the district to separate children because of language differences.

The battle was rejoined in 1931, when a principal at an elementary school near San Diego, California, barred the door against Mexican American students, instructing them to go to a separate, two-room facility for "Americanization." In *Alvarez v. the Board of Trustees of the Lemon Grove School District,* a local judge ruled that there was no basis in California law for segregating students of Mexican ancestry from whites, and he ordered their readmission into the school. Although this case did not serve as a legal precedent for later cases, many consider it the country's first ruling in favor of desegregation.

The 1947 case *Mendez v. Westminster School District,* which originated in Orange County, California, set a more important precedent. This suit was brought by a group of Hispanic parents angered by four districts that segregated Hispanic American students from white students, even if they were proficient in English. The defendants contended that the facilities were equal, and therefore permissible under *Plessy.* The plaintiffs won in federal district court and the judgment was confirmed on appeal. Indeed, the appeals judge rebuked the districts for their actions, declaring that "nowhere in any California law is there a suggestion that any segregation can be made of children within one of the great races." This case inspired California governor Earl Warren, who would later oversee the *Brown* ruling as chief justice of the Supreme Court, to lead the state to repeal laws segregating Asian and Native American children.

After the *Brown* ruling overturned legal segregation in 1954, Hispanic Americans continued their fight against *de facto* segregation. The 1970 federal case *Cisneros v. Corpus Christi Independent School District* was a landmark in this regard, for it extended the protections of the *Brown* decision to Mexican Americans, defining them as an identifiable minority with a history of discrimination. The judge added that "desegregating" schools by placing African Americans with similarly disadvantaged Latino students did not comply with *Brown.* The Supreme Court affirmed this view three years later in its *Keyes v. School District No. 1* decision.

Although these decisions extended the legal rights of *Brown* to Hispanic Americans, Latino students in many parts of the country are today confronted with the same resegregation trend seen in black communities. In fact, as Gary Orfield noted in *The Unfinished Agenda of Brown v. Board of Education,* Latinos are "segregated more than blacks both from whites and from the middle class and increasingly facing linguistic segregation." The educational challenges facing African Americans in the twenty-first century thus pose similar problems for Hispanic Americans, who in 2003 became the largest ethnic minority in the United States.

more conservative than their predecessors, led the Court to adopt a more cautious approach in addressing segregation. The first step in reducing court involvement came in 1974, in the *Milliken v. Bradley* case. This case originated in Michigan, where "white flight" to the suburbs had left the city of Detroit's schools heavily segregated. A federal district judge decided that involving the surrounding suburbs was the only way to desegregate Detroit's schools, so he ordered the creation of a busing program that would involve some 310,000 students from 53 suburbs.

This court order was roundly condemned by many parents. Several suburbs challenged the ruling, citing the logistical complexities of such a program and raising the specter of bus rides of an hour or more for numerous students. In a 5-4 decision, the Supreme Court ruled in favor of the suburbs. The majority determined that since the suburban districts had not engaged in segregation, they were not obligated to participate in efforts to find a remedy for Detroit's ills.

Not all the justices felt this way, however, as the close vote indicated. Justice Thurgood Marshall, the former NAACP lawyer who had joined the Court in 1967, wrote a heartfelt dissent in the case:

> Today's holding, I fear, is more a reflection of a perceived public mood that we have gone far enough in enforcing the Constitution's guarantee of equal justice than it is the product of neutral principles of law. In the short run, it may seem to be the easier course to allow our great metropolitan areas to be divided up each into two cities—one white, the other black—but it is a course, I predict, our people will ultimately regret.

Marshall's words were prophetic, for after *Milliken* the nation experienced a surge in *de facto* segregation caused by white migration to the suburbs. By the 1980s, urban school districts in the North were nearly as segregated as they had been before the 1954 *Brown v. Board of Education* ruling. Ironically, the South became the region with the fewest segregated schools. The percentage of African Americans in the region attending mostly black schools (schools with black populations greater than 90 percent) dropped from 77.5 percent in 1968 to 26.5 percent in 1992. Conversely, the decline in the Midwest was much smaller (from 58 percent in 1968 to 39.4 percent in 1992), and the number of African Americans attending mostly black schools actually increased in the Northeast, from 42.7 percent of all students in 1968 to 49.9 percent in 1992. In the West, increased population diversity drove a drop in segregation from 50.9 percent to 26.6 percent over the same time period.

In 1991 a key Supreme Court ruling gave further momentum to the "resegregation" trend. Back in 1972 the Oklahoma City school district had been ordered to implement a desegregation plan. The district used widespread busing to reduce segregation, and in 1977 the court ruled the district was in compliance and gave an order terminating the case. Eight years later, the school district decided to end its elementary school busing program and create neighborhood schools. Under this scheme, families still had the option to transfer a child to a school where they would be in the minority. Because of residential patterns, however, the new system meant that eleven schools would have African American populations of greater than 90 percent. Alarmed at this development, the NAACP mounted a legal challenge to the plan. The case eventually made its way all the way to the Supreme Court.

The Supreme Court ruled by a 5-3 vote in *Board of Education of Oklahoma City v. Dowell* that school districts were not responsible for changing social and economic conditions that resulted in *de facto* segregation. Thurgood Marshall once again dissented, noting that "in a district with a history of state-sponsored school segregation, racial separation, in my view, remains inherently unequal." Nevertheless, the Court reaffirmed its opinion on this issue one year later, in *Freeman v. Pitts*.

These rulings paved the way for communities to adopt a variety of "choice" and "neighborhood" enrollment programs that further accelerated the resegregation of American schools. The architects of these programs were not being racist. In fact, many of these programs were created with the express purpose of improving educational opportunities for minorities. But "choice" programs have been very controversial. "On one side are those who claim that poor kids in ghettos and barrios have the right (and ought to receive public money) to leave crummy schools and seek a quality education elsewhere," wrote Ellis Cose in *Beyond* Brown v. Board. "On the other side are those who say that vouchers will not appreciably increase the options of children attending wretched schools but will instead deprive public schools of resources they can ill afford to lose." In any case, the realities of "white flight" and the continuing socioeconomic divide between whites and minorities have produced myriad schools that are virtually one-race in character.

## Affirmative Action

When the Supreme Court began restricting remedies for *de facto* segregation, activists cast about for other ways to improve learning opportunities for minority students. In a 1977 revisiting of *Milliken v. Bradley* (known as *Milliken II*), the Supreme Court said that courts could order "compensatory or remedial educational programs for schoolchildren who have been subjected to past acts of *de jure* segregation." These remedies, designed to equalize what had become racially segregated facilities, could range from mandated reductions in class sizes to spending money on additional specialists and facilities.

The Supreme Court was not willing to authorize unlimited spending, however. In 1995 the justices considered *Missouri v. Jenkins*. This case involved the school district of Kansas City, Missouri, which had spent almost $800 million between 1985 and 1995 in an attempt to create "magnet" schools that would attract white students to segregated areas. The district succeeded in creating prime facilities, but white students still stayed away, and African Americans did not show appreciable improvements in student achievement. An appeals court mandated that the state of Missouri invest more money in the school district, but in a 5-4 vote the Supreme Court overturned the decision. Noting that many factors besides segregation affect student performance, the Court ruled that the level of student body integration could not be used as the sole yardstick for determining compliance with *Brown* and other integration laws. "While a mandate for significant educational improvement, both in teaching and in facilities, may have been justified originally, its indefinite extension is not," Chief Justice William Rehnquist wrote in his majority opinion.

Another remedy for the effects of segregation was "affirmative action," a phrase first coined by John F. Kennedy. This approach became government policy when Lyndon B. Johnson signed an executive order in 1965 requiring federal contractors to document that they had taken "affirmative action" in seeking minority employees. In education, affirmative action came to refer to admission policies, particularly at the university level, that sought to increase minority enrollment through quotas or preferential admissions. When slots in choice programs were reserved for African Americans and other minorities, a white backlash developed.

In 1978 the Supreme Court was called on to assess the constitutionality of these affirmative action programs. In *Bakke v. Regents of the University of*

*California* the Court ruled 5-4 that the quota system used by the medical school of the University of California at Davis was unconstitutional. But the Court also ruled, by another 5-4 vote, that the university was free to consider race as a factor in the admissions process. In the aftermath of this ruling, educational institutions around the country scrambled to find methods of increasing minority enrollment that would satisfy standards of constitutionality.

Several of these methods were questioned in court, particularly as anti-affirmative action forces grew in strength in the 1990s. In 1996, a U.S. Court of Appeals considered the admissions system at the University of Texas's Law School, which maintained different standards for white and minority candidates. In *Hopwood v. Texas* the appeals court found this dual-track system unconstitutional, and the Supreme Court declined to hear the appeal.

This development left many universities wondering just what kind of admission systems were acceptable. In 2003 the Supreme Court clarified the matter somewhat with a pair of cases from the University of Michigan. In *Gratz v. Bollinger*, the Court looked at the policy the university used for undergraduate admissions: candidates were granted points for various qualifications, including grades, test scores, alumni relationships, and minority status. In *Grutter v. Bollinger*, the Court examined the policy of Michigan's Law School, which considered race as one of several factors contributing to diversity. In *Gratz*, the Court held 6-3 that the automatic granting of points for race was too formulaic to be constitutional. In *Grutter*, however, a 5-4 majority ruled that the law school's "narrowly tailored" policy was permissible, for "student body diversity is a compelling state interest in the context of university admissions."

The 2003 Supreme Court rulings indicated the judiciary's belief that there was still a place for affirmative action in American education. Many states no longer agree, however. California and Washington both enacted bans on affirmative action in the late 1990s, and the early 2000s saw similar voter initiatives moving towards the ballot in other states.

## Reassessing *Brown* and School Desegregation

In the fifty years since *Brown*, the decision has received both high praise and deep condemnation. Its basic position—that segregation is morally wrong and inherently unequal—is almost universally acknowledged as correct.

*Brown I*'s declaration that segregation is unconstitutional "is no longer open to debate," Michael J. Klarman observed in the *Nation.* "Conservative legal commentators and prospective judicial nominees still criticize many landmark decisions of the Warren Court, but not *Brown.* No constitutional theory or theorist failing to support the result in *Brown* will be taken seriously today."

The "all deliberate speed" component of the *Brown II* decision, however, has been widely criticized. Even Justice Hugo Black acknowledged in 1969 that "'all deliberate speed' has turned out to be only a soft euphemism for delay." Writing in *Silent Covenants,* scholar Derrick Bell explained how the *Brown II* decision undercut the potential of the original *Brown v. Board of Education* ruling:

> Having promised much in its first *Brown* decision, the Court in *Brown II* said in effect that its landmark earlier decision was more symbolic than real.... Its advocates expected that the *Brown* decision would cut through the dark years of segregation with laserlike intensity. The resistance, though, was open and determined. At best, the *Brown* precedent did no more than cast a half-light on that resistance, enough to encourage its supporters but not bright enough to reveal just how long and difficult the road to equal educational opportunity would prove to be.

With the advent of resegregation, several scholars have even debated whether *Brown's* ruling mandating school desegregation was truly in the best interests of minority students. Supreme Court Justice Clarence Thomas, who in 1991 became the second African American to join the court, attacked the underlying assumption of *Brown* in his concurring opinion in *Missouri v. Jenkins:* "The court has read our cases to support the theory that black students suffer an unspecified psychological harm from segregation that retards their mental and educational development. This approach not only relies upon questionable social science research rather than constitutional principle, but it also rests on an assumption of black inferiority."

*Brown* also has been criticized for assuming that changing a child's school would address "the underlying social, political, and material inequalities that [*Brown*] did not and perhaps could not tackle head on," Regina Austin observed in the *Journal of Appellate Practice and Process.* "Segregated

## Segregation Still a Part of Alabama's State Constitution

A half-century after the *Brown v. Board of Education* ruling, federal laws ensured the existence of integrated schools in the state of Alabama. But the state constitution actually still contained segregation-era language requiring separate schools for "white and colored children." In addition, the Alabama constitution still contained references to the use of poll taxes once imposed to prevent blacks from voting.

Neither of these provisions had been enforced for years, but critics felt that the continued presence of this language was a shameful stain on the state's reputation. With this in mind, a proposed amendment to the state constitution erasing these references to segregation and poll taxes was put before Alabama voters on November 2, 2004. Since the presidential election was the same day, high voter turnout for the amendment was assured.

When the vote count was tallied up, the state announced that voters had defeated the amendment by a very slim margin. A mandatory statewide recount confirmed that the proposal to remove the segregation-era language was defeated by 0.13 percent (1,850 votes out of more than 1.3 million cast).

Some observers asserted that the amendment's defeat was due in part to voter distrust of all constitutional amendments and unsubstantiated concerns that the amendment's passage might trigger higher taxes to pay for public school improvements. Afterward, some leading opponents of the amendment insisted that they would accept a differently worded amendment removing the constitution's references to segregated schools. But many disappointed supporters of the proposed amendment expressed a deep conviction that persistent racism was the chief reason that the amendment went down to defeat.

schools were not just determiners of those inequalities; they were a reflection of them." These and other critics argue that until the underlying social inequities facing African Americans are addressed, desegregated schools will provide only limited help in breaking the centuries-old cycle of oppression, poverty, and ignorance created by racism in America.

Fifty years after *Brown,* the goal of providing truly equal educational opportunities for children of all races continues to frustrate and perplex educators, parents, and politicians. Other trends have complicated this challenge as well. These include the robust growth in the population of other minority groups, including Latinos and Asian Americans; the growing income gap between poor Americans and middle- and upper-class Americans; and patterns of migration within the country that influence enrollment and education funding.

Yet despite all this, the Supreme Court's 1954 *Brown v. Board of Education* ruling continues to be widely recognized as a landmark in American history—a giant stride forward in the nation's never-ending effort to live up to its stated ideals. "Taking stock of the current state of public education, it is clear that *Brown* has not achieved its primary purpose of guaranteeing equal educational opportunity for children of color," observed Robert Carter, one of the lawyers to litigate the original *Brown* case, in a *Nation* article commemorating its fiftieth anniversary. Nevertheless, he concluded,

> in making equality for all people a fundamental tenet in our society, *Brown* provides the foundation for activists and scholars committed to fulfilling its promise to pursue that goal. I am optimistic or fatuous enough to believe that at some future point in time, America will give credence to that unfulfilled promise.

# Chapter Eight

# BROWN'S LEGACY IN CIVIL RIGHTS

[After *Brown*,] Blacks were no longer supplicants seeking, pleading, begging to be treated as full-fledged members of the human race; no longer were they appealing to morality, to conscience, to white America's better instincts. They were entitled to equal treatment as a right under the law; when such treatment was denied, they were being deprived—in fact robbed—of what was legally theirs. As a result, the Negro was propelled into a stance of insistent militancy. Now he was demanding—fighting to secure and possess what was rightfully his.

—NAACP Legal Defense and Education Fund Counsel Robert Carter, writing about the *Brown* case in 1968

Although the *Brown v. Board of Education* case only addressed segregation in public school education, the legal precedent it set spelled doom for the entire institutionalized segregation system known as Jim Crow. Indeed, the Supreme Court's May 1954 decision changed the social and cultural landscape of the United States decisively and irrevocably. "Had there been no May 17, 1954, I'm not sure there would have been a Little Rock," said civil rights leader and U.S. Representative John Lewis in a 2002 speech commemorating the Supreme Court ruling. "I'm not sure there would have been a Martin Luther King Jr., or Rosa Parks, had it not been for May 17, 1954. It created an environment for us to push, for us to pull. We live in a different country, a better country, because of what happened here [in Topeka, Kansas] in 1954. And we must never forget it. We must tell the story, over and over and over."

## *Brown* Ruling Spurs Widespread Legal Changes

In the same term that the Supreme Court announced *Brown,* it remanded other cases involving segregated universities, a junior college, and a city amphitheater to lower courts "for consideration in light of the Segregation Cases ... and conditions that now prevail." The Court would also use *Brown* as a precedent in several *per curiam* ("by the court," or non-opinion) orders to desegregate public facilities including hospitals, city buses, parks, theaters, swimming pools, beaches, and golf courses. In many cases, lower courts used *Brown* as justification for overturning segregation, and the Supreme Court did not even bother to hear oral arguments before upholding these rulings.

In other cases, the Supreme Court cited *Brown* in overturning an array of segregation statutes. In 1960's *Wolfe v. North Carolina,* the Court overturned the arrest of a group of African Americans who persisted in playing on a city golf course after being denied admission. Three years later, in *Johnson v. Virginia,* the Court similarly overturned the contempt conviction of an African American who refused to move from the "white" seating section of a courtroom. In a *per curiam* ruling, the Court cited *Brown* as evidence that "it is no longer open to question that a State may not constitutionally require segregation of public facilities." That same year, in *Watson v. Memphis,* the Court ordered the immediate desegregation of public parks in Memphis, Tennessee. In 1967 the Supreme Court overturned so-called "miscegenation" laws—those statutes outlawing interracial marriage. The Court's 9-0 vote in *Loving v. Virginia,* breaking the South's greatest taboo, would have been virtually unthinkable before the *Brown* decision.

These rulings underscored the degree to which the *Brown v. Board of Education* decision "not only legally ended segregation, it deprived segregationist practices of their moral legitimacy as well," wrote David Halberstam in *The Fifties:*

> It was therefore perhaps the single most important moment in the decade, the moment that separated the old order from the new and helped create the tumultuous era just arriving.... This had a profound effect on the growing and increasingly powerful communications industry in the United States. Because of *Brown,* reporters for the national press, print and now television, felt emboldened to cover stories of racial prejudice.... *Brown v. Board of Education* was just the beginning of

a startling new period of change, not just in the area of civil
rights, but in all aspects of social behavior. One era was ending
and another beginning.

## The Birth of the Civil Rights Movement

Nevertheless, this groundbreaking decision was not enough to guarantee
African Americans equal rights under the law. "To gain their due, black Americans soon discovered, they would have to go on the march, under the banner
of lawful entitlement, and not wait to be gifted with the nation's long with-
held kindness," as Richard Kluger observed in *Simple Justice.*

The start of the civil rights movement in the mid-1950s confirmed
Nathan Margold's prediction in his 1931 NAACP report that "the psychological effect [of a court victory] upon Negroes themselves will be that of stirring
the spirit of revolt among them." The first sign came on December 1, 1955,
just months after *Brown II,* when an NAACP secretary named Rosa Parks
sparked the Montgomery Bus Boycott by refusing to give up her seat to a
white man. Over the next year, African Americans shunned city bus lines in
favor of car pools and taxi services. Despite harassment from Montgomery
police, arrests of the boycott's leaders, and bombings of black homes and
churches, the African American community continued the boycott. In
December 1956, a federal court order—combined with the financial impact
of the boycott—forced Montgomery to desegregate the city's buses.

Meanwhile, a new generation of civil rights leaders came to the fore.
These individuals, buoyed by the *Brown v. Board* ruling and other signs that
America's walls of racial discrimination were crumbling, brought energy and
hope to black communities across the country. One of those leaders was the
Reverend Martin Luther King, Jr., who helped found the Southern Christian
Leadership Conference (SCLC), an organization dedicated to nonviolent
protest against discriminatory laws.

The next major step in the fight for civil rights began in February 1960,
when the first sit-in of a segregated lunch counter was staged in Greensboro,
North Carolina, by students from North Carolina A&T University. Within two
weeks, these sit-in protests had spread to fifteen other cities. Many of these sit-
ins were guided by the Congress of Racial Equality (CORE), a civil rights
advocacy group founded by an interracial group of Chicago students in 1942.
CORE's strategy was for members arrested for participating in sit-ins to accept

Violence against buses carrying "freedom riders" became so widespread that national guardsmen were deployed to protect passengers from harm.

jail sentences rather than pay bail—a decision that both emphasized the righteousness of their cause and brought publicity to it. In 1961 CORE sponsored its first "freedom rides," interracial attempts to desegregate interstate buses and bus stations. Voter registration drives also became a priority of CORE and other civil rights organizations. Such efforts were often met with ugly violence by segregationists, but these attacks served to increase public sympathy for the civil rights cause.

Besides engaging in civil disobedience against segregation laws, African Americans began participating in public marches to agitate for change. The first and most famous of these was the 1963 March on Washington, which gathered some 250,000 black and white people together in peaceful protest at the nation's capital. The march brought together African American labor leaders and activists from the NAACP, SCLC, CORE, the Urban League, and other organizations, and it focused on issues ranging from fair employment to fighting segregation laws. The most notable event of the day was King's historic "I Have a Dream" speech, which was broadcast live to the entire nation.

Another march would prove to be just as influential, but for more shocking reasons. In 1965 a group led by John Lewis of the SNCC organized a march from Selma, Alabama, to the state capital of Montgomery to lobby for voting rights for African Americans. The group had scarcely left Selma when it was confronted by the local sheriff and state troopers. When the marchers refused their order to disperse, the police used tear gas, clubs, whips, and horses against the crowd. The televised footage of ordinary black citizens being brutalized in this manner shocked television audiences around the country. Other peaceful protests in the South, broken up by police with dogs and fire hoses, similarly broadened public opinion against anti-civil rights forces. This change in public perception made it much easier for presidents Kennedy and Johnson to propose new federal laws against discrimination.

*"Brown was about far more than schools. The whole Martin Luther King Jr. phase of the civil rights movement would never have happened without Brown. Brown was the breakthrough."*

## The Renewal of Civil Rights Legislation

Congress had first passed civil rights laws during the Reconstruction era, but later Supreme Court decisions had gutted their effectiveness by handing enforcement over to the states. With the Court's decision in *Brown*, however, civil rights advocates saw a chance to re-establish statutes against discrimination that could be more easily enforced under federal law.

The first such legislation was the Civil Rights Act of 1957, which primarily dealt with voting rights. Southern opponents succeeded in making this a mostly toothless law, but the act did create a permanent Commission on Civil Rights to investigate and report on incidents of discrimination. The Commission's findings and recommendations would strongly influence later civil rights legislation. Another Civil Rights Act was approved in May 1960 to address some of the deficiencies of the 1957 Act. This legislation made it a federal crime to obstruct a desegregation order, and it mandated that election officers preserve federal voting records for use in investigations by the Attorney General.

In 1963 President Johnson pressed for an ambitious new slate of civil rights legislation. He encountered fierce resistance in the South, especially from

The Civil Rights Act of 1968 was passed one week after the assassination of Martin Luther King Jr., seen here delivering his "I Have a Dream Speech" at the Lincoln Memorial.

members of his own Democratic Party. But the president convinced enough Republican senators to vote his way that the Senate overcame a Southern filibuster and passed the Civil Rights Act of 1964 into law. The act was far-reaching, with eleven provisions, or titles. The most important provision banned racial discrimination in "places of public accommodation," which included almost every restaurant, hotel, and theater in the country. The act also gave the Department of Justice the ability to bring civil actions against discrimination, and tied federal funding to compliance with desegregation regulations.

Further civil rights legislation was passed under the Johnson Administration as well. Spurred on by public outrage against the violence in Selma, Congress passed the Voting Rights Act of 1965. The act prohibited poll taxes, literacy taxes, and other methods used over the years to disenfranchise African Americans. In addition, it placed the burden of proof in voter intimidation cases on the state, not the individual. The final significant piece of legislation from this era was the Civil Rights Act of 1968, also known as the Fair Housing Act, which outlawed discrimination in the sale, rental, or financing of housing. Although there was some debate in Congress over the bill, the tragic assassination of Martin Luther King, Jr. on April 4, 1968, made it much more difficult for opponents to defend their position. The legislation passed quickly without amendments, and President Johnson signed the bill into law just a week after King's death.

## Modern Assessments of *Brown*

In May 2004 people all across the United States commemorated the fiftieth anniversary of the historic *Brown v. Board of Education* decision. One of the most significant events recognizing the occasion was the grand opening of a

The *Brown v. Board of Education* National Historic Site opened in Topeka, Kansas, on May 17, 2004, on the fiftieth anniversary of the famous ruling.

museum at the *Brown v. Board of Education* National Historic Site in Topeka. During this period, many observers noted the groundbreaking nature of the decision and credited it with changing the nation. "Sometimes history serves as a magnifying mirror—making momentous what actually was not," remarked Ellis Cose in *Beyond* Brown v. Board. "But *Brown v. Board of Education of Topeka, Kansas,* is the real thing: a Supreme Court decision that fundamentally and forever changed America. It jump-started the modern civil-rights movement and excised a cancer eating a hole in the heart of the Constitution" (See Reflecting on *Brown* v. *Board of Education,* Fifty Years Later, p. 223). Civil rights scholar Leland Ware offered an even more succinct summary of *Brown's* importance in *Black Issues in Higher Education:* "*Brown* was about far more than schools. The whole Martin Luther King Jr. phase of the civil rights movement would never have happened without *Brown. Brown* was the breakthrough."

Other scholars have observed that *Brown* also reflected evolving American attitudes towards race. "The Justices in *Brown* did not think they were creating a movement for racial reform; they understood that they were working with, not against, historical forces," remarked *Nation* contributor Michael

J. Klarman. Writing in the *Journal of Southern History,* history professor Raymond Wolters offered a similar perspective, asserting that:

> *Brown* was accepted because several other forces had prepared the way: scientific racism had been called into question by recent scholarship and discredited by the excesses of Adolf Hitler; the Great Migration of blacks out of the South had led to black voting in urban areas and in some cities black control of the balance of political power; the Cold War had brought about competition for influence in the Third World; and African Americans had mobilized their own resources—their churches, colleges, and racial betterment organizations—and created a powerful civil rights movement. Had these other factors not been present, the *Brown* Court would not have prevailed against official apartheid.

*Brown* also created new perceptions of the Supreme Court. In their study *Brown v. Board of Education: Caste, Culture, and the Constitution,* Robert J. Cottrol, Raymond T. Diamond, and Leland B. Ware noted that

> *Brown* would also come to change the way many Americans would view the courts and their proper role in American governance. *Brown* was initially criticized by many as a severe kind of judicial overreaching, the forging of a constitutional mandate not originally intended by the framers of the Fourteenth Amendment. That view still exists in some quarters. But for many, *Brown* has become exhibit A in the case for a more activist judiciary, an argument that courts, because of their relative insulation from political pressures, might in fact be better vehicles to resolve knotty social problems.

## A Challenge to American Ideals

Cheryl Brown Henderson, daughter of the plaintiff who originally gave his name to the *Brown* case, also sees the *Brown* ruling as a landmark defense of individual rights for all Americans, whatever their ethnic heritage. In *The Unfinished Agenda of Brown v. Board of Education,* Henderson remarked that

> When the Supreme Court used the Fourteenth Amendment to render its decision, *Brown v. Board* became important for every

citizen, not just African Americans. It showed that we all had sovereign rights that could not be restricted by state and local governments. That decision impacted the lives of women, people with disabilities, blacks, whites, Hispanics, Asians, everyone living in this country. Before the *Brown* decision we were still living in a system of states' rights, where some of our rights were honored and respected while some were not, depending on where you lived.

Indeed, the *Brown v. Board of Education* decision dared Americans to live up to the noble ideals of their country's founding, including its central tenet that "all men are created equal." As Cottrol, Diamond, and Ware commented:

The decision posed a direct challenge to the way millions of ordinary white Americans lived their lives. More significantly, *Brown* posed a direct challenge to the values of millions of ordinary white Americans, to their beliefs, their deeply rooted prejudices, their views concerning how proper lives should be lived, and of course the proper places of blacks and whites in America.

Today, half a century after the Warren Court handed down the *Brown* decision, the quest to make America a land of truly equal opportunity for all of its children continues. And although many of the most important steps in this journey have taken place in courtrooms, the outcome ultimately will be determined in the nation's homes, schools, factories, and places of worship. As Jack Greenberg, one of the LDF lawyers in the original *Brown* case, concluded in his memoir *Crusaders in the Courts:* "Altogether, school desegregation has been a story of conspicuous achievements, flawed by marked failures, the causes of which lie beyond the capacity of lawyers to correct. Lawyers can do right, they can do good, but they have their limits. The rest of the job is up to society."

# BIOGRAPHIES

## Daisy Bates (1914-1999)
*Civil Rights Activist and Advisor to the Little Rock Nine*

Daisy Bates was born Daisy Lee Gatson on November 11, 1914, in Huttig, Arkansas. She was adopted at a young age by Orlee Smith, a lumber grader, and his wife Susan. Bates believed these were her real parents until the age of eight. At that time she learned that her biological mother had been raped and murdered by three white men. After the local sheriff did nothing to find the killers, Bates's father had been so demoralized he left town, leaving his daughter with the Smiths.

The discovery of the circumstances surrounding her adoption colored young Daisy's perceptions of the world. This information, combined with the indignities she and other African Americans suffered in segregated Arkansas, led her to develop a deep hatred for white people. She rejected a little white girl who had previously been her friend and spurned the kindness of white neighbors. Her parents sent her to spend time with family and friends further north, including some time in Canada and Memphis, Tennessee. Daisy's experiences in these places taught her that not all white people were racists. Her perspective on this issue was also influenced by a deathbed challenge from her adoptive father, as she recalled in her memoir *The Long Shadow of Little Rock:*

> Don't hate white people just because they're white. If you hate, make it count for something. Hate the humiliations we are living under in the south. Hate the discrimination that eats away at the soul of every black man and woman. Hate the insults hurled at us by white scum—then try to do something about it, or your hate won't spell a thing.

In 1941 Daisy Gatson married Lucius Christopher "L. C." Bates, a family friend she had first met at the age of fifteen. L. C. Bates was a journalist who

125

had lost his job during the Great Depression and turned to insurance sales to make ends meet. He had a college degree in journalism, however, and wanted to return to the field. After their marriage, the couple moved to Little Rock, Arkansas, and used their savings to lease a printing plant. On May 9, 1941, L. C. and Daisy Bates published the first issue of the *Arkansas State Press*.

## Building a Respected Activist Newspaper

The Bateses worked together to write, edit, and publish the weekly editions of the *State Press*. They focused on issues important to the African American community, and within a few months their circulation had grown to 10,000 readers. To acquire more skills, Bates took business and public relations classes at Shorter College, a local school founded by the African Methodist Episcopal (AME) Church. She also took flying lessons, although the rising cost of her insurance premiums forced her to halt the lessons just as she was on the verge of earning her pilot's license.

After the United States entered World War II in December of 1941, a military base was opened near Little Rock. Camp Robinson had a large number of black soldiers, and many of them spent their weekends in the city. The Bateses documented several incidents of police brutality against these visiting African Americans in the *State Press,* including the shooting death of an African American sergeant by a local policeman. Daisy Bates came to the crime scene and filed a report in the *State Press;* later articles documented how nothing was done to prosecute the policeman by either the U.S. Army or Little Rock officials. The coverage stirred the local black community to protest, but it also angered local businessmen. They were concerned that the bad publicity would cost them business, and most of them withdrew their advertising support from the newspaper. Faced with potential ruin, the Bateses worked extra hours to take their paper directly to the people. After a year they had doubled their circulation to 20,000 and reclaimed many advertisers. The *State Press* continued to cover incidents of discrimination and brutality against African Americans, and it soon became the leading black newspaper in the state.

After World War II, Bates wrote articles detailing the persecution black veterans faced in returning to the South; she also covered the community's need for improved economic and social conditions. The paper's advocacy helped prompt significant changes in city policies, including the hiring of

African Americans to police black neighborhoods. As a result, Bates recalled in her memoir, Little Rock had earned "a reputation as a liberal Southern city" by the late 1940s.

Bates's role at the paper continued to grow as well. In 1946 her husband took a long-needed vacation, and during his absence Daisy wrote, edited, and published the weekly editions herself. After his return, she continued chasing controversial stories. During a local oil worker strike, she covered the conflict that led to the murder of a striker by a replacement worker. When the murderer was acquitted and three onlooking strikers were arrested on trumped-up charges, Bates criticized the local judge who oversaw the trials. The article led the judge to order the Bateses arrested for contempt. The couple appealed the decision, and their conviction was eventually overturned by Arkansas's Supreme Court.

## Spurs Desegregation in Little Rock

Besides her work on the State Press, Bates was involved in many community groups, including the local branch of the National Association for the Advancement of Colored People (NAACP). In 1952 she was elected president of the state conference of NAACP branches, a position she would hold for the next seven years. That period of time saw great changes in Little Rock. Bates's efforts contributed to the desegregation of Little Rock's bus system in 1956, but it was her role in ending school segregation that brought her national attention.

After the Brown v. Board of Education decision in 1954, Bates and Little Rock NAACP president J. C. Crenshaw put pressure on the local school board to begin desegregation. Bates began escorting African American children to white schools to register them as students; when they were denied because of their race, she documented the incidents in the State Press.

Little Rock's school board eventually drew up plans to desegregate the city's schools, but Bates and Crenshaw believed the plan moved too slowly. They filed suit with the NAACP Legal Defense and Education Fund in 1955, and a federal judge ruled that Little Rock had to begin executing their plan in the fall of 1957. The Blossom Plan, named after Superintendent Virgil Blossom, called for desegregation to begin in the high schools. Out of eighty black applicants, seventeen were chosen to attend Central High School and nine decided to accept the transfers. These students—Minnijean Brown, Elizabeth Eckford, Ernest Green, Thelma Mothershed, Melba Patillo, Gloria Ray, Terrence Roberts, Jefferson Thomas, and Carlotta Walls—became known as the Little Rock Nine.

As a highly visible advisor to—and advocate for—the Little Rock Nine, Bates faced harassment even before the school year began. In August 1957 a rock crashed through the front window of the Bates home, the first in a series of missiles, gunshots, and bombs targeting her home. She was forced to keep her telephone off the hook because of the constant calls she received threatening violence against her and the Little Rock Nine. Nevertheless, Bates promised to look after the Nine and keep them safe. This promise proved difficult to keep. On September 4, 1957, for example, Elizabeth Eckford did not get Bates's message to meet the escort of interracial ministers she had arranged for the Nine on their first day of school. She was surrounded by a mob and only escaped with the help of a sympathetic white bystander.

The school year began without the Nine, who were prevented from entering the facility by state National Guardsmen called out by Arkansas Governor Orval Faubus. Bates arranged for the students to receive private tutoring from a group of local professors. The students finally were able to take their seats on September 25, after President Dwight D. Eisenhower sent federal troops to Little Rock to protect the Nine.

Once they had been placed at Central High, the Nine often met at Bates's home, where they received both academic and emotional support. When the Nine suffered harassment in school, Bates attended meetings with their parents and school administrators. She also secured personal bodyguards for the Nine by threatening to withdraw them from Central High and blame the Army for failing to protect them. Her dedication to the Little Rock Nine was evident to all. "I can see why Mrs. Bates was successful as president of the state NAACP. She was a good infighter, persistent, intelligent, unintimidated—a woman who made a choice of this career fully aware of its dangers to her person and also its rewards in the prestige and service of her people," wrote Elizabeth Huckaby, the school's vice-principal for girls, in her memoir *Crisis at Central High.*

Bates not only faced physical threats and harassment for her work on behalf of the Little Rock Nine, she endured government persecution. In October 1957 she was arrested and charged with failing to provide NAACP membership lists to the city council, contrary to a recently enacted city ordinance. Bates refused to comply with the order, knowing that if the NAACP's membership was made public, its members could face discrimination and intimidation from segregationists. She was fined, but the NAACP helped her appeal the charges. They took the fight all the way to the Supreme Court, which overturned her conviction in 1960's *Bates v. Little Rock;* the justices unanimously ruled that the city's law was an unconstitutional restriction on freedom of assembly.

## Devotes Herself to Civil Rights

Bates sacrificed a great deal to help the Little Rock Nine desegregate Central High School. Businesses that had supported the *Arkansas State Press* withdrew their advertising under threat of boycott by the segregationist community. With little revenue coming in, the Bateses were forced to close their newspaper in 1959. L. C. Bates subsequently took a position with the NAACP, and Daisy Bates spent the next two years writing her memoir, *The Long Shadow of Little Rock,* which was published in 1962. When the book was reprinted in 1988, it won an American Book Award from the Before Columbus Foundation.

Bates lived in New York City and Washington, D.C. after the *State Press* went out of business. During the early 1960s she traveled the country on behalf of the Democratic National Committee. She then worked on President Lyndon Johnson's "War on Poverty" program until suffering a stroke in 1965. She returned to Arkansas, where she contributed to revitalization projects aimed at African American communities. She retired in 1974, but remained involved in various charities and advocacy groups. Her husband L.C. died in 1980, and four years later she re-established the *Arkansas State Press* in his honor. The first issue of the paper sold out, but Bates sold her interest in the paper in 1987.

In total, Bates received some two hundred honors and awards over her lifetime, including the NAACP's prestigious Spingarn Medal, which she shared with the Little Rock Nine in 1958. Bates died on November 4, 1999, just a week before the Little Rock Nine received the Congressional Gold Medal, the nation's highest civilian honor. She lay in state for public viewing, the first African American to be so honored by the city of Little Rock. At her memorial service, President Bill Clinton eulogized the civil rights pioneer for a long and fruitful life: "I like Daisy Bates, not only because of what she did at Little Rock, but because of the way she lived right to the end," Clinton said. "And when she lost things that are painful for any person to lose, somehow what was left became more pure, more strong—almost like a diamond that was chipped away in form and shines more brightly." In 2001 the state of Arkansas declared a state holiday honoring Bates, to be observed on President's Day each February.

## Sources

Bates, Daisy. *The Long Shadow of Little Rock.* New York: McKay, 1962.

Bennett, Lerone, Jr. "Chronicles of Black Courage: The Little Rock 10." *Ebony,* December 1997.

"Clinton Joins in Little Rock Memorial Service Honoring Civil Rights Heroine Daisy Bates." *Jet,* May 15, 2000.

"Fighter for Integration: Daisy Gatson Bates." *New York Times,* September 24, 1957.

Huckaby, Elizabeth. *Crisis at Central High School: Little Rock, 1957-1958.* Baton Rouge: Louisiana State University Press, 1980.

Hughes, Langston. *Fight for Freedom: The Story of the NAACP.* New York: W.W. Norton, 1962.

Martin, Douglas. "Daisy Bates, Civil Rights Leader, Dies at 84." *New York Times,* November 5, 1999.

## Kenneth B. Clark (1914–2005)

*Psychologist, Social Scientist, and Professor Who Researched Effects of Segregation on African Americans*

Kenneth Bancroft Clark was born on July 24, 1914, in the Panama Canal Zone. He was the son of Arthur Bancroft and Miriam (Hanson) Clark, both natives of Jamaica. Arthur Clark had a steady job in Panama as a superintendent of cargo for the United Fruit Company, but his wife wanted Kenneth and his sister to be raised in America, believing they would have more opportunities there. The elder Clark, however, did not want to leave his management job to move to a country where he would be unlikely to find an equal position. Young Kenneth was only four years old when the family left his father behind in Panama and moved to New York City. His mother found a job as a seamstress and settled down in the uptown region of Manhattan known as Harlem.

Clark grew up in Harlem, which during the 1920s was an ethnically diverse neighborhood with a growing African American population. Many black writers, musicians, artists, and scholars came to prominence during this time, which was later called the "Harlem Renaissance." It was in this positive culture of African American success that Clark came of age. He attended schools with majority white populations, and recalled that his teachers held him to the same standards of excellence that they expected of other students. This experience would have a profound influence on Clark's future research and career.

Clark did experience racism during his youth, however. His mother battled to make sure he attended an academic high school, refusing the school system's efforts to funnel him into a vocational training program. At George Washington High School, Clark performed well in all his subjects, especially economics, but became disenchanted with the field when a teacher refused to give him an award for excellence because of his race.

## Drawn to Psychology

When he entered Howard University, the country's most prominent African American university, Clark intended to become a physician. A second-year psychology class soon changed his mind, however. Intrigued by the complexities of human behavior and the origins of racism and other emotions, he decided to major in psychology.

Clark received his bachelor's degree in 1935 and a master's degree the following year. During his time at Howard, he also edited the school paper and organized a group of students to picket the Capitol because its restaurants did not serve African Americans.

Clark could have pursued a doctorate at Howard, but his professors encouraged him to seek a more prestigious program. He gained admittance to Columbia University, an Ivy League school in New York City. In 1940 he became the first African American to receive a doctorate in psychology at Columbia. He was soon followed by his wife, Mamie Phipps Clark, whom he had met at Howard and married in 1938. She also completed bachelor's and master's degrees in the field of psychology at Howard before receiving her doctorate in psychology from Columbia in 1943. She was the second African American (after her husband) and first African American woman to do so.

## Investigating Racism and Its Effects

After receiving his doctorate, Clark spent one year teaching at the Hampton Institute, a black college in Virginia, then worked another year as a social science analyst for the U.S. Office of War Information. In 1942 Clark began a long tenure in the psychology department at the City College of New York (CCNY). He started as an instructor in 1942, became a full professor in 1960, and taught there until his retirement as professor emeritus in 1975. His early years at CCNY were filled with pioneering research, as Clark and his wife explored the effects of segregation on kindergarten students in Washington, D.C. Over the course of a decade, the couple published several articles in major journals and became well-respected experts in the field.

It was Clark's work at the 1950 Midcentury White House Conference on Children and Youth that brought him to wider prominence. Clark wrote a summary of existing research on segregation and its negative psychological effect on American children for that conference; his report was later revised and published as *Prejudice and Your Child* in 1955. This report came to the attention of NAACP Associate Counsel Robert Carter. Intrigued by the work the Clarks had done in demonstrating the damage that segregation did to children's self-esteem, Carter invited the psychologist to assist the NAACP Legal Defense and Education Fund (LDF) in preparing its school segregation cases. Clark accepted the invitation. "I had some doubts about the effectiveness of the legal approach in curing the basic problems," he later admitted to Richard Kluger in *Simple Justice,* "but I guess I was envious that they were actually doing something specific to improve things while I was off in the scholarly area, vaguely wishing to be part of what they were doing."

Clark played an important role in the LDF's preparations for court. In addition to his testimony as an expert witness, he helped prepare social science material for the legal briefs and brought other experts into the fight. For *Briggs v. Elliott* (one of five cases that were eventually considered by the U.S. Supreme Court under the banner of *Brown v. Board of Education*), Clark traveled to Clarendon County, South Carolina, to administer the famous "doll test" he and his wife had developed to assess the self-perception and self-esteem of African American children. The test involved giving both black and white dolls to children and asking them to identify the dolls that looked most like themselves. Clark also asked them to attach "nice" and "bad" labels to the dolls and vote for the dolls they like best. All of the tested black children correctly identified the dolls' race. But almost half picked the white dolls as "most like themselves," and more than half called the white doll "nice" and the black one "bad."

These results clearly showed that many black children had absorbed—and come to believe—societal messages that blacks were inferior to whites. On the witness stand, Clark confidently interpreted these results for the court: "These children in Clarendon County, like other human beings who are subjected to an obviously inferior status in the society in which they live, have been definitely harmed in the development of their personalities." The three-judge panel ultimately decided *Briggs* in favor of the defendants, but the testimony of Clark and other social scientists clearly influenced dissenting judge J. Waties Waring, who issued an opinion condemning how segregation "poisoned" the minds of children.

Clark also testified in two other preliminary school segregation trials: Delaware's *Gebhart v. Belton* and Virginia's *Davis v. County School Board of Prince Edward County* (both of which eventually were folded into the Supreme Court's *Brown v. Board* decision). In both cases Clark conducted tests or interviews with children from the district in question, and in both cases he testified that they had been adversely affected by segregation. In the Delaware case, Clark's testimony contributed to Chancellor Collins Seitz's finding that segregation "creates a mental health problem in many Negro children with a resulting impediment to their educational progress" and his subsequent order to admit the plaintiffs to white schools. In the Virginia case, the ruling went against the NAACP and Clark, but the psychological testimony they presented became a part of the record and had to be reckoned with in future rulings.

When the NAACP legal team began preparing briefs for the Supreme Court's *Brown v. Board* hearing, it asked Clark to help prepare a survey of current social science opinion on the issue. The document he produced in collaboration with former CCNY colleague Isidor Chein and Stuart W. Cook, the chairman of psychology at New York University, was submitted as an appendix to the NAACP's Supreme Court brief. Although Clark did not take part in the Supreme Court trial—only arguments, not testimony, are heard before the Court—his work clearly played a part in the Court's decision to hold school segregation unconstitutional. In explaining that segregation's harmful effects are "amply supported by modern authority," the first source Chief Justice Earl Warren cited was Clark's work from 1950's Midcentury White House Conference on Children and Youth.

## Continues Research and Fights against Poverty

Clark and his wife contributed to the black community in other ways as well. During their research, they had documented the paucity of social services provided to residents of Harlem. When the city refused to expand existing services into the neighborhood, the Clarks founded the Northside Testing and Consultation Center (later named the Northside Center for Child Development) in 1946 to provide mental health and social services to Harlem's children. Mamie Clark served as its executive director until she retired in 1980, while Kenneth Clark was its research director for twenty years.

In 1962 Clark used federal funds to found Harlem Youth Opportunities Unlimited (HARYOU), an anti-delinquency program designed to help disadvantaged youth. Two years into the program, he produced a farsighted report that called for community-based strategies to combat poverty and violence and to help students achieve. Twenty years later, this type of approach would become enormously popular in community revitalization programs. At the time, however, Clark's suggestions were undermined by local politics and few were implemented.

Clark's work brought him national attention once again during the 1960s, when the civil rights movement and President Lyndon Johnson's "War on Poverty" brought those issues to the forefront of American thought. In 1965 he published *Dark Ghetto: Dilemmas of Social Power,* a groundbreaking study of life in impoverished African American neighborhoods. The psychologist took a novel approach to the study, disdaining the role of objective observer for an impassioned call for social justice. This "cry of a social psychologist, controlled in part by the concepts and language of social science," as the author described it in his introduction, brought the author nationwide recognition. When race riots broke out in northern cities in the late 1960s, many Americans turned to *Dark Ghetto* to gain a better understanding of black perspectives on racial issues and American society.

Over the next two decades, Clark continued working for change in impoverished communities, lobbying for increased economic, educational, and emotional support to inner-city residents. In 1966 he was appointed to the New York State Board of Regents. He served on this state educational supervisory body for twenty years. In 1967 he founded the Metropolitan Applied Research Center, Inc. (MARC Corp.), a social science research firm that advised the District of Columbia school system on a new educational program in 1970. Again, political considerations prevented many of his recommendations from being implemented, but Clark remained devoted to the concept of integration even as many radical African American activists were suggesting separatist solutions to social problems.

In 1975 Clark retired from City College of New York to found the psychological research firm Clark, Phipps, Clark & Harris with his wife, Mamie, and their two children, Kate and Hilton. He lent his expertise to various business and government groups, often helping design minority hiring programs. He also published another book, 1974's *Pathos of Power.* He continued his contributions to various organizations even after the death of his wife and partner Mamie in 1983.

Over his career Clark was honored by numerous professional groups and universities, receiving honorary doctorates from institutions such as Princeton University and Johns Hopkins University. He served as president of the American Psychological Association (APA), the American Association for the Advancement of Science, and the Society for the Psychological Study of Social Issues. In 1961 the NAACP awarded him their prestigious Spingarn Medal for his contributions to the civil rights movement, and in 1985 he received the Franklin Delano Roosevelt Four Freedoms Award from the Franklin and Eleanor Roosevelt Institute.

Despite such acclaim, Clark expressed pessimism over the issue of race relations in America in recent years. Although the civil rights movement gained victories in the legal arena, he felt that impoverished African Americans had made little social progress. This perceived lack of progress, Clark told the *Washington Post,* led him to regard his professional life as "a series of glorious defeats."

Nevertheless, as Michael Meyers and John P. Nidiry observed in the *Antioch Review,* Clark carved out a significant place for himself in the history of African American civil rights. "[He] will be remembered for his superior intellect, passion for equality, and for his personal courage and temerity to challenge the color lines of his times, and ours." Some day, the authors continued, Americans "may yet discover, and then internalize, the simple truth about the lie of 'race' that Kenneth Clark labored so mightily and intelligently to convey."

## Sources

Clark, Kenneth B. *Toward Humanity and Justice: The Writings of Kenneth B. Clark, Scholar of the* Brown v. Board of Education *Decision.* Edited by Woody Klein. Westport, CT: Praeger, 2004.

Hentoff, Nat. "The Integrationist." *The New Yorker,* August 23, 1982.

Keppel, Ben. *The Work of Democracy: Ralph Bunche, Kenneth B. Clark, Lorraine Hansberry, and the Cultural Politics of Race.* Cambridge, MA: Harvard University Press, 1995.

Kluger, Richard. *Simple Justice: The History of* Brown v. Board of Education *and Black America's Struggle for Equality.* New York: Knopf, 1975.

Maraniss, David. "Icon of Integration and the Durability of Racism." *Washington Post,* March 4, 1990.

Markowitz, Gerald E., and David Rosner. *Children, Race, and Power: Kenneth and Mamie Clark's Northside Center.* Charlottesville: University of Virginia Press, 1996.

Meyers, Michael, and John P. Nidiry. "Kenneth Bancroft Clark: The Uppity Negro Integrationist." *Antioch Review,* Spring 2004.

Roberts, Sam. "An Integrationist to This Day, Believing All Else Has Failed." *New York Times,* May 7, 1995.

## John W. Davis (1873-1955)
*Lead Counsel for South Carolina before the*
*Supreme Court in the* Brown *cases*

John William Davis was born on April 13, 1873, in Clarksburg, West Virginia, the fifth of six children of John J. and Anna (Kennedy) Davis. The senior Davis was a lawyer and former Congressman for West Virginia, while his wife had a college degree and was known for her love of learning. She imparted this love to her only son, teaching him to read and appreciate literature and music. Davis was educated at home until the age of ten, when he attended a class for potential teachers; his fellow students were much older, but Davis performed so well his instructors suggested he take the teacher qualification exam. At the age of twelve he attended a local day school, and two years later he was sent off to Pantops Academy, a preparatory school in Virginia.

Davis entered Washington & Lee University in Lexington, Virginia, at age sixteen. A bright, hard-working student, Davis involved himself in a wide range of extracurricular activities until he discovered he had diabetes. He received a bachelor's degree in 1892 and hoped to enter law school, but his family did not have the funds for his tuition. Instead, Davis took a position as a private tutor to fifteen children in the extended family of a West Virginia landowner. In the ensuing months he began a courtship with the family's second daughter, Julia McDonald. They would eventually marry on June 20, 1899.

After one year of tutoring, Davis joined his father's practice as a legal assistant. In 1894 he enrolled in Washington & Lee's law school. He graduated a year later, having been named "Class Orator," and began practicing with his father. After losing his first three cases he was ready to quit, but a speech from his father inspired him to continue. His performance in the courtroom improved to the point that Washington & Lee asked him to take an assistant professorship at their law school. He agreed in order to pay off school-related debts but gave up the position after a year in favor of the "rough and tumble" of private practice.

Davis spent the next decade expanding his practice. He proved particularly adept at attracting clients from the growing coal, lumber, and railroad industries of West Virginia, and cultivated a reputation as a civic-minded member of the community. In the summer of 1900 his wife contracted a fatal fever after giving birth to a daughter, Julia McDonald Davis.

## Begins Political Career

Davis's father had served as a congressman in both the West Virginia and U.S. houses, so it was natural for his son to enter politics as well. In 1898 the younger Davis was drafted by the Democratic Party to run for the West Virginia House of Delegates; he felt obligated to accept his party's nomination and served one term. He then continued his involvement in party politics, serving as a local Democratic Party chairman and attending the 1904 Democratic National Convention as a delegate.

In 1910 Davis was once again drafted into running for election to a seat in the U.S. House of Representatives. After winning election, party leaders decided to use his legal expertise by giving him a coveted assignment to the House Judiciary Committee. Although he found the work draining, he ran for re-election in 1912 and won by a very slight margin. That same year he married Ellen "Nell" Graham Bessell, the daughter of a rival Charlottesville lawyer.

In 1913 newly elected President Woodrow Wilson offered Davis the job of U.S. Solicitor General. He spent the next five years as the trial attorney representing the United States in court cases. Davis appeared before the Supreme Court as solicitor general sixty-seven times over this period of time, winning forty-eight times. His cases included antitrust victories against Standard Oil, U.S. Steel, and International Harvester; defenses of government child labor and minimum wage laws (he lost the former); and victories in overturning Alabama's convict labor laws and Oklahoma's "grandfather clause," used to deny African Americans the vote. His mastery of facts, calm delivery, and pleasant voice distinguished him before the Court; every justice reputedly told President Wilson they would be pleased to see Davis join the Court someday.

Although Davis excelled in his position as the government's trial lawyer, he grew weary of the workload and chafed at the loss of lucrative opportunities in the private sector. When Wilson asked him in 1918 to become ambassador to Great Britain, Davis accepted the position at the urging of his wife. The position was important, as the two countries were key World War I allies. During his tenure in London, his engaging manner, tact, and empathy for his hosts endeared him to many in the British government. Davis not only smoothed over disagreements between the two countries over the proposed League of Nations, he participated in some of the postwar negotiations.

Despite his success as an ambassador, Davis was eager to return home and resume private law practice after the war. Shortly after Republican Warren Harding took over the presidency in 1921, Davis sailed for New York, where he took a job with the prominent Wall Street legal firm of Stetson, Jennings & Russell. A short time later he was named to the boards of the Rockefeller Foundation and the Carnegie Endowment. In 1922 he was named president of the American Bar Association; that year he also refused an appointment to the Supreme Court, describing it as a "life sentence to monastic seclusion."

In 1924 Davis was drawn back into national politics. That year, he emerged as a compromise presidential candidate at the Democratic Party's national convention in New York. The party had become split between rural and urban constituencies, with neither side able to muster the two-thirds majority needed to secure the nomination for their candidate. Davis's solid reputation made him acceptable to leaders of both camps, so he became the Democratic candidate for president on the convention's 103rd ballot. Nebraska Governor Charles W. Bryan was named his running mate.

The presidential campaign was a difficult one for Davis, who took a leave of absence from his firm during the election season. The Democratic Party was deeply divided and Davis's political views were more conservative than his party's on most issues, although he did denounce the Ku Klux Klan during the campaign. In addition, he faced a popular Republican incumbent, Calvin Coolidge, who had succeeded to the office upon Harding's death in August of 1923. When the votes were tallied, Davis lost by more than 25 percent of the popular vote, carrying only the Confederate South and Oklahoma. He even placed third behind Coolidge and Progressive Party candidate Robert LaFollette in twelve states. The result was not unexpected, however, given the Democrats' disarray. Once the election was over, Davis expressed eagerness to return to his legal practice.

## Returning to the National Stage

During the 1930s and 1940s Davis remained one of the most respected and well-known attorneys in the country. "Of all the persons who appeared before the Court in my time," declared Supreme Court Justice Oliver Wendell Holmes, "there was never anybody more elegant, more clear, more concise or more logical than John W. Davis." Devoted to his work, he was noted for his ability to find the core of the most complex legal matters. He had particular expertise in appellate law (appeals cases) and appeared before the Supreme Court 141 times, more than any other lawyer of his generation (he also prepared briefs and strategies for over 100 additional Supreme Court cases.) Davis also was a strict constructionist who strongly favored a narrow interpretation of the Constitution, limited federal power, and strong civil liberties and states' rights.

In 1952, an impending strike by steel workers so threatened the nation's economy that President Harry S. Truman threatened to take control of plants and force a compromise between the industry's management and union work force. Representing steel company owners, Davis argued against government intervention before the Supreme Court. He called Truman's action an "usurpation" of power that was "alien to the spirit of the Constitution." Three months later, the Court rendered a 6-3 decision in favor of Davis and his clients.

Davis would have no such luck with the last case he argued before the Supreme Court. South Carolina Governor James F. Byrne asked him to represent the state in the appeal of *Briggs v. Elliott,* a school desegregation case scheduled for the Supreme Court as part of the *Brown v. Board of Education* slate of desegregation cases in 1952. Davis took the case free of charge, an indication of his strong conviction that individual states had the right to determine their own system of education.

Davis coordinated his briefs with the attorneys of the defendants in the other four cases under the *Brown* banner. When the Court ordered reargument in 1953 the justices interrupted him only once during his oral presentation, a sign of the great respect they had for his abilities. Davis's efforts proved futile, however, as the Court ruled 9-0 to declare segregation unconstitutional in the 1954 *Brown* decision. "If he lost the School Segregation case, it was only because in 1954 no lawyer could have won it," wrote Yale Kamisar in *Argument.* "And although he lost, he left no doubt why he was reputed to be *the* leading advocate of his time.... Davis' argument was carefully organized, and his urbaneness and splendid rhetoric is shown again and again in the record. When one adds what all observers call the magic of his voice, the total effect was almost—almost—irresistible."

Disheartened and in failing health, Davis retired to Charleston, South Carolina, where he had maintained a winter cottage for twenty years. His wife had preceded him in death in 1943, but his daughter Julia was by his bedside when he died on March 24, 1955.

## Sources

"John W. Davis." *Dictionary of American Biography, Supplement 5: 1951-1955.* New York: Scribner for American Council of Learned Societies, 1977.

Harbaugh, William H. *Lawyer's Lawyer: The Life of John W. Davis.* New York, Oxford University Press, 1973.

Kamisar, Yale. "The School Desegregation Cases in Retrospect: Some Reflections on Causes and Effects." In *Argument: The Oral Argument before the Supreme Court in* Brown v. Board of Education, *Topeka, 1952-55.* Edited by Leon Friedman. New York: Chelsea House, 1969.

Ranson, Edward. "'A Snarling Roughhouse:' The Democratic Convention of 1924." *History Today,* July 1994.

Thompson, Sydnor. "John W. Davis and His Role in the Public School Segregation Cases—A Personal Memoir." *Washington and Lee Law Review,* Winter 1996.

## Dwight D. Eisenhower (1890-1969)
*34th President of the United States*

Dwight David Eisenhower was born on October 14, 1890, in Denison, Texas. He was the third of seven sons of David and Ida (Stover) Eisenhower. Called "Ike" from an early age, Eisenhower grew up in Abilene, Kansas. Although his father had a steady job in a creamery, the family had to work hard to make ends meet: Ike and his five brothers (the sixth died in infancy) helped their mother work the family's small farm. A good student who excelled in history and math, Eisenhower also enjoyed sports and outdoor activities like camping. He graduated from Abilene High School in 1909, then spent two years working with his father at the local creamery before entering West Point, the U.S. Army's training academy, in 1911.

Eisenhower was an average student at West Point and received his commission as a second lieutenant upon his graduation in 1915. The following year he married Mamie Doud, a Denver native. Their first child, Doud Dwight, died of scarlet fever at the age of three, but their second child, John, survived into adulthood.

When the United States entered World War I in 1917, Eisenhower was assigned to train troops at home. By the time he was scheduled to assume a European command, the war had ended. Eisenhower spent most of the 1920s as an executive officer, working in the Panama Canal Zone and later for the assistant secretary of war. He also continued his military education at the Army War College and the Army Industrial College, graduating first in his class in Army Command and General Staff School. Although the career soldier hoped for a command in the field, his administrative skills made him more valuable as a military aide. In 1929 he was appointed to the staff of General George V. Mosely, Assistant Secretary of War.

In 1933 Eisenhower became chief military aide to General Douglas MacArthur. He followed MacArthur to the Philippine Islands in the Pacific, where the general was in charge of military defense for the area, and in 1936 he gained a promotion to lieutenant colonel. Five years later he was promoted to colonel, and in September 1941 he became a brigadier general.

When the United States entered World War II in 1941, Eisenhower was called back from the Philippines and posted to the War Department in Washington, D.C. There he worked under Army Chief of Staff General George C. Marshall as chief of the War Plans Division. His experience in the Philippines proved invaluable in devising military strategies for the Pacific, and he also contributed to the Allies' overall military strategy in Europe and North Africa.

## Leads Allies to Victory in Europe

In the summer of 1942 Marshall appointed Eisenhower chief of the European theater of operations, and the new major general went to London to consult with the British. His outgoing personality and patient manner earned him many friends, including British Prime Minister Winston Churchill. In late 1942 Eisenhower oversaw a successful invasion of North Africa, called Operation Torch, which enabled Allied Troops to invade Italy the following year. His greatest triumph, however, was the Allied invasion of France. On "D-Day," June 6, 1944, thousands of Allied troops crossed the English Channel or parachuted into Normandy, France, supported by thousands of ships and planes. It was a monumental undertaking, but within a week Allied forces had gained control of a large area of Northern France. It was the turning point of the war in Europe, and on May 7, 1945, Eisenhower accepted Germany's unconditional surrender.

After the war's conclusion, President Harry S. Truman named General Eisenhower as his Army chief of staff. He served in that capacity until 1948, when he retired from the military. Although both political parties asked him to run for president that year, Eisenhower declined. Instead, he wrote a best-selling book about the war, *Crusade in Europe,* and accepted the presidency of Columbia University in New York. When President Truman asked him to coordinate the Allied military of the new North Atlantic Treaty Organization (NATO), Eisenhower took a leave of absence from Columbia in 1950 and moved to Paris, France.

In 1950 the United States entered the Korean War, which had flared to life after an invasion of South Korea by Communist North Korea. As the war progressed, an already significant isolationist movement within the United States gained further strength. Eisenhower was alarmed by this trend because he believed that withdrawing from involvement in international affairs would jeopardize U.S. security. He also felt a strong sense of duty, and believed he should serve the American people in any capacity they chose. After he polled well in early primaries as a write-in candidate, Eisenhower announced he was leaving his NATO post to campaign for the Republican nomination for president.

Eisenhower edged out conservative Ohio Senator Robert A. Taft for the nomination. Turning his attention to the general election, he focused on the fight against Communism and new limits on federal government programs and authority. Eisenhower's moderate domestic positions and military experience appealed to an American public worried about the Korean conflict and the ideological Cold War with Soviet Russia. He won 442 electoral votes to Democratic candidate Adlai Stevenson's 89 and carried every state outside the heavily-Democratic South.

## Serves as Popular President

After his election, Eisenhower made good on a campaign promise to visit the Korean front. He devoted much of his attention to international affairs after his January 1953 inauguration. During his first term, the Eisenhower administration negotiated a cease-fire in Korea and approved aid packages to French forces fighting insurgents in Vietnam. In general, Eisenhower's foreign policy involved the development of American military strength, particularly in nuclear weapons, while avoiding direct military action. He built on America's alliances with Western Europe and also stressed the importance for countries to have self-rule.

On the home front, Eisenhower was mostly quiet about the Congressional investigations led by Republican Senator Joseph McCarthy to find purported Communists lurking in the U.S. government and media outlets. He maintained a balanced budget, even as he expanded the New Deal program of Social Security. He also approved the creation of the Department of Health, Education, and Welfare, and signed legislation establishing the interstate highway system.

In 1956 Eisenhower easily won re-election, despite having suffered a heart attack the previous year. In his second term he continued his support of NATO but kept the U.S. out of several international conflicts, including a war between Egypt and Israel, a revolt against Russian rule in Hungary, and the Communist revolution in Cuba. On the domestic front, he approved the creation of the National Aeronautics and Space Administration (NASA).

## Eisenhower's Civil Rights Record

Eisenhower was one of the first presidents to name African Americans to important administration posts, including Ernest Wilkins as an assistant secretary of labor. He also made a number of decisions that had a profound effect on the early civil rights movement. In 1953 he named California Governor Earl Warren as Chief Justice of the Supreme Court after the sudden death of Fred Vinson. It was Warren's leadership that led to the unanimous decision overturning segregation in *Brown v. Board of Education* the following year. Four years later, Eisenhower called up federal troops to enforce desegregation after Arkansas Governor Orval Faubus defied a court order to desegregate Little Rock's Central High School. This convinced many Southerners they had no choice but to comply with desegregation. Eisenhower also signed the Civil Rights Acts of 1957 and 1960, designed to strengthen voting rights for African Americans, and signed orders desegregating public facilities in the District of Columbia.

Nevertheless, Eisenhower's record on civil rights is generally regarded as mediocre at best. During his years in the Oval Office he rarely spoke on the issue, and civil rights was not a priority of his administration. Many historians have subsequently criticized him for his record of passivity on civil rights. As Stephen E. Ambrose noted in *Eisenhower,* the president "missed a historic opportunity to provide moral leadership … on the most fundamental social problem of his time."

After leaving the presidency in 1961, Eisenhower retired from public life, although he did write three volumes of memoirs. He spent time in Gettysburg, Pennsylvania, and Palm Springs, California, but after a series of heart attacks in 1968 he went to the Walter Reed Hospital in Washington, D.C. He died there of congestive heart failure on March 28, 1969. He was buried in his hometown of Abilene, Kansas, where there is now a presidential library and memorial.

### Sources

Ambrose, Stephen E. *Eisenhower.* 2 vols. New York: Simon & Schuster, 1983-1984.

"Dwight D. Eisenhower." *Dictionary of American Biography, Supplement 8: 1966-1970.* New York: Scribner, for American Council of Learned Societies, 1988.

"Dwight D. Eisenhower Library and Museum." http://www.eisenhower.utexas.edu.

Eisenhower, Dwight D. *The White House Years.* 2 vols. Garden City, NY: Doubleday, 1963-1965.

Perret, Geoffrey. *Eisenhower.* New York: Random House, 1999.

Richardson, Elmo. *The Presidency of Dwight D. Eisenhower.* Lawrence, KS: The University of Kansas Press, 1979.

Wicker, Tom. *Dwight D. Eisenhower.* New York: Henry Holt, 2002.

## Orval E. Faubus (1910-1994)
*Governor of Arkansas During the 1957 Little Rock School Crisis*

Orval Eugene Faubus was born January 7, 1910, in a log cabin in the Ozark Mountains, near Greasy Creek, Arkansas. He was the first of seven children of John Samuel ("Sam") and Addie (Joslin) Faubus. Sam Faubus was a farmer who often had to supplement his income by working temporary jobs as a railroad section hand, a harvester, or a miner.

As a youngster Orval enjoyed reading, but he did not finish eighth grade until the age of seventeen because of the need to help support his family. At eighteen he passed the state teacher's exam and spent the next decade teaching in rural schoolhouses in his home of Madison County. He took high school classes in his spare time, and he earned his diploma at age twenty-four. One of his students was Alta Haskins, whom he married in 1931. Their first two children were stillborn, but in 1939 Alta Faubus gave birth to a healthy son, Farrell.

### Early Political Career

In 1936 Faubus waged his first political campaign. He aligned himself with the Democratic Party, which was dominant not only in Arkansas but across the South during this period. His bid for the Democratic nomination to a seat in the Arkansas House of Representatives fell short by only four votes, but his refusal to request a recount earned him the gratitude of local Democrats. Two years later, party support helped him win election as Madison County clerk and recorder. He moved to the county seat of Huntsville and continued his education by taking night classes. He won re-election in 1940 and was unopposed for the position of county judge in 1942, but Faubus withdrew his name prior to the election in order to join the Army and fight in World War II. He took part in the invasion of Normandy, France, and served as an intelligence officer in the Third Army during the Battle of the Bulge. By the time he returned home in 1946, he had been awarded a Bronze Star and attained the rank of major.

Faubus hoped to quickly resume his political career—he had kept his name in the public eye by writing letters to the editor of the local paper during his service—but he lost the 1946 election for county judge. A friend appointed him postmaster of Huntsville and in 1947 he bought a small newspaper, the *Madison County Record*. He published liberal-leaning editorials advocating public control of Arkansas's electrical grid and supportive of Governor Sidney McMath. The governor rewarded him with a highway commissioner's job and then a post on his own staff. Faubus made many political contacts throughout the state as a member of the governor's staff, and after McMath was defeated in the 1952 election he decided to launch his own bid for the office.

The 1954 campaign against incumbent Francis Cherry was hotly contested, but Faubus's campaign promises to hold the line on property taxes and utility rates and oppose cuts in welfare benefits earned him enough votes to force a two-person runoff against Cherry in the Democratic primary. As the campaign intensified, Cherry accused Faubus of being a Communist because he briefly attended Commonwealth College, a left-wing Socialist institution, in 1935. Faubus downplayed his study at the school and accused Cherry of red-baiting tactics. The accusations boomeranged against the governor when moderates threw their support to Faubus, who won by more than 6,000 votes in the August primary. He went on to win the general election by a margin of almost two to one.

## Political Winds Prompt Embrace of Segregation

Faubus was sworn in as Arkansas's governor in January 1955. Upon taking office, he extended welfare and unemployment benefits, revamped the property tax system to increase funds for education, started a conservation program that created state parks and promoted tourism, and appointed Republican businessman Winthrop Rockefeller to head a industrial development task force.

On racial issues Faubus initially adopted a moderate position. He appointed African Americans to state posts, integrated the state's Democratic Party organization, and made early preparations to desegregate the state's public schools in accordance with the Supreme Court's 1954 *Brown* decision.

The school system in Hoxie, Arkansas, even became the focus of a 1955 *Life* article on successful desegregation.

In the 1956 gubernatorial primary for the Democratic nomination, however, Faubus faced Jim Johnson, the state director of the Arkansas White Citizens Council and sponsor of a state amendment to "nullify" the Supreme Court's *Brown* decision. Johnson's stridently racist and segregationist rhetoric attracted strong support from whites. Determined to neutralize Johnson's campaign strategy, Faubus rolled out his own strong segregationist message. He proposed his own interposition amendment to nullify the Court decision and touted a student placement plan that would allow white parents to move their children out of desegregated schools. By pledging that "no school district will be forced to mix the races as long as I am governor of Arkansas," Faubus easily won the 1956 election.

Faubus began his second term by convincing the legislature to raise sales, income, and severance taxes in order to improve the state's public school system. The funds improved higher education facilities and allowed all primary schools in the state to operate a full nine-month school term. This success, however, was tempered by growing anger and anxiety over court-ordered desegregation. In the fall of 1957 Faubus pandered to white opponents of desegregation, calling out the Arkansas National Guard to prevent Central High School in Little Rock from carrying out a court-ordered desegregation plan. Warning that "blood would run in the streets" if the plan were carried out, Faubus instructed the guardsmen to keep nine African American students enrolled at Central High from entering the school. His defiance kept the so-called "Little Rock Nine" out of Central High until September 25, when President Dwight D. Eisenhower sent in federal troops to enforce the court's desegregation decree.

The conflict at Little Rock came to define Faubus's career, but he never disavowed his actions as other segregationists later did. For the rest of his life, Faubus firmly maintained he acted only to keep the peace. Others, though, saw his actions as a craven attempt to boost his political popularity at a time when leadership could have made integration much easier to accomplish.

Faubus's actions at Little Rock increased his popularity in many regions of the state. He won four more elections as governor, during which time he reformed the state's mental health system, improved state hospitals, created vocational technical schools, improved teacher salaries, and set up a bond system to encourage industrial development. But his administration was also rocked by a series of scandals, and by 1966 he concluded that he would probably be unable to win another term.

Faubus left the governor's mansion in 1967. Two years later he divorced his wife Alta in order to marry Beth Westmoreland, a Democratic Party organizer from New England who was almost thirty years his junior. Criticism of his divorce and remarriage harmed his attempt at a political comeback in 1970, when he mounted an unsuccessful bid to reclaim the governorship. Two later comebacks were equally unsuccessful, and Faubus spent the rest of his life in debt and decline. His only child committed suicide in 1976, and his estranged wife Beth was murdered in 1983 by a drifter in Houston, Texas.

Faubus enjoyed a brief return to the public spotlight in 1980, when he helped Republican Frank White defeat Arkansas Governor Bill Clinton. He subsequently took a position heading the state's Office of Veteran's Affairs in the White administration. He lost the job, however, when Clinton regained the governorship, and he eventually was forced to take a job as a bank teller to support himself. He married teacher Janice Wittenburg in 1986 and was diagnosed with prostate cancer in 1991. The disease eventually spread to his bones and spine, and Faubus died on December 14, 1994, in Conway, Arkansas.

## Sources

Kirk, John A. "Arkansas, the *Brown* Decision, and the 1957 Little Rock School Crisis: A Local Perspective," in *Understanding the Little Rock Crisis: An Exercise in Remembrance and Reconciliation.* Elizabeth Jacobway and C. Fred Williams, editors. Fayetteville, AR: The University of Arkansas Press, 1999.

Old State House Museum, Department of Arkansas Heritage. "Orval Eugene Faubus (1955-67)." http://www.oldstatehouse.com/exhibits/virtual/governors/from_the_forties_to_faubus/faubus.asp.

Peltason, J. W. *Fifty-Eight Lonely Men: Southern Federal Judges and School Desegregation,* new edition. Urbana, IL: University of Illinois Press, 1971.

Reed, Roy. "The Contest for the Soul of Orval Faubus," in *Understanding the Little Rock Crisis: An Exercise in Remembrance and Reconciliation.* Elizabeth Jacobway and C. Fred Williams, editors. Fayetteville, AR: University of Arkansas Press, 1999.

Reed, Roy. *Faubus: The Life and Times of an American Prodigal.* Fayetteville, AR: University of Arkansas Press, 1997.

Roy, Beth. *Bitters in the Honey: Tales of Hope and Disappointment across Divides of Race and Time.* Fayetteville, AR: The University of Arkansas Press, 1999.

### Charles Hamilton Houston (1895-1950)
*Counsel to the NAACP and Architect of NAACP Desegregation Strategy*

Charles Hamilton Houston was born on September 3, 1895, in Washington, D.C., the only child of William LePre and Mary Ethel (Hamilton) Houston. Houston grew up in a comfortable, middle-class household. His father was a government clerk and lawyer who later became an assistant U.S. attorney general. Houston's mother had been a teacher before her marriage, but afterwards worked as a hairdresser and seamstress. Houston's parents shielded him from the discrimination of the era as best they could, emphasizing instead their pride in their African American heritage.

Charles Houston was a bright child, and his parents encouraged his love of music and learning. He entered Washington's M Street High School (later named Paul Laurence Dunbar High School), the first black high school in the country and one noted for its focus on academics. He graduated in 1911 at age fifteen with the top grades in his class. He was offered a scholarship to the University of Pittsburgh, but his parents encouraged him to seek admission to a more prestigious school. With his family's financial support, Houston entered Amherst College in Massachusetts. The only African American in his class, he graduated with Phi Beta Kappa honors as one of six valedictorians in 1915.

After Amherst, Houston was unsure what career to pursue. He dreamed of being a concert pianist, but also considered teaching or the diplomatic service. As he pondered his options, he supported himself by working as an English instructor at Washington, D.C.'s Howard University, the country's most prestigious college for African Americans.

When the United States entered World War I in 1917, Houston joined a group of young black college graduates in lobbying the government for a black officer training program. The program was approved, and Houston was commissioned as a first lieutenant in October 1917. He encountered discrimination throughout his service in the army, and when Houston was called to serve as an advocate for two black soldiers accused of disorderly conduct, the racism he encountered during the trial inspired his future career: "I made up my mind that I would never get caught again without knowing something about my rights; that if luck was with me, and I got through this war, I would study law and use my time fighting for men who could not strike back."

Houston was honorably discharged in 1919, and that fall he entered Harvard University Law School. During his years there he organized a law club for non-white and non-Protestant students, helping them gain access to outside legal activities. He excelled in his classes, and became the first African American elected to the *Harvard Law Review.* He graduated in the top five percent of his class in 1922, and then earned a scholarship to continue studying at Harvard. Working under Felix Frankfurter, a future Supreme Court justice, Houston earned his doctorate in 1923. He also won Harvard's prestigious Sheldon Traveling Fellowship, which enabled him to study in Europe at the University of Madrid. Over the ensuing year Houston earned another doctorate, in civil law, and traveled throughout Italy, France, and North Africa—places he found to be refreshingly free of racial prejudice.

## Upgrades Howard University Law School

Houston returned to Washington, D.C. and joined his father's law practice in 1924, the same year he married Gladys Margaret "Mag" Moran. The new lawyer also began teaching law classes at Howard University, which at the time offered a part-time law program for working students. Unfortunately, Howard's law program had few facilities and a very small library, and it had not been accredited by either the American Bar Association (ABA) or the American Association of Law Schools (AALS). When the law school asked Houston to survey the state of African American lawyers, he traveled the country looking at various law schools and examining the black community's need for lawyers. He worked so hard he became ill and had to take a year off from teaching.

When Howard Law School's dean, Fenton Booth, was selected for a federal judgeship in 1929, the university asked Houston to become vice-dean. Houston accepted and immediately set about revamping the school's law program. He set higher admission standards, closed down night classes in favor of a full-time program, improved the library, created a more challenging curriculum, and sought out full-time faculty members and distinguished guest lecturers. Within three years, Howard Law School had been fully accredited by the ABA and the AALS and its civil rights law program was well-known across the country. This focus on civil rights law reflected Houston's oft-stated belief that "a lawyer is either a social engineer or he's a parasite." The foundation was thus laid for Howard Law School to prepare a generation of black lawyers, including Thurgood Marshall and Oliver Hill, for the civil rights struggles of the mid-twentieth century.

Houston himself accepted several civil rights cases in the 1930s. He helped the NAACP prepare its Supreme Court brief in 1932's *Nixon v. Condon* case, which overturned Texas's all-white primary election as unconstitutional. He also participated in the successful appeal of the conviction of the Scottsboro Boys, a group of black Alabama teenagers who were originally sentenced to death by an all-white jury for raping two white women. In addition, Houston was a valuable resource for the NAACP's legal committee. Working on behalf of the NAACP's Legal Defense and Education Fund (LDF), Houston explored discrimination in employment, appeared before Congress to lobby for anti-lynching laws, and defended other African Americans unfairly charged with or convicted of crimes. In 1934 he took a leave of absence from his father's practice and moved to New York to join the NAACP full-time as its first black legal counsel.

### Implements NAACP Plan to Overturn Segregation

When Houston came on board as NAACP special counsel, he subtly changed the organization's previous legal strategy, which focused on challenging segregation's constitutionality in the federal courts. Instead, he used the NAACP's resources to fight for equal funding for black institutions, equal salaries for black teachers, and equal access to higher education for black students. Houston believed that by forcing states to meet the "equal" provision of the "separate but equal" doctrine, he could make it too expensive for states to maintain segregated systems.

Houston's civil rights work focused on education because he believed that "education is a preparation for the competition of life." As he noted in a 1935 speech: "In the United States the Negro is economically exploited, politically ignored and socially ostracized. His education reflects his condition; the discriminations practiced against him are no accident." Houston took this message to the black community, traveling 25,000 miles in his first year alone to give speeches and raise funds.

In 1935 one of Houston's former students, Thurgood Marshall, brought him the case of Donald Murray, who had been denied a place in the University of Maryland's Law School because of his race. Taking Murray as a client, Houston argued the initial case (*Pearson v. Murray*) in a Maryland court and won; he then oversaw Marshall's successful defense of the initial judgment in a state appeals court.

Houston knew, however, that the key to improving black educational opportunities depended on a favorable ruling from the U.S. Supreme Court. With this in mind, he took the case of Lloyd Gaines, who had been rejected by the University of Missouri Law School because of his race. Instead, the law school had offered him a scholarship to attend a school outside the state. In 1938 the Supreme Court ruled in *Gaines v. Canada* that the scholarship offered by the law school did not give Gaines an "equal opportunity" to an education. In 1940 Houston secured a victory for black teachers when U.S. courts formally approved the concept of equal pay for equal work.

Houston was also involved in other civil rights cases for the NAACP. In 1935, for example, he became the first African American working for the NAACP to win a case before the Supreme Court. In this case, *Hollins v. Oklahoma*, Houston successfully argued that a black man convicted of rape and sentenced to death by an all-white jury had been denied due process.

Houston found his work for the NAACP rewarding, but in 1940 he left the organization due to family considerations. His father had been appointed an assistant U.S. attorney general, and the demands of the position left him with little time to tend to the family law practice. In addition, Houston had a new family to support. He had separated from his first wife in 1934 and they divorced in 1937. Later that year Houston married Henrietta Williams, his father's secretary, with whom he eventually had one son, Charles Hamilton Houston, Jr.

## Continues Fight for Equality

Although he devoted much of his time to his family's practice, Houston never stopped working on civil rights issues. In 1944 Houston was appointed to the federal government's Fair Employment Practices Committee, although he eventually quit in protest over government inaction on the issue. He also litigated several prominent discrimination cases. In 1944, for example, he won the Supreme Court case *Steele v. Louisville & Nashville Railroad* when the court ruled that a labor union must fairly represent all workers, regardless of race. The following year he won a judgment against a public library that tried to deny a black woman admission into a government-funded training class. In 1948 Houston helped litigate another precedent-setting ruling by the Supreme Court against restrictive covenants—property contracts that included provisions against selling to African Americans. Houston's brief in *Hurd v. Hodge,* a companion case to the precedent-setting *Shelley v. Kraemer,* foreshadowed the NAACP school desegregation briefs in its use of sociological data to document the psychological damage wreaked on African Americans by segregation.

Houston continued giving advice to the NAACP in its school desegregation cases but he did not become directly involved in one until 1947. That year he took the case of a group of black District of Columbia parents who were protesting crowded—and thus "unequal"—conditions in their children's schools. He worked on the case until 1949, when he became too ill to continue. He referred the parents to Howard law professor James Nabrit, Jr., who agreed to take the case if they challenged segregation itself. That new case, filed in 1951 as *Bolling v. Sharpe,* became one of the five cases the Supreme Court used to overturn segregation in the *Brown v. Board of Education* decision of 1954. Houston did not live to see this triumph, however. He died of heart failure on April 22, 1950, in his hometown of Washington.

After his death, Houston was remembered for his unfailing scholarship and devotion to civil rights. The NAACP posthumously awarded him its prestigious Spingarn Medal, and Supreme Court Justice William O. Douglas described Houston as "a veritable dynamo of energy guided by a mind that had as sharp a cutting edge as any I have known." Speaking at his funeral, colleague William Hastie offered a fitting assessment of Houston's legacy:

> He guided us through the legal wilderness of second-class citizenship. He was truly the Moses of that journey. He lived to see us close to the promised land of full equality under the law, closer than even he dared hope when he set out on that journey and so much closer than would have been possible without his genius and his leadership.

### Sources

Arnesen, Eric, "Charles Hamilton Houston," *Footsteps,* March/April 2003.
"Charles Hamilton Houston." *Encyclopedia of World Biography,* 2nd ed. 17 vols. Farmington Hills, MI: Gale Research, 1998.

Cobb, William Jelani. "Past Imperfect: *Brown*'s Overlooked Architect," *Africana,* May 24, 2004. http://www.africana.com.

Cottrol, Robert J., Raymond T. Diamond, and Leland B. Ware. *Brown v. Board of Education: Caste, Culture, and the Constitution.* Lawrence, KS: University of Kansas Press, 2003.

Greenberg, Jack. *Crusaders in the Courts: How a Dedicated Band of Lawyers Fought for the Civil Rights Revolution.* New York: Basic Books, 1994.

Hughes, Langston. *Fight for Freedom: The Story of the NAACP.* New York: W.W. Norton, 1962.

Kluger, Richard. *Simple Justice: The History of* Brown v. Board of Education *and Black America's Struggle for Equality.* New York: Knopf, 1975.

McNeil, Genna Rae. *Charles Hamilton Houston and the Struggle for Civil Rights.* Philadelphia: University of Pennsylvania Press, 1983.

Tushnet, Mark V. *The NAACP's Legal Strategy against Segregation, 1925-1950.* Chapel Hill, NC: The University of North Carolina Press, 1987.

### Thurgood Marshall (1908-1993)
*Lead LDF Attorney for* Brown v. Board *and First African American Supreme Court Justice.*

Thurgood Marshall was born on July 2, 1908, in Baltimore, Maryland, the second child of William Canfield and Norma Arica (Williams) Marshall. He had originally been named Thoroughgood after his paternal grandfather, but he shortened it to Thurgood while in grade school. Marshall grew up in Baltimore, which he called the "most segregated city in the United States," but his family was part of the city's African American elite: both grandfathers owned grocery stores; his mother was an elementary school teacher; and his father was head steward at an exclusive yachting club.

Although William Marshall had little formal education, he loved political debate and had been the first African American to sit on a Baltimore grand jury. He sometimes took Thurgood and his older brother Aubrey to observe court proceedings in the city, and he often turned the family dinner table into a debate club. Blue-eyed and light-skinned, William Marshall taught his sons to take pride in their African heritage, telling them, "If anyone calls you nigger, you not only got my permission to fight him—you got my orders to fight him."

Marshall's parents expected their sons to attend college, and Thurgood followed his older brother to Lincoln University, an all-black college in Pennsylvania with an excellent reputation. Thurgood majored in American literature and philosophy, and he graduated with honors in 1930. Rejected by the University of Maryland Law School because of his race, Marshall commuted to Howard University in Washington, D.C. He and his new wife, Vivian "Buster" Burey, whom he had married in 1929, lived with his parents while he finished school.

## Drawn to Civil Rights Law

At Howard, Marshall became the protégé of Dean Charles Houston, who had transformed the school into a nationally respected and accredited institution over the previous few years. Houston had also made civil rights law the focus of the school's programs, and Marshall excelled in his studies. The top-ranked student in his class, he earned a job in the law library that not only paid for school but brought him into daily contact with Houston. As the months passed by, he took to heart Houston's conviction that lawyers should work as "social engineers" fighting for justice. When he graduated first in his class in 1933, he turned down a fellowship to attend Harvard University in order to begin his practice at once. He passed the Maryland Bar and opened a law office in Baltimore.

Establishing a new law practice during the Great Depression was diffi-cult. Marshall even had to take a second job as a clerk to support his family for a time. But his willingness to take civil rights cases for little or no fee brought him to the attention of community and business leaders, and his practice soon expanded. His work on behalf of the local NAACP also raised his profile in the black community. These activities included an investigation of lynchings in the eastern part of Maryland and organization of a boycott against stores that refused to hire African Americans even when the stores' survival depended on purchases from the black community.

Marshall also took his first swing against school segregation during this time, suing the University of Maryland on behalf of an African American seeking admission to its school of pharmacy. He lost the case on a technicali-ty, but the experience taught him some important lessons about choosing plaintiffs and garnering community support.

In 1935 he agreed to represent Donald Murray, a black student who had been denied a place at the University of Maryland's law school because of his race. Working with his mentor Houston, who was now special counsel to the NAACP, Marshall won the case in state court. Then, under Houston's guid-ance, Marshall successfully defended the verdict before the Maryland Court of Appeals. This marked the first time in U.S. history that a court ordered a white university to admit African Americans. Marshall followed this triumph by forcing Maryland to equalize its salary structures for white and black teachers.

## Heads the NAACP Fight for Civil Rights

Marshall's dedication—combined with his proven ability to secure legal advances for African Americans—convinced Houston to offer him a job as assistant counsel at the NAACP in 1936.

Marshall promptly moved to New York City, and he spent the next few years working side by side with Houston. "We tried our cases one by one," Marshall recalled. "We had no plan, because you couldn't make a plan. You were limited by money, and you were also limited by people who wanted you to file suits."

One of those people was Lloyd Gaines, a black man whose attempts to gain admittance to the University of Missouri's law school had been repeatedly rebuffed. Instead, the university offered to provide Gaines with a full scholarship to attend an integrated school out of state. Marshall helped Houston prepare the legal briefs for the NAACP's appeal of *Missouri ex rel. Gaines v. Canada* before the Supreme Court. In 1938 the Court ruled that Missouri had to provide a law school for African Americans. This was a very important ruling, for although it did not address the constitutionality of educational segregation, it clearly indicated that the Court was determined to start enforcing the "equal" provision of the "separate but equal" doctrine.

That same year Houston left the NAACP to return to private practice and Marshall was named as his replacement. When the NAACP created the Legal Defense and Education Fund (LDF) in 1939 to handle legal issues, the organization made Marshall its first director counsel. He traveled the country, often risking his own safety, to investigate cases and speak to local branches. As LDF Associate Counsel Jack Greenberg recalled in *Crusaders in the Courts,* Marshall "was more in demand as a speaker than anyone in the Association. In a mass meeting he could bring an audience to its feet, clapping and stomping. In court, he was conversational and usually lectured as a professor might, although sometimes there were emotional riffs full of vivid imagery."

Marshall also coordinated the LDF's growing legal staff as it pursued justice in the courts over the next decade. In 1944 he and William Hastie secured a judgment from the U.S. Supreme Court (in *Smith v. Allwright*) that Texas's all-white political primaries were unconstitutional. Two years later, Marshall and Hastie won another victory in *Morgan v. Virginia,* in which the Supreme Court overturned a Virginia law requiring segregation on interstate transportation. And in 1948, Marshall reveled in a third major Supreme Court victory (*Shelley v. Kraemer*) when the Court overturned restrictive covenants—housing agreements forbidding the sale of property to African Americans. These successes earned Marshall the nickname of "Mr. Civil Rights" and convinced the NAACP to award him the Spingarn Medal in 1946.

### *Brown* Ruling Ends Segregation

During this time, Marshall and the LDF shifted their legal strategy toward direct attacks on segregation as an unconstitutional violation of African American rights. School segregation was a major focus of this strategy. In 1950 Marshall and the LDF achieved landmark rulings in *Sweatt v. Painter* and *McLaurin v. Oklahoma State Regents*. In the former case, the Supreme Court cited "intangible" factors in ruling that a separate law school for African Americans could not provide an education equal to that at the all-white University of Texas. In the *McLaurin* case, the Court ruled that a school could not admit an African American student and then segregate him from his fellow students. These two rulings provide key precedents for the Court when *Brown v. Board of Education* appeared on the court docket two years later.

Marshall spent time in 1951 investigating the treatment of African American soldiers who had been unfairly court-martialed in Korea and Japan. In several cases Marshall and other legal allies were able to reduce their sentences. After returning to America, he coordinated the LDF's preparation for four of the five cases that would come before the Supreme Court as *Brown v. Board of Education*. When oral arguments before the Court commenced, Marshall himself argued the *Briggs v. Elliott* case from South Carolina. His opponent in the case was former U.S. Solicitor General John W. Davis.

After two arguments before the Supreme Court, Marshall and the LDF emerged victorious. On May 17, 1954, the Supreme Court handed down a unanimous ruling that school segregation was unconstitutional. Almost twenty years of litigating cases and building precedents had finally paid off. "I really believed we couldn't be held down any longer and that right would win out and people would realize that we weren't just fighting for Afro-Americans," recalled Marshall in a 1990 interview with *Ebony*. "We were fighting for the heart of the entire nation."

The professional triumph of *Brown* was tempered by personal tragedy, however. In February 1955 Marshall's wife Vivian died of cancer. After a period of mourning, Marshall married Cecilia "Cissy" Burat, a NAACP secretary of Filipino heritage, in December 1955. They eventually had two sons, Thurgood Jr. and John.

Marshall also resumed his professional life, winning other important cases for the LDF before the Supreme Court. These included *Lucy v. Adams,* a 1955 decision ordering the desegregation of the University of Alabama; *Coop-*

*er v. Aaron,* the 1958 ruling ordering Little Rock to continue desegregation plans in the face of community resistance; and *NAACP v. Alabama,* a 1959 case overturning an Alabama injunction against the NAACP's operations in that state. He also contributed to the LDF brief for *Garner v. Louisiana,* a 1961 case which ruled that sit-ins were a protected form of free speech. All in all, Marshall came away with twenty-nine victories in the thirty-two civil rights cases that he and the LDF brought before the Supreme Court.

## Blazes Trails as Federal Judge and Lawyer

After more than twenty years leading the LDF, Marshall began to feel he had contributed all he could to the organization and began considering alternative employment. In 1960 he spent time in Kenya, and the following year he helped draw up a constitution for this former British colony. When John F. Kennedy began his presidency in 1961, Marshall lobbied for an appointment to the federal bench. The administration initially offered Marshall a district court judgeship, but he held out for a seat on the U.S. Court of Appeals, believing his extensive appellate experience suited him for the job.

In early 1961 the administration honored Marshall's wishes and nominated him to the Second Court of Appeals, which covered New York, Vermont, and Connecticut. One year later, after Senate confirmation, he became only the second African American, after William H. Hastie, to serve on the U.S. Court of Appeals. Marshall served on the appellate bench for four years.

In 1965 President Lyndon Johnson asked Marshall if he would leave his lifetime appointment and take a pay cut to serve as U.S. Solicitor General, the lawyer who represents the government before the Supreme Court. Marshall agreed, becoming the first African American to serve as the government's top lawyer. Over the next two years, Marshall won fourteen of the nineteen cases he argued on behalf of the federal government, including a successful defense of the Voting Rights Act of 1965. In recalling those times, Marshall later said that "Stanley Reed, on [the Supreme] Court, who used to be solicitor general, said it was the greatest job he ever had. I think I agree with him. You're on the top of everything all the time. You know what I mean? You stay on the top of everything. As soon as you get through with [one case], there is another right there."

Nevertheless, Marshall left his post as Solicitor General in 1967 when President Johnson nominated him to serve on the U.S. Supreme Court. "I believe he has already earned his place in history, but I think it will be greatly enhanced by his service on the Court," Johnson declared. "I believe he earned that appointment; he deserves the appointment. He is best qualified by training and by very valuable service to the country. I believe it is the right thing to do, the right time to do it, and the right man and the right place." Although there was some opposition from Southern congressmen, it only took two months for Marshall to be confirmed as the first African American to serve on the Supreme Court.

## Liberal Pillar of the Supreme Court

As a member of Chief Justice Earl Warren's liberal-leaning court, Marshall was initially considered moderate in his views. As the Court filled with Republican appointees during the Nixon administrations (1969-1974), however, he became a leading liberal voice on the Court. He strongly opposed the death penalty, for example, calling it a violation of the Eighth Amendment's ban on "cruel and unusual punishment." He also was a fierce defender of civil liberties, including freedom of speech and religion, and a woman's right to abortion.

Although he was not considered a distinguished legal scholar, Marshall did write some important opinions. In the 1969 case *Stanley v. Georgia* he wrote the majority opinion that held that private possession of pornographic material was protected under the First Amendment. In 1972's *Furman v. Georgia*, which overturned three death sentences as violations of cruel and unusual punishment, Marshall prepared an exhaustive concurring opinion noting that "in striking down capital punishment, this Court does not malign our system of government. On the contrary, it pays homage to it. Only in a free society could right triumph in difficult times, and could civilization record its magnificent advancement. In recognizing the humanity of our fellow beings, we pay ourselves the highest tribute."

Despite health problems that included recurring pneumonia, heart attacks, blood clots, and glaucoma, Marshall served on the Court throughout the 1980s. By this time his stature in American jurisprudence was unquestioned. "If you study the history of Marshall's career, the history of his rulings on the Supreme Court, even his dissents, you will understand that when he speaks, he is not speaking just for Black Americans but for Americans of all times," said scholar John Hope Franklin in *Ebony*. "He reminds us constantly of the great promise this country has made of equality, and he reminds us that it has not been fulfilled. Through his life he has been a great watchdog, insisting that this nation live up to the Constitution."

## "The Great Dissenter"

As the Court turned out increasingly conservative opinions on civil liberties, affirmative action, the death penalty, and the rights of criminal defendants, Marshall found himself in the minority and earned the nickname "The Great Dissenter." "Maybe I am just crying in the wilderness," he told a legal conference in 1988, "but as long as I have breath in me I am going to cry."

In 1991 failing health forced Marshall to announce his retirement from the nation's highest court. Making his announcement, the justice noted: "I don't know what legacy I left. It's up to the people. I guess you could say, 'He did what he could with what he had.' I have given fifty years to it, and if that is not enough, God bless them." Despite this self-effacing comment, many Americans rushed to pay homage to his long and distinguished career as a lawyer and judge. As Donald Baer reported in the *U.S. News & World Report,* "No American lawyer in this century of lawyers, probably no judge in America's history, has given more life to the law than Marshall. Now the nation faces yet another court confirmation fight that eventually will cast up someone to take Thurgood Marshall's seat. Finding someone to take his place as an inspiration—for all Americans—is a much more daunting task."

Less than two years after his retirement, on January 24, 1993, Thurgood Marshall died in Bethesda, Maryland. His body was laid in state in the nation's capital and nearly 20,000 people visited to pay their respects on the first day alone. The government erected a Washington federal judiciary building in his honor, and Texas Southern University named its law school and library after him.

## Sources

Baer, Donald. "Embracing a Great Man's Gift to America," *U.S. News & World Report,* July 8, 1991.

Davis, Michael D., and Hunter R. Clark. *Thurgood Marshall: Warrior at the Bar, Rebel on the Bench.* New York: Birch Lane Press, 1992.

Greenberg, Jack. *Crusaders in the Courts: How a Dedicated Band of Lawyers Fought for the Civil Rights Revolution.* New York: Basic Books, 1994.

Kluger, Richard. *Simple Justice: The History of* Brown v. Board of Education *and Black America's Struggle for Equality.* New York: Knopf, 1975.

Marshall, Thurgood. *Thurgood Marshall: His Speeches, Writings, Arguments, Opinions, and Reminiscences.* Edited by Mark V. Tushnet. Chicago, IL: Lawrence Hill Books, 2001.

Rowan, Carl T. *Dream Makers, Dream Breakers: The World of Justice Thurgood Marshall.* Boston: Little, Brown, 1993.

"The Tension of Change." *Time,* September 19, 1955.

Tushnet, Mark. *Making Civil Rights Law: Thurgood Marshall and the Supreme Court, 1936-1961.* New York: Oxford University Press, 1994.

Williams, Juan. *Thurgood Marshall: American Revolutionary.* New York: Times Books, 1998.

Williams, Juan. "The Thurgood Marshall Nobody Knows; First Black Supreme Court Justice Recalls His Life on the Front Line of the Civil Rights Issue." *Ebony,* May 1990.

**Earl Warren (1891-1974)**
*Chief Justice of the Supreme Court for the*
Brown *decisions*

Earl Warren was born on March 9, 1891, in Los Angeles, California. He was the second of two children born to Methias "Matt" and Christine Hernlund Warren, first-generation immigrants from Scandinavia. Matt Warren (the family name was altered from "Varran") was a repairman for the Southern Pacific Railroad when he participated in an 1894 strike. Fired and blacklisted by the railway, he moved his family east to Bakersfield, California, where Earl and his sister grew up.

Earl Warren was a better than average student who took music lessons and participated in sports. He worked summer and after school jobs during his teenage years, including a stint as a call boy at his father's employer, rounding up railway crews. He later said the experience taught him how a large company "dominated the economic and political life of the community. I saw that power exercised and the hardship that followed in its wake." This sympathy for the underdog would inform Warren's later career.

After graduating from high school in 1908, Warren attended the University of California at Berkeley, where his father wanted him to study mining. Warren, however, decided to pursue a career in law. He received his bachelor's degree in political science in 1912 and his law degree two years later. After graduation he was admitted to the bar and began working as an assistant counsel for a San Francisco oil company, a job which exposed him to the city's rampant political corruption. He left after a year and joined an Oakland law firm. After eighteen months he began laying the groundwork to start his own practice, but when the United States entered World War I in 1917 he felt compelled to join the Army. He began as an enlisted man but soon qualified for officers' training; commissioned as a second lieutenant, he spent the war training draftees in Virginia.

## A Dedicated District Attorney

Warren returned to California after the war ended in November 1918 and took a temporary position as clerk to the California Assembly's influential Judiciary Committee. The position introduced him to California state politics as well as various job opportunities. When the session ended in 1919, Warren found a job in the Oakland city attorney's office. A year later he joined the district attorney's office of Alameda County, which included the cities of Oakland and Berkeley. The job gave him a broader spectrum of criminal and civil cases to experience, and by 1924 he had become assistant district attorney. The following year he was appointed to finish the term of the retiring district attorney. In 1925 he also married Nina Palmquist Meyers, a young widow with a six-year-old son. He adopted the boy, Jim, and the couple went on to have five more children: Virginia, Earl Jr., Dorothy, Nina Elizabeth, and Robert.

As district attorney, Warren immediately implemented a program to increase criminal investigations and reduce corruption, particularly in the county's bail bondsman program. He fought illegal gambling and bootlegging and investigated fraud in the Berkeley school system. In 1926 he won election to the office of district attorney in his own right, winning in a landslide despite funding his campaign almost entirely with his own money.

Warren's independence from political patrons enabled him to investigate corruption in the county sheriff's office and other areas of government, and he became adept at using the media to generate public pressure on uncooperative officials. Warren easily won re-election in 1930, and the following year a national survey named him the best district attorney in the entire country. In 1934 he won a third term as district attorney of Alameda County. Around this same time he successfully ran for election as head of the state's Republican Assembly.

## Enters California State Politics

In 1938 the incumbent attorney general of California stepped down and Warren quickly declared his candidacy for the vacancy. He resigned his post as a Republican national committeeman in hope of appealing to voters of both parties. His campaign, meanwhile, emphasized his devotion to fighting crime and protecting civil liberties. Warren's solid reputation and his moderate message enabled him to emerge from the primary election with the backing of Republicans, Progressives, and Democrats (at the time, California allowed candidates to "cross-file" for all party nominations). From there he cruised to victory in the general election. The only dark cloud for Warren during the campaign season was the murder of his father, a crime that went unsolved.

As attorney general for the state of California, Warren quickly got down to business. On his first day he ordered an investigation into allegations that the outgoing governor had sold pardons to convicted criminals. He also tackled organized gambling and improved cooperation between the state's various local law enforcement agencies. It was as state attorney general, however, that Warren took the one action in his political career he would later regret: he advocated the evacuation of more than 110,000 Japanese Americans to internment camps after the United States declared war on Japan in 1942.

Years later, Warren expressed great regret about his involvement in the internment. In 1972 he broke down in tears when he was interviewed on the subject, and in his *Memoirs,* he said that the internment "was not in keeping with our American concept of freedom and the rights of citizens," adding that "it was wrong to react so impulsively, without positive evidence of disloyalty, even though we felt we had a good motive in the security of our state."

In 1942 the Republican Party sought to capitalize on Warren's statewide popularity by urging him to run for governor. He agreed despite some misgivings, and over the next several months his nonpartisan direction of the attorney general's office and plainspoken ways made a deep impression on California voters. He ended up defeating incumbent Democratic Governor Culbert Olson with 57 percent of the vote, and he was inaugurated in a simple ceremony in January 1943.

As governor, Warren worked to enact improvements to the state's prison and mental health systems, and he unsuccessfully lobbied for the creation of a state health insurance program. When he ran for re-election in 1946, he was nominated by both the Republicans and the Democrats and handily won a second term.

As the popular governor of a large and economically important state, Warren also became prominent in national politics. At the 1948 Republican National Convention New York Governor Thomas A. Dewey emerged as the choice for president. When Dewey offered him a spot as his vice-president, Warren felt compelled to accept. Throughout the ensuing campaign, many observers believed that the Dewey-led ticket would unseat incumbent President Harry S. Truman, but Truman kept the White House by a razor-thin margin.

Warren returned to his post as governor and devoted himself to furthering the state's development. He easily won election to an unprecedented third term in 1950, although the victory was tempered by his daughter Nina's bout with polio and a car accident involving his daughter Dorothy that left her with broken ribs and a punctured lung. These events inspired the governor to once again propose hospitalization insurance legislation. By the end of his third term he had also sponsored the continuing operation of child care centers for working mothers and a juvenile court system to rehabilitate young offenders—all the while keeping taxes stable and maintaining a balanced budget.

As the 1952 presidential election approached, Warren's name once again figured prominently on the short list of candidates for the Republican nomination. At the Republican Convention, however, General Dwight D. Eisenhower and Ohio Senator Robert Taft emerged as the party favorites for the nomination. When it became clear that his prospects for the nomination looked hopeless, Warren released his California delegates to vote for Eisenhower, ensuring his nomination. The grateful candidate later told Warren that he would appoint him to the next vacancy on the Supreme Court if he won the general election. A few months later, Eisenhower won the election by a comfortable margin over Democratic candidate Adlai Stevenson.

## Heads the Supreme Court

By 1953 Warren had already decided not to run for a fourth term as governor of California. That summer, Eisenhower asked him to serve as his administration's solicitor general. Warren accepted, but a short time later Supreme Court Chief Justice Fred M. Vinson unexpectedly died of a heart attack. Although Eisenhower had not envisioned appointing Warren to the Supreme Court's top position (Warren had never served on a judicial bench at any level), the president was impressed with his administrative ability, experience as a prosecutor, and aura of "statesmanship." On September 30 the president announced Warren's appointment as Chief Justice of the United States to the approval of most observers, both Republican and Democrat.

Warren scarcely had time to settle in and learn the routine when the Supreme Court was faced with one of its most controversial cases: *Brown v. Board of Education*. It was the second time the Court had heard the arguments concerning the issue of school segregation, and Warren knew the public ramifications of the Court's eventual decision would be huge, no matter what it decided.

Warren approached the case already convinced that segregation was morally wrong. As California's governor he had pushed the assembly to repeal laws that segregated Asian and Native American schoolchildren, supported antidiscrimination legislation, spearheaded the creation of a Fair Employment Practices Commission, and appointed the first African American and Japanese American judges to the California bench.

Warren was pleased to find during initial discussions with his colleagues that a majority were in favor of overturning segregation. But the chief justice knew that it was in the nation's best interests for the Court to craft a unanimous decision striking down segregation. Any dissenting opinion would be seized on by segregationists in the South and give their defiance a patina of legitimacy.

With this in mind, Warren worked furiously to craft a unanimous decision. Under Chief Justice Vinson, personality clashes and differing philosophies had created a deeply divided Court. Warren, however, skillfully bridged the differences between the various justices. For example, instead of taking an early vote on the case—which might force justices to stake out positions that they would later be reluctant to change—he allowed discussion to develop slowly. He also embraced Justice Felix Frankfurter's suggestion that the Court decide the issue of relief at a later date to build a consensus on the principle of segregation.

In the end, Warren drafted a short but straightforward opinion ruling that segregation was unconstitutional. Seven of his colleagues signed on, two of them forgoing concurring opinions that might have prompted objections from the others. The last holdout, Justice Stanley Reed, capitulated after Warren convinced him that a unanimous decision was in the best interests of the country. When the Chief Justice read the opinion on May 17, 1954, the country heard one voice proclaiming that "in the field of public education the doctrine of 'separate but equal' has no place."

## The Warren Court

The *Brown* decision bore all the hallmarks of a "Warren Court" decision. Over the years the chief justice became known both for his ability to achieve consensus and his inclination to decide an issue and then seek the legal justification for the decision. He became known as a liberal champion of individual rights and civil liberties, much to the consternation of Eisenhower, who later called his appointment "the biggest damned-fool mistake I ever made."

The "Super Chief," as Warren was dubbed by his colleague William Brennan, presided over several important court precedents: *Engel v. Vitale* (1962), which outlawed mandatory prayer in schools; *Baker v. Carr* (1962) and *Reynolds v. Sims* (1964), which ruled state legislatures had to apportion representatives equally among urban and rural areas; *Griswold v. Connecticut* (1965), which overturned a law banning contraception; and *Loving v. Virginia* (1967), which overturned bans on interracial marriage. The former prosecutor also oversaw a revolution in protecting the rights of accused criminals: *Mapp v. Ohio* (1961) forbade prosecutors to use evidence found during an illegal search; *Gideon v. Wainwright* (1963) required the state to provide a lawyer to poor defendants; and *Miranda v. Arizona* (1966) required police to inform defendants of their rights.

Warren rendered one other service to his country during his years on the Supreme Court. On November 22, 1963, President John F. Kennedy was shot and killed in Dallas, Texas. Two days later his assassin, Lee Harvey Oswald, was likewise shot dead while being transferred to the county jail. Rumors of a conspiracy quickly arose, and the new president, Lyndon B. Johnson, asked the chief justice to lead a commission to investigate Kennedy's death. Warren, who had befriended Kennedy and delivered one of the eulogies at his funeral, reluctantly accepted the job. The Warren Commission, as it came to be called, spent ten months conducting an independent investigation of the assassination. The Commission's report, released in September 1964, concluded that both Oswald and his murderer, Jack Ruby, had acted alone. Although conspiracy theorists criticized the final Warren Commission Report as incomplete, Warren refused to be drawn into further debate, noting only that "we achieved as much proof as could be achieved."

In 1968 Warren informed President Johnson that he was ready to retire whenever the president could find a suitable replacement. Johnson nominated Associate Justice Abe Fortas for the position, but some financial irregularities in Fortas's background derailed his nomination and led to his resignation. As a result, conservative Republican President Richard Nixon—a vocal critic of some of the Warren Court's decisions over the years—ended up naming Warren's replacement, U.S. Appeals Judge Warren E. Burger. Warren left the Court in July 1969 and spent his retirement traveling, giving speeches, and working on his memoirs (published posthumously in 1977). He died on July 9, 1974, in Washington, D.C. He was buried in Washington's Arlington National Cemetery.

Although many of the Warren Court's decisions were controversial—some were later weakened or overturned—even his detractors admitted that Warren was a man of great integrity who brought needed leadership to the Court during a time of turmoil in the nation. Many observers consider him one of the nation's finest chief justices, despite his lack of rigorous legal scholarship. "He lacked an articulated judicial philosophy beyond the penetrating and constant query, 'Is is fair?'" Ed Cray observed in *Chief Justice.* "He had only an abiding sense of the public good—that, and a respect for personal values considered old-fashioned or even irrelevant to the business of governing. Those two qualities, coupled with his own sense of purpose, made him a great leader."

## Sources

Cray, Ed. *Chief Justice: A Biography of Earl Warren.* New York: Simon & Schuster, 1997.

Pollack, Jack Harrison. *Earl Warren: The Judge Who Changed America.* Englewood Cliffs, NJ: Prentice-Hall, 1979.

Schwarz, Frederic D. "1953: The Warren Court." *American Heritage,* August-September 2003.

Warren, Earl. *The Memoirs of Earl Warren.* Garden City, NY: Doubleday, 1977.

# PRIMARY SOURCES

# A Black Man Recalls Attending a Segregated School in the South

*In this oral history collected in* Remembering Jim Crow, *William J. Coker, Jr. recalls attending all-black schools in Norfolk, Virginia, in the 1940s and early 1950s. Not only does he tell of inadequate facilities, filled with hand-me-downs from white schools, he relates how shades of skin color and family backgrounds affected the way some black teachers treated students.*

I was able to ease into school at five years old, but I got the whooping cough. This was before we moved to Norfolk. I got the whooping cough, and didn't finish the year. So when I came to Norfolk, well, I was six, I started in the first grade. The first school [I attended] was Waterford Elementary School in south Norfolk, Virginia. This was an eight-room building without a library. We had books without backs on them, pages torn out of them, and some of the pages were marked and a part of the book marked. What we got was the books from the white schools, which they had probably used for four or five years and then passed on to us.

We never got a new desk. We had a basement cafeteria, for a small school—except for the fact that it was very hot down there. Kids are resilient. Kids don't complain. But today no parent would send their child to that kind of thing.

The teachers were a mixture. They were all dedicated, I'm sure, but some of them—how shall I say this to be delicate? Some of them did not treat the lower class, for lack of a better word, children in the best manner, and I was very aware of this. As a child, I was very aware of it. I guess I've been a fighter for the underdog by being an underdog all of my life. Children from certain neighborhoods, children who did not have the advantage of being able to dress in a reasonable manner, or maybe even children who didn't have that 10, 15 cents in their pocket for lunch—by some teachers [such children] were treated atrociously in my way of thinking.

This is going to blow your mind. I've only started talking about this recently, and the reason I'm talking about it is not to lambaste anyone, but we must assure ourselves on an intragroup basis that this must never happen

---

again. We can't expect [help from] external forces. You must learn to do some of the things that need to be done for your particular grouping yourself.

First grade. The very first day the teacher placed you in what was to be your permanent seat. All of the little fair-skinned, curly-haired girls and boys were placed on the first, second, then maybe some of them in the third row, according to how well they dressed and their skin complexion. There were no dark-skinned children on these three rows. Even if they were from wealthy families—and there weren't that many wealthy families, but there were some who did better than others.

It was very well stratified. Being middle complexioned and being well dressed, I was on the fourth row. For the next three years, I would be on the fourth or fifth row, which naturally meant that the [teacher's] attention would presumably be given to the children closer to her, since her desk was in the front.

I remember a girl, and I haven't seen her since 1950. [She] had black velvet skin, coarse long black hair. A beautiful girl. Quiet—subdued into being quiet, perhaps—and brilliant. Okay? She was never called on. She was almost voiceless. Her seat for [the] eight years I went to school with was the seat nearest the door. So when class was over, she can get out of that door and get home and will not have to be called names. Of course, since the teacher didn't do anything to—we're kind when we say "build her self-esteem," but that really wasn't a question. Something was projected to this girl.

She didn't dress in a stylish or elaborate manner, but her dresses were starched like cardboard. She was a beautiful kid. She was an only child, and her parents were quiet churchgoing people, and you never heard anything negative about them. There wasn't any reason for this girl not to have been one of the leading students in the class, called upon, looked upon, and so forth, but instead she was treated as a reject.

There was a neighborhood, a very rough neighborhood, of boys and girls—A Avenue, B Avenue, several other avenues. They all centered around hip joints and gambling houses, and of course, kids were born. If you want to speak of absolute rejects, those were the children. They couldn't have bought their way past the sixth or seventh row in the class, heading toward the back. Very few of them made it through high school. Most of them dropped out after the eighth grade.

This has been stuck in my craw for a very long time. It's painful. It hurts, because I was the kind of kid who was outgoing and I played with everybody, I talked with everybody. I'd get on my bicycle after school and go over to another section to talk to guys and girls. I was never interested in sports. Music, reading, and just going and talking to people, were always the things that I was interested in, even old people, believe it or not.

After the eighth grade—we didn't have a high school. There was a [white] high school within a mile and a half from my house. They bused us to another town, from Norfolk to Portsmouth, which is about 10 miles, and named the school Norfolk County High. Now, what they did was purely political, because they didn't know which way the integration [issue] was going to go. So good political minds of the South said, "We'd better build some high schools, some black high schools," and that's precisely what they did.

But in the meantime, we've got all these kids, what are we going to do with them? Now, you can imagine, before 1952, in south Norfolk, Virginia, there was no high school. People lied and claimed to live in Norfolk [so they could attend Booker T. Washington High School]. If they had an aunt or cousin, anybody, they used that address. That's what my sister did. And there was St. Joseph's [a private high school]. They did the same thing. [South Norfolk] had what they called a high school, which was based on the old-time standard of two years. At any rate, that was the school they had.

By the time I came around, by the time I finished the eighth grade, there was a political issue called the desegregation of the schools on the docket. They knew they had to do something, or they didn't want to take a gambler's chance of not doing anything. So they decided to build some schools. [George Washington Carver High School] cost $350,000, thereabouts, and when it was completed—a year after they started building Oscar Smith [a white school], which at the time cost more than $1 million.

So [meanwhile] they bused us to Norfolk County High School, which was in Portsmouth, Virginia. There were government buildings that were built over there during World War II for the Navy, and these were the buildings that we were using. Cold in the winter, hot in the summer, but they bused us over there, and we went to school there in January of 1950, I believe it was. We stayed there until, '50, '51, and [then I] started to Carver High—George Washington Carver High. They completed our school in south Norfolk.

Still, it was furnished and supplied by the old system, and no library again. There was a library room, but apparently no allocation for it. So they just grabbed some old books that may have been floating around at several of the other schools and threw them in there. You see, this was all a part of the system that you're not 100 percent proud of. My dad paid as much taxes as any workingman there, and yet we did not get the benefits of it. I say my dad, but hundreds of other people did likewise.

The school was built and supplied in a manner that [said], "Well, now they got their school." Okay? But the school was not a school, a high school, as we know a high school now. We were in no ways comparable to Oscar Smith High, which was the white high school.

It's sad. It's sad, because it was a place you go to in the morning, and you leave in the early evening and go back the next day. The school was supposed to be second to home and church, but it wasn't. It wasn't. I think in systems like this, we lose too many good people. We lose too many people.

I walked past an elementary school that was exactly two blocks from my house, and walked a mile to school, from the first through eighth grade. You talk about paying dues. What mother will take as a choice of putting her six-year-old son or daughter to walk a mile to school, across traffic spots and so forth, in the rain, in the snow, in the cold, etc., etc.? Not many. So anyone who would take the stand of, "Well, you people have to work harder," as someone said a few weeks ago, doesn't know. You've given blood, sweat, and tears, the best of everything that you have had *traditionally.*

Now, what more can you give? How much longer do you have to wait for your slice of the pie? It is not a gift. Your slice of the pie would not be a gift. It would be the same thing that all men get, and the same thing that the cattle-men get in some regions of the country, and other industries, and other groups, as a matter of fact. There is no greater welfare than the tax breaks and all the considerations that's given toward business. So "welfare" has become a dirty word, and certainly it needed some changes. It never should have drifted to this, but why penalize the recipient? Because they're the ones that's locked into it and least likely to be able to do anything about it.

Source: Coker, William J. Jr., "Lessons Well Learned." In *Remembering Jim Crow: African Americans Tell about Life in the Segregated South.* New York: New Press, 2001, pp. 157-161.

176

# "The Effects of Segregation and the Consequences of Desegregation: A Social Science Statement"

*The NAACP Legal Defense and Education Fund (LDF) team had some success in using psychological and sociological testimony in early hearings of the school desegregation cases. When it was time to submit briefs for the Supreme Court's hearing in* Brown v. Board of Education, *the LDF team decided to include an appendix presenting sociological evidence on segregation. The team asked New York psychologist Kenneth B. Clark to prepare a summary of current research on how segregation affected African Americans. Working with former City College of New York psychology colleague Isidor Chein and Stuart W. Cook, the chairman of psychology at New York University, Clark produced the following "social science statement," which was co-signed by thirty-five of the most prominent social scientists in the country.*

I

The problem of the segregation of racial and ethnic groups constitutes one of the major problems facing the American people today. It seems desirable, therefore, to summarize the contributions which contemporary social science can make toward its resolution. There are, of course, moral and legal issues involved with respect to which the signers of the present statement cannot speak with any special authority and which must be taken into account in the solution of the problem. There are, however, also factual issues involved with respect to which certain conclusions seem to be justified on the basis of the available scientific evidence. It is with these issues only that this paper is concerned. Some of the issues have to do with the consequences of segregation, some with the problems of changing from segregated to unsegregated practices. These two groups of issues will be dealt with in separate sections below. It is necessary, first, however, to define and delimit the problem to be discussed.

## Definitions

For purposes of the present statement, *segregation* refers to that restriction of opportunities for different types of associations between the members of one racial, religious, national or geographic origin, or linguistic group and those of other groups, which results from or is supported by the action of any official body or agency representing some branch of government....

Where the action takes place in a social milieu in which the groups involved do not enjoy equal social status, the group that is of lesser social status will be referred to as the *segregated* group.

177

In dealing with the question of the effects of segregation, it must be recognized that these effects do not take place in a vacuum, but in a social context. The segregation of Negroes and of other groups in the United States takes place in a social milieu in which "race" prejudice and discrimination exist.... The imbeddedness of segregation in such a context makes it difficult to disentangle the effects of segregation *per se* from the effects of the context.... We shall, however, return to this problem after consideration of the observable effects of the total social complex in which segregation is a major component.

II

At the recent Mid-century White House Conference on Children and Youth, a fact-finding report on the effects of prejudice, discrimination and segregation on the personality development of children was prepared as a basis for some of the deliberations.[1] This report brought together the available social science and psychological studies which were related to the problem of how racial and religious prejudices influenced the development of a healthy personality. It highlighted the fact that segregation, prejudices and discriminations, and their social concomitants potentially damage the personality of all children—the children of the majority group in a somewhat different way than the more obviously damaged children of the minority group.

The report indicates that as minority group children learn the inferior status to which they are assigned—as they observe the fact that they are almost always segregated and kept apart from others who are treated with more respect by the society as a whole—they often react with feelings of inferiority and a sense of personal humiliation. Many of them become confused about their own personal worth. On the one hand, like all other human beings they require a sense of personal dignity; on the other hand, almost nowhere in the larger society do they find their own dignity as human beings respected by others. Under these conditions, the minority group child is thrown into a conflict with regard to his feelings about himself and his group. He wonders whether his group and he himself are worthy of no more respect than they receive. This conflict and confusion leads to self-hatred and rejection of his own group....

Some children, usually of the lower socio-economic classes, may react by overt aggressions and hostility directed toward their own group or members of the dominant group.[2] Anti-social and delinquent behavior may often be interpreted as reactions to these racial frustrations. These reactions are self-destructive in that the larger society not only punishes those who commit them, but often interprets such aggressive and antisocial behavior as justification for continuing prejudice and segregation.

Middle class and upper class minority group children are likely to react to their racial frustrations and conflicts by withdrawal and submissive behavior. Or, they may react with compensatory and rigid conformity to the prevailing middle class values and standards and an aggressive determination to succeed in these terms in spite of the handicap of their minority status.

The report indicates that minority group children of all social and economic classes often react with a generally defeatist attitude and a lowering of personal ambitions. This, for example, is reflected in a lowering of pupil morale and a depression of the educational aspiration level among minority group children in segregated schools. In producing such effects, segregated schools impair the ability of the child to profit from the educational opportunities provided him.

Many minority group children of all classes also tend to be hypersensitive and anxious about their relations with the larger society. They tend to see hostility and rejection even in those areas where these might not actually exist. The report concludes that while the range of individual differences among members of a rejected minority group is as wide as among other peoples, the evidence suggests that all of these children are unnecessarily encumbered in some ways by segregation and its concomitants.

With reference to the impact of segregation and its concomitants on children of the majority group, the report indicates that the effects are somewhat more obscure. Those children who learn the prejudices of our society are also being taught to gain personal status in an unrealistic and non-adaptive way. When comparing themselves to members of the minority group, they are not required to evaluate themselves in terms of the more basic standards of actual personal ability and achievement. The culture permits and, at times, encourages them to direct their feelings of hostility and aggression against whole groups of people the members of which are perceived as weaker than themselves. They often develop patterns of guilt feelings, rationalizations and other mechanisms which they must use in an attempt to protect themselves from recognizing the essential injustice of their unrealistic fears and hatreds of minority groups.[3]

The report indicates further that confusion, conflict, moral cynicism, and disrespect for authority may arise in majority group children as a consequence of being taught the moral, religious and democratic principles of the brotherhood of man and the importance of justice and fair play by the same persons and institutions who, in their support of racial segregation and related practices, seem to be acting in a prejudiced and discriminatory manner. Some individuals may attempt to resolve this conflict by intensifying their hostility toward the minority group. Others may react by guilt feelings which are not necessarily reflected in more humane attitudes toward the minority group. Still others react by developing an unwholesome, rigid, and uncritical idealization of all authority figures—their parents, strong political and economic leaders. As described in *The Authoritarian Personality*[4] they despise the weak, while they obsequiously and unquestioningly conform to the demands of the strong whom they also, paradoxically, subconsciously hate....

Conclusions similar to those reached by the Mid-century White House Conference Report have been stated by other social scientists who have concerned themselves with this problem. The following are some examples of these conclusions:

Segregation imposes upon individuals a distorted sense of social reality.[5]

Segregation leads to a blockage in the communications and interaction between the two groups. Such blockages tend to increase mutual suspicion, distrust and hostility.[6]

Segregation not only perpetuates rigid stereotypes and reinforces negative attitudes toward members of the other group, but also leads to the development of a social climate within which violent outbreaks of racial tensions are likely to occur.[7]

We return now to the question, deferred earlier, of what it is about the total society complex of which segregation is one feature that produces the effects described above—or, more precisely, to the question of whether we can justifiably conclude that, as only one feature of a complex social setting, segregation is in fact a significantly contributing factor to these effects.

To answer this question, it is necessary to bring to bear the general fund of psychological and sociological knowledge concerning the role of various environmental influences in producing feelings of inferiority, confusions in personal roles, various types of basic personality structures and the various forms of personal and social disorganization.

On the basis of this general fund of knowledge, it seems likely that feelings of inferiority and doubts about personal worth are attributable to living in an underprivileged environment only insofar as the latter is itself perceived as an indicator of low social status and as a symbol of inferiority. In other words, one of the important determinants in producing such feelings is the awareness of social status difference. While there are many other factors that serve as reminders of the differences in social status, there can be little doubt that the fact of enforced segregation is a major factor.[8]

This seems to be true for the following reasons among others: (1) because enforced segregation results from the decision of the majority group without the consent of the segregated and is commonly so perceived; and (2) because historically segregation patterns in the United States were developed on the assumption of the inferiority of the segregated.

In addition, enforced segregation gives official recognition and sanction to these other factors of the social complex, and thereby enhances the effects of the latter in creating the awareness of social status differences and feelings of inferiority.[9] The child who, for example, is compelled to attend a segregated school may be able to cope with ordinary expressions of prejudice by regarding the prejudiced person as evil or misguided; but he cannot readily cope with symbols of authority, the full force of the authority of the State—the school or the school board, in this instance—in the same manner. Given both the ordinary expression of prejudice and the school's policy of segregation, the former takes on greater force and seemingly becomes an official expression of the latter.

Not all of the psychological traits which are commonly observed in the social complex under discussion can be related so directly to the awareness of status differences—which in turn is, as we have already noted, materially contributed to by the practices of segregation. Thus, the low level of aspiration and defeatism so commonly observed in segregated groups is undoubtedly related to the level of self-evaluation; but it is also, in some measure, related among other things to one's expectations with regard to opportunities for achievement and, having achieved, to the opportunities for making use of these achievements. Similarly, the hyper-sensitivity and anxiety displayed by many minority group children about their relations with the larger society probably reflects their awareness of status differences; but it may also be influenced by the relative absence of opportunities for equal status contact which would provide correctives for prevailing unrealistic stereotypes.

The preceding view is consistent with the opinion stated by a large majority (90%) of social scientists who replied to a questionnaire concerning the probable effects of enforced segregation under conditions of equal facilities. This opinion was that, regardless of the facilities which are provided, enforced segregation is psychologically detrimental to the members of the segregated group....[10]

It may be noted that many of these social scientists supported their opinions on the effects of segregation on both majority and minority groups by reference to one or another or to several of the following four lines of published and unpublished evidence.[11] First, studies of children throw light on the relative priority of the awareness of status differentials and related factors as compared to the awareness of differences in facilities. On this basis, it is possible to infer some of the consequences of segregation as distinct from the influence of inequalities of facilities. Second, clinical studies and depth interviews throw light on the genetic sources and causal sequences of various patterns of psychological reaction; and, again, certain inferences are possible with respect to the effects of segregation per se in situations where one finds both segregation and unequal facilities.

III

Segregation is at present a social reality. Questions may be raised, therefore, as to what are the likely consequences of desegregation.

One such question asks whether the inclusion of an intellectually inferior group may jeopardize the education of the more intelligent group by lowering educational standards or damage the less intelligent group by placing it in a situation where it is at a marked competitive disadvantage. Behind this question is the assumption, which is examined below, that the presently segregated groups actually are inferior intellectually.

The available scientific evidence indicates that much, perhaps all, of the observable differences among various racial and national groups may be adequately explained in terms of environmental differences.[12] It has been found, for instance, that the differences between the average intelligence test scores of Negro and white children decrease, and the overlap of the distributions increases, proportionately to the number of years that the Negro children have lived in the North.[13] Related studies have shown that this change cannot be explained by the hypothesis of selective migration.[14] It seems clear, therefore, that fears based on the assumption of innate racial differences in intelligence are not well founded.

It may also be noted in passing that the argument regarding the intellectual inferiority of one group as compared to another is, as applied to schools, essentially an argument for homogeneous groupings of children by intelligence rather than by race.... [M]any educators have come to doubt the wisdom of class groupings made homogeneous solely on the basis of intelligence.[15] Those who are opposed to such homogeneous grouping believe that this type of segregation, too, appears to create generalized feelings of inferiority in the child who attends a below average class, leads to undesirable emotional consequences in the education of the gifted child, and reduces learning opportunities which result from the interaction of individuals with varied gifts.

A second problem that comes up in an evaluation of the possible consequences of desegregation involves the question of whether segregation prevents or stimulates interracial tension and conflict and the corollary question of whether desegregation has one or the other effect.

The most direct evidence available on this problem comes from observations and systematic study of instances in which desegregation has occurred. Comprehensive reviews of such instances[16] clearly establish the fact that desegregation has been carried out successfully in a variety of situations although outbreaks of violence had been commonly predicted. Extensive desegregation has taken place without major incidents in the armed services in both Northern and Southern installations and involving officers and enlisted men from all parts of the country, including the South.[17] Similar changes have been noted in housing[18] and in industry.[19] During the last war, many factories both in the North and South hired Negroes on a non-segregated, non-discriminatory basis. While a few strikes occurred, refusal by management and unions to yield quelled all strikes within a few days.[20]

Relevant to this general problem is a comprehensive study of urban race riots which found that race riots occurred in segregated neighborhoods, whereas there was no violence in sections of the city where the two races lived, worked and attended school together.[21]

Under certain circumstances desegregation not only proceeds without major difficulties, but has been observed to lead to the emergence of more favorable attitudes and friendlier relations between races....

Much depends, however, on the circumstances under which members of previously segregated groups first come in contact with others in unsegregated situations. Available evidence suggests, first, that there is less likelihood of unfriendly relations when the change is simultaneously introduced into all units of a social institution to which it is applicable—*e.g.,* all of the schools in a school system or all of the shops in a given factory.[22] When factories introduced Negroes in only some shops but not in others the prejudiced workers tended to classify the desegregated shops as inferior, "Negro work." Such objections were not raised when complete integration was introduced.

The available evidence also suggests the importance of consistent and firm enforcement of the new policy by those in authority.[23] It indicates also the importance of such factors as: the absence of competition for a limited number of facilities or benefits;[24] the possibility of contacts which permit individuals to learn about one another as individuals;[25] and the possibility of equivalence of positions and functions among all of the participants within the unsegregated situation.[26] These conditions can generally be satisfied in a number of situations, as in the armed services, public housing developments, and public schools.

IV

The problem with which we have here attempted to deal is admittedly on the frontiers of scientific knowledge. Inevitably, there must be some differences of opinion among us concerning the conclusiveness of certain items of evidence, and concerning the particular choice of words and placement of emphasis in the preceding statement. We are nonetheless in agreement that this statement is substantially correct and justified by the evidence, and the differences among us, if any, are of a relatively minor order and would not materially influence the preceding conclusions.

[1] Clark, K.B., *Effect of Prejudice and Discrimination on Personality Development,* Fact Finding Report Mid-century White House Conference on Children and Youth, Children's Bureau, Federal Security Agency, 1950 (mimeographed).

[2] Brenman, M., The Relationship Between Minority Group Identification in a Group of Urban Middle Class Negro Girls, *J. Soc. Psychol.,* 1940, 11, 171-197; Brenman, M., Minority Group Membership and Religious, Psychosexual and Social Patterns in a Group of Middle-Class Negro Girls, *J. Soc. Psychol.,* 1940, 12, 179-196; Brenman, M., Urban Lower-Class Negro Girls, *Psychiatry,* 1943, 6, 307-324; Davis, A., The Socialization of the American Negro Child and Adolescent, *J. Negro Educ.,* 1939, 8, 264-275.

[3] Adorno, T.W.; Frenkel-Brunswik, E.; Levinson, D.J.; Sanford, R.N., *The Authoritarian Personality,* 1951.

[4] Adorno, T.W.; Frenkel-Brunswik, E.; Levinson, D.J.; Sanford, R.N., *The Authoritarian Personality,* 1951.

[5] Reid, Ira, What Segregated Areas Mean; Brameld, T, Educational Cost, *Discrimination and National Welfare*, Ed. by MacIver, R.M., 1949.

[6] Frazier, E., *The Negro in the United States*, 1949; Krech, D. & Crutchfield, R. S., *Theory and Problems of Social Psychology*, 1948; Newcomb, T., *Social Psychology*, 1950.

[7] Lee, A. McClung and Humphrey, N.D., *Race Riot*, 1943.

[8] Frazier, E., *The Negro in the United States*, 1949; Myrdal, G., *An American Dilemma*, 1944.

[9] Reid, Ira, What Segregated Areas Mean, *Discrimination and National Welfare*, Ed. by MacIver, R.M., 1949.

[10] Deutscher, M. and Chein, I., The Psychological Effects of Enforced Segregation: A Survey of Social Science Opinion, *J. Psychol.*, 1948, 26, 259-287.

[11] Chein, I., What Are the Psychological Effects of Segregation Under Conditions of Equal Facilities?, *International J. Opinion and Attitude Res.*, 1949, 2, 229-234.

[12] Klineberg, O. *Characteristics of American Negro*, 1945; Klineberg, O., *Race Differences*, 1936.

[13] Klineberg, O. *Negro Intelligence and Selective Migration*, 1935.

[14] Klineberg, O. *Negro Intelligence and Selective Migration*, 1935.

[15] Brooks, J.J., Interage Grouping on Trial-Continuous Learning, Bulletin #87, *Association for Childhood Education*, 1951; Lane, R.H., Teacher in Modern Elementary School, 1941; Educational Policies Commission of the National Education Association and the American Association of School Administration Report in *Education For All Americans*, published by the N.E.A. 1948.

[16] Delano, W., Grade School Segregation: The Latest Attack on Racial Discrimination, *Yale Law Journal*, 1952, 61, 5, 730-744; Rose, A, The Influence of Legislation on Prejudice; Chapter 53 in *Race Prejudice and Discrimination*, Ed. by Rose, A., 1951; Rose, A, *Studies in the Reduction of Prejudice*, Amer. Council on Race Relations, 1948.

[17] Kenworthy, E.W., The Case Against Army Segregation, *Annals of the American Academy of Political and Social Science*, 1951, 275, 27-33; Nelson, Lt. D.D., *The Integration of the Negro in the U.S. Navy*, 1951; Opinions About Negro Infantry Platoons in White Companies in Several Divisions, *Information and Education Division, U.S. War Department, Report No. B-157*, 1945.

[18] Conover, R.D., *Race Relations at Codornices Village, Berkeley-Albany, California: A Report of the Attempt to Break Down the Segregated Pattern on a Directly Managed Housing Project*, Housing and Home Finance Agency, Public Housing Administration, Region I, December 1947 (mimeographed); Deutch, M. and Collins, M.E., *Interracial Housing, A Psychological Study of a Social Experiment*, 1951; Rutledge, E., *Integration of Racial Minorities in Public Housing Projects: A Guide for Local Housing Authorities on How to Do It*, Public Housing Administration, New York Field Office (mimeographed).

[19] Minard, R.D., The Pattern of Race Relationships in the Pocahontas Coal Field, *J. Social Issues*, 1952, 8, 29-44; Southall, S.E., *Industry's Unfinished Business*, 1951; Weaver, G. L-P, *Negro Labor, A National Problem*, 1941.

[20] Southall, S.E., *Industry's Unfinished Business*, 1951; Weaver, G. L-P, *Negro Labor, A National Problem*, 1941.

[21] Lee, A. McClung and Humphrey, N.D., *Race Riot*, 1943; Lee, A. McClung, Race Riots Aren't Necessary, *Public Affairs Pamphlet*, 1945.

[22] Minard, R.D., The Pattern of Race Relationships in the Pocahontas Coal Field, *J. Social Issues,* 1952, 8, 29-44; Rutledge, E., *Integration of Racial Minorities in Public Housing Projects: A Guide for Local Housing Authorities on How To Do It,* Public Housing Administration, New York Field Office (mimeographed).

[23] Deutsch, M. and Collins, M.E., *Interracial Housing, A Psychological Study of a Social Experiment,* 1951; Feldman, H., The Technique of Introducing Negroes Into the Plant, *Personnel,* 1942,19, 461-466; Rutledge, E., *Integration of Racial Minorities in Public Housing Projects: A Guide for Local Housing Authorities on How To Do It,* Public Housing Administration, New York Field Office (mimeographed); Southall, S.E., *Industry's Unfinished Business,* 1951; Watson, G., *Action for Unity,* 1947.

[24] Lee, A. McClung and Humphrey, N.D., *Race Riot,* 1943; Williams, R, Jr., *The Reduction of Intergroup Tensions,* Social Science Research Council, New York, 1947; Windner, AE., *White Attitudes Towards Negro-White Interaction in An Area of Changing Racial Composition.* Paper Delivered at the Sixtieth Annual Meeting of the American Psychological Association, Washington, September 1952.

[25] Wilner, D.M.; Walkley, R.P.; and Cook, S.W., Intergroup Contact and Ethnic Attitudes in Public Housing Projects, *J. Social Issues,* 1952, 8, 45-69.

[26] Allport, G.W., and Kramer, B., Some Roots of Prejudice, *J. Psychol.,* 1946, 22, 9-39; Watson, J., Some Social and Psychological Situations Related to Change in Attitude, *Human Relations,* 1950, 3, 1.

Source: Philip B. Kurland and Gerhard Casper, eds., *Landmark Briefs and Arguments of the Supreme Court of the United States: Constitutional Law,* vol. 49. Arlington, VA: University Publications of America, 1975. Reprinted in *Brown v. Board of Education: A Brief History of Documents.* Edited with introduction by Waldo E. Martin, Jr. Boston: Bedford/St. Martin's, 1998.

# The U.S. Government's *Amicus Curiae* Brief in the *Brown v. Board* Case

*When the Supreme Court decided to hear several school segregation cases together in the fall of 1952, most observers knew that the case might finally address the constitutionality of school segregation. In addition to briefs from the two sides litigating the issue, the Supreme Court received several amicus curiae ("friend of the court") briefs. Many organizations offered arguments supporting the NAACP, including labor groups such as the Congress of Industrial Organizations (CIO) and civil rights groups such as the American Jewish Congress and the Japanese American Citizens League. The federal government also weighed in on the case, with civil rights advocates within the Truman administration seeing it as a last opportunity to achieve real progress before leaving office in January 1953. The following excerpts from the government amicus brief reflect the country's struggle to assume a new role as leader of the "free world," a struggle undermined by "existing flaws in our democracy."*

Because of the national importance of the constitutional questions presented in these cases, the United States considers it appropriate to submit this brief as *amicus curiae.* We shall not undertake, however, to deal with every aspect of the issues involved. Comprehensive briefs have been submitted by the parties and other *amici curiae;* and, so far as possible, this brief will avoid repetition of arguments and materials contained in those briefs. We shall try to confine ourselves to those aspects of the cases which are of particular concern to the Government or within its special competence to discuss.

I

## The interest of the United States

In recent years the Federal Government has increasingly recognized its special responsibility for assuring vindication of the fundamental civil rights guaranteed by the Constitution. The President has stated: "We shall not ... finally achieve the ideals for which this Nation was founded so long as any American suffers discrimination as a result of his race, or religion, or color, or the land of origin of his forefathers.... The Federal Government has a clear duty to see that constitutional guaranties of individual liberties and of equal protection under the laws are not denied or abridged anywhere in our Union."[1]

Recognition of the responsibility of the Federal Government with regard to civil rights is not a matter of partisan controversy, even though differences of opinion may exist as to the need for particular legislative or executive action. Few Americans believe that government should pursue a *laissez-faire* policy in the field of civil rights, or that it adequately discharges its duty to the people so long as it does not itself intrude on their civil liberties. Instead, there is general acceptance of an affirmative government obligation to insure respect for fundamental human rights.

The constitutional right invoked in these cases is the basic right, secured to all Americans, to equal treatment before the law. The cases at bar do not involve isolated acts of racial discrimination by private individuals or groups. On the contrary, it is contended in these cases that public school systems established in the states of Kansas, South Carolina, Virginia, and Delaware, and in the District of Columbia, unconstitutionally discriminate against Negroes solely because of their color.

This contention raises questions of the first importance in our society. For racial discriminations imposed by law, or having the sanction or support of government, inevitably tend to undermine the foundations of a society dedicated to freedom, justice, and equality. The proposition that all men are created equal is not mere rhetoric. It implies a rule of law—an indispensable condition to a civilized society—under which all men stand equal and alike in the rights and opportunities secured to them by their government. Under the Constitution every agency of government, national and local, legislative, executive, and judicial, must treat each of our people as an *American,* and not as a member of a particular group classified on the basis of race or some other constitutional irrelevancy. The color of a man's skin—like his religious beliefs, or his political attachments, or the country from which he or his ancestors came to the United States—does not diminish or alter his legal rights. "Our Constitution is color-blind, and neither knows nor tolerates classes among citizens."[2]

The problem of racial discrimination is particularly acute in the District of Columbia, the nation's capital. This city is the window through which the world looks into our house. The embassies, legations, and representatives of all nations are here, at the seat of the Federal Government. Foreign officials and visitors naturally judge this country and our people by their experiences and observations in the nation's capital; and the treatment of colored persons here is taken as the measure of our attitude toward minorities generally. The President has stated that "The District of Columbia should be a true symbol of American freedom and democracy for our own people, and for the people of the world."[3] Instead, as the President's Committee on Civil Rights found, the District of Columbia "is a graphic illustration of a failure of democracy."[4] The findings Committee summarized its findings as follows:

> For Negro Americans, Washington is not just the nation's capital. It is the point at which all public transportation into the South becomes "Jim Crow." If he stops in Washington, a Negro may dine like other men in the Union Station, but as soon as he steps out into the capital, he leaves such democratic practices behind. With very few exceptions, he is refused service at downtown restaurants, he may not attend a downtown movie or play, and he has to go into the poorer section of the city to find a night's lodging. The Negro who decides to settle in the District must often find a home in an overcrowded, substandard area. He must often take a job below the level of his ability. He must send his children to the inferior public schools set aside for Negroes and entrust his family's health to medical agencies which give inferior service. In addition, he must endure the countless daily humiliations that the system of segregation imposes upon the one-third of Washington that is Negro....
>
> The shamefulness and absurdity of Washington's treatment of Negro Americans is highlighted by the presence of many dark-skinned foreign visitors. Capital custom not only humiliates colored citizens, but is a source of considerable embarrassment to these visitors.... Foreign officials are often mistaken for American Negroes and refused food, lodging and entertainment. However, once it is established that they are not Americans, they are accommodated.[5]

It is in the context of the present world struggle between freedom and tyranny that the problem of racial discrimination must be viewed. The United States is trying to prove to the people of the world, of every nationality, race, and color, that a free democracy is the most civilized and most secure form of government yet devised by man. We must set an example for others by showing firm determination to remove existing flaws in our democracy.

The existence of discrimination against minority groups in the United States has an adverse effect upon our relations with other countries. Racial discrimination furnishes grist for the Communist propaganda mills, and it raises doubts even among friendly nations as to the intensity of our devotion to the democratic faith. In response to the request of the Attorney General for an authoritative statement of the effects of racial discrimination in the United States upon the conduct of foreign relations, the Secretary of State has written as follows:

> … I wrote the Chairman of the Fair Employment Practices Committee on May 8, 1946, that the existence of discrimination against minority groups was having an adverse effect upon our relations with other countries. At that time I pointed out that discrimination against such groups in the United States created suspicion and resentment in other countries, and that we would have better international relations were these reasons for suspicion and resentment to be removed.
>
> During the past six years, the damage to our foreign relations attributable to this source has become progressively greater. The United States is under constant attack in the foreign press, over the foreign radio, and in such international bodies as the United Nations because of various practices of discrimination against minority groups in this country. As might be expected, Soviet spokesmen regularly exploit this situation in propaganda against the United States, both within the United Nations and through radio broadcasts and the press, which reaches all corners of the world. Some of these attacks against us are based on falsehood or distortion; but the undeniable existence of racial discrimination gives unfriendly governments the most effective kind of ammunition for their propaganda warfare. The hostile reaction among normally friendly peoples, many of whom are particularly sensitive in regard to the status of non-European races, is growing in alarming proportions. In such countries the view is expressed more and more vocally that the United States is hypocritical in claiming to be the champion of democracy while permitting practices of racial discrimination here in this country.

The segregation of school children on a racial basis is one of the practices in the United States that has been singled out for hostile foreign comment in the United Nations and elsewhere. Other peoples cannot understand how such a practice can exist in a country which professes to be a staunch supporter of freedom, justice, and democracy. The sincerity of the United States in this respect will be judged by its deeds as well as by its words.

Although progress is being made, the continuance of racial discrimination in the United States remains a source of constant embarrassment to this Government in the day-to-day conduct of its foreign relations ; and it jeopardizes the effective maintenance of our moral leadership of the free and democratic nations of the world.[6]...

## CONCLUSION

The subordinate position occupied by Negroes in this country as a result of governmental discriminations ("second-class citizenship," as it is sometimes called) presents an unsolved problem for American democracy, an inescapable challenge to the sincerity of our espousal of the democratic faith.

In these days, when the free world must conserve and fortify the moral as well as the material sources of its strength, it is especially important to affirm that the Constitution of the United States places no limitation, express or implied, on the principle of the equality of all men before the law. Mr. Justice Harlan said in his dissent in the *Plessy* case (163 U. S. at 562):

We boast of the freedom enjoyed by our people above all other peoples. But it is difficult to reconcile that boast with a state of the law which, practically, puts the brand of servitude and degradation upon a large class of our fellow-citizens, our equals before the law.

The Government and people of the United States must prove by their actions that the ideals expressed in the Bill of Bights are living realities, not literary abstractions. As the President has stated:

If we wish to inspire the people of the world whose freedom is in jeopardy, if we wish to restore hope to those who have already lost their civil liberties, if we wish to fulfill the promise that is ours, we must correct the remaining imperfections in our practice of democracy.

We know the way. We need only the will.[7]

Respectfully submitted.
JAMES P. McGRANERY, Attorney General.
PHILIP ELMAN, Special Assistant to the Attorney General.
DECEMBER 1952.

---

[1] Message to the Congress, February 2, 1948, H. Doc. No. 516, 80th Cong., 2d sess., p. 2.

[2] Mr. Justice Harlan in *Plessy v. Feguson,* 163 U.S. 537, 559. Regrettably, he was speaking only for himself, in dissent.

[3] Message to the Congress, note 1, *supra,* p. 5.

[4] *To Secure These Rights,* Report of the President's Committee on Civil Rights (1947), p. 89.

[5] *Ibid.,* pp. 89, 95.

[6] Letter to the Attorney General, dated December 2, 1952. The earlier letter of May 8, 1946, referred to by the Secretary, is quoted in *To Serve These Rights,* note 4, *supra,* pp. 146-147.

[7] Message to the Congress, note 1, *supra,* p. 7.

Source: United States Supreme Court Records and Briefs, *Brown v. Board of Education I,* 347 U.S. 483 (1954), http://curiae.law.yale.edu/pdf/347-483/022.pdf.

# The U.S. Supreme Court's Decision in *Brown v. Board of Education*

*After considering arguments from both sides in* Brown v. Board of Education, *the Supreme Court finally came to a decision: "We conclude that in the field of public education the doctrine of 'separate but equal' has no place." Drafting a simple, straightforward opinion that eschewed sentiment or blame, newly appointed Chief Justice Earl Warren was able to gain unanimous approval for the decision from his eight colleagues.*

347 U.S. 483

BROWN ET AL. v. BOARD OF EDUCATION OF TOPEKA ET AL.

Appeal from the United States District Court for the District of Kansas.

*No. 1. Argued December 9, 1952. Reargued December 8, 1953. Decided May 17, 1954.

Segregation of white and Negro children in the public schools of a State solely on the basis of race, pursuant to state laws permitting or requiring such segregation, denies to Negro children the equal protection of the laws guaranteed by the Fourteenth Amendment—even though the physical facilities and other "tangible" factors of white and Negro schools may be equal.

(a) The history of the Fourteenth Amendment is inconclusive as to its intended effect on public education.

(b) The question presented in these cases must be determined, not on the basis of conditions existing when the Fourteenth Amendment was adopted, but in the light of the full development of public education and its present place in American life throughout the Nation.

(c) Where a State has undertaken to provide an opportunity for an education in its public schools, such an opportunity is a right which must be made available to all on equal terms.

(d) Segregation of children in public schools solely on the basis of race deprives children of the minority group of equal educational opportunities, even though the physical facilities and other "tangible" factors may be equal.

(e) The "separate but equal" doctrine adopted in *Plessy v. Ferguson,* 163 U.S. 537, has no place in the field of public education.

(f) The cases are restored to the docket for further argument on specified questions relating to the forms of the decrees.

MR. CHIEF JUSTICE WARREN delivered the opinion of the Court.

These cases come to us from the States of Kansas, South Carolina, Virginia, and Delaware. They are premised on different facts and different local conditions, but a common legal question justifies their consideration together in this consolidated opinion.[1]

In each of the cases, minors of the Negro race, through their legal representatives, seek the aid of the courts in obtaining admission to the public schools of their community on a nonsegregated basis. In each instance, they had been denied admission to schools attended by white children under laws requiring or permitting segregation according to race. This segregation was alleged to deprive the plaintiffs of the equal protection of the laws under the Fourteenth Amendment. In each of the cases other than the Delaware case, a three-judge federal district court denied relief to the plaintiffs on the so-called "separate but equal" doctrine announced by this Court in *Plessy v. Ferguson,* 163 U.S. 537. Under that doctrine, equality of treatment is accorded when the races are provided substantially equal facilities, even though these facilities be separate. In the Delaware case, the Supreme Court of Delaware adhered to that doctrine, but ordered that the plaintiffs be admitted to the white schools because of their superiority to the Negro schools.

The plaintiffs contend that segregated public schools are not "equal" and cannot be made "equal," and that hence they are deprived of the equal protection of the laws. Because of the obvious importance of the question presented, the Court took jurisdiction.[2] Argument was heard in the 1952 Term, and reargument was heard this Term on certain questions propounded by the Court.[3]

Reargument was largely devoted to the circumstances surrounding the adoption of the Fourteenth Amendment in 1868. It covered exhaustively consideration of the Amendment in Congress, ratification by the states, then existing practices in racial segregation, and the views of proponents and opponents of the Amendment. This discussion and our own investigation convince us that, although these sources cast some light, it is not enough to resolve the problem with which we are faced. At best, they are inconclusive. The most avid proponents of the post-War Amendments undoubtedly intended them to remove all legal distinctions among "all persons born or naturalized in the United States." Their opponents, just as certainly, were antagonistic to both the letter and the spirit of the Amendments and wished them to have the most limited effect. What others in Congress and the state legislatures had in mind cannot be determined with any degree of certainty.

An additional reason for the inconclusive nature of the Amendment's history, with respect to segregated schools, is the status of public education at that time.[4] In the South, the movement toward free common schools, supported by general taxation, had not yet taken hold. Education of white children was largely in the hands of private groups. Education of Negroes was almost nonexistent, and practically all of the race were illiterate. In fact, any education of Negroes was forbidden by law in some states. Today, in contrast, many Negroes have achieved outstanding success in the arts and sciences as well as in the business and professional world. It is true that public school education at the time of the Amendment had advanced further in the North, but the effect of the Amendment on Northern States was generally ignored in the congressional debates. Even in the North, the conditions of public education did not approximate those existing today. The curriculum was usually rudimentary; ungraded schools were common in rural areas; the school term was but three months a year in many states; and compulsory school attendance was virtually unknown. As a consequence, it is not surprising that there should be so little in the history of the Fourteenth Amendment relating to its intended effect on public education.

In the first cases in this Court construing the Fourteenth Amendment, decided shortly after its adoption, the Court interpreted it as proscribing all state-imposed discriminations against the Negro race.[5] The doctrine of "separate but equal" did not make its appearance in this Court until 1896 in the case of *Plessy v. Ferguson,* supra, involving not education but transportation.[6] American courts have since labored with the doctrine for over half a century. In this Court, there have been six cases involving the "separate but equal" doctrine in the field of public education.[7] In *Cumming v. County Board of Education,* 175 U.S. 528, and *Gong Lum v. Rice,* 275 U.S. 78, the validity of the doctrine itself was not challenged.[8] In more recent cases, all on the graduate school level, inequality was found in that specific benefits enjoyed by white students were denied to Negro students of the same educational qualifications. *Missouri ex rel. Gaines v. Canada,* 305 U.S. 337 ; *Sipuel v. Oklahoma,* 332 U.S. 631 ; *Sweatt v. Painter,* 339 U.S. 629 ; *McLaurin v. Oklahoma State Regents,* 339 U.S. 637 . In none of these cases was it necessary to re-examine the doctrine to grant relief to the Negro plaintiff. And in *Sweatt v. Painter,* supra, the Court expressly reserved decision on the question whether *Plessy v. Ferguson* should be held inapplicable to public education.

In the instant cases, that question is directly presented. Here, unlike *Sweatt v. Painter,* there are findings below that the Negro and white schools involved have been equalized, or are being equalized, with respect to buildings, curricula, qualifications and salaries of teachers, and other "tangible" factors.[9] Our decision, therefore, cannot turn on merely a comparison of these tangible factors in the Negro and white schools involved in each of the cases. We must look instead to the effect of segregation itself on public education.

In approaching this problem, we cannot turn the clock back to 1868 when the Amendment was adopted, or even to 1896 when *Plessy v. Ferguson* was written. We must consider public education in the light of its full development and its present place in American life throughout the Nation. Only in this way can it be determined if segregation in public schools deprives these plaintiffs of the equal protection of the laws.

Today, education is perhaps the most important function of state and local governments. Compulsory school attendance laws and the great expenditures for education both demonstrate our recognition of the importance of education to our democratic society. It is required in the performance of our most basic public responsibilities, even service in the armed forces. It is the very foundation of good citizenship. Today it is a principal instrument in awakening the child to cultural values, in preparing him for later professional training, and in helping him to adjust normally to his environment. In these days, it is doubtful that any child may reasonably be expected to succeed in life if he is denied the opportunity of an education. Such an opportunity, where the state has undertaken to provide it, is a right which must be made available to all on equal terms.

We come then to the question presented: Does segregation of children in public schools solely on the basis of race, even though the physical facilities and other "tangible" factors may be equal, deprive the children of the minority group of equal educational opportunities? We believe that it does.

In *Sweatt v. Painter,* supra, in finding that a segregated law school for Negroes could not provide them equal educational opportunities, this Court relied in large part on "those qualities which are incapable of objective measurement but which make for greatness in a law school." In *McLaurin v. Oklahoma State Regents,* supra, the Court, in requiring that a Negro admitted to a white graduate school be treated like all other students, again resorted to intangible considerations: "...his ability to study, to engage in discussions and exchange views with other students, and, in general, to learn his profession." Such considerations apply with added force to children in grade and high schools. To separate them from others of similar age and qualifications solely because of their race generates a feeling of inferiority as to their status in the community that may affect their hearts and minds in a way unlikely ever to be undone. The effect of this separation on their educational opportunities was well stated by a finding in the Kansas case by a court which nevertheless felt compelled to rule against the Negro plaintiffs:

> "Segregation of white and colored children in public schools has a detrimental effect upon the colored children. The impact is greater when it has the sanction of the law; for the policy of separating the races is usually interpreted as denoting the inferiority of the negro group. A sense of inferiority affects the motivation of a child to learn. Segregation with the sanction of law, therefore, has a tendency to [retard] the educational and mental development of negro children and to deprive them of some of the benefits they would receive in a racial[ly] integrated school system."[10]

Whatever may have been the extent of psychological knowledge at the time of *Plessy v. Ferguson,* this finding is amply supported by modern authority.[11] Any language in *Plessy v. Ferguson* contrary to this finding is rejected.

We conclude that in the field of public education the doctrine of "separate but equal" has no place. Separate educational facilities are inherently unequal. Therefore, we hold that the plaintiffs and others similarly situated for whom the actions have been brought are, by reason of the segregation complained of, deprived of the equal protection of the laws guaranteed by the Fourteenth Amendment. This disposition makes unnecessary any discussion whether such segregation also violates the Due Process Clause of the Fourteenth Amendment.[12]

Because these are class actions, because of the wide applicability of this decision, and because of the great variety of local conditions, the formulation of decrees in these cases presents problems of considerable complexity. On reargument, the consideration of appropriate relief was necessarily subordinated to the primary question—the constitutionality of segregation in public education. We have now announced that such segregation is a denial of the equal protection of the laws. In order that we may have the full assistance of the parties in formulating decrees, the cases will be restored to the docket, and the parties are requested to present further argument on Questions 4 and 5 previously propounded by the Court for the reargument this Term.[13] The Attorney General of the United States is again invited to participate. The Attorneys General of the states requiring or permitting segregation in public education will also be permitted to appear as amici curiae upon request to do so by September 15, 1954, and submission of briefs by October 1, 1954.[14]

It is so ordered.

---

[*] Together with No. 2, *Briggs et al. v. Elliott et al.,* on appeal from the United States District Court for the Eastern District of South Carolina, argued December 9-10, 1952, reargued December 7-8, 1953; No. 4, *Davis et al. v. County School Board of Prince Edward County, Virginia, et al.,* on appeal from the United States District Court for the Eastern District of Virginia, argued December 10, 1952, reargued December 7-8, 1953; and No. 10, *Gebhart et al. v. Belton et al.,* on certiorari to the Supreme Court of Delaware, argued December 11, 1952, reargued December 9, 1953.

[1] In the Kansas case, *Brown v. Board of Education,* the plaintiffs are Negro children of elementary school age residing in Topeka. They brought this action in the United States District Court for the District of Kansas to enjoin enforcement of a Kansas statute which permits, but does not require, cities of more than 15,000 population to maintain separate school facilities for Negro and white students. Kan. Gen. Stat. 72-1724 (1949). Pursuant to that authority, the Topeka Board of Education elected to establish segregated elementary schools. Other public schools in the community, however, are operated on a nonsegregated basis. The three-judge District Court, convened under 28 U.S.C. 2281 and 2284, found that segregation in public education has a detrimental effect upon Negro children, but denied relief on the ground that the Negro and white schools were substantially equal with respect to buildings, transportation, curricula, and educational qualifications of teachers. 98 F. Supp. 797. The case is here on direct appeal under 28 U.S.C. 1253. In the South Carolina case, *Briggs v. Elliott,* the plaintiffs are Negro children of both elementary and high school age residing in Clarendon County. They brought this action in the United States District Court for the Eastern District of South Carolina to enjoin enforcement of provisions in the state constitution and statutory code which require the segregation of Negroes and whites in public schools. S. C. Const., Art. XI, 7; S. C. Code 5377 (1942). The three-judge District Court, convened under 28 U.S.C. 2281 and 2284, denied the requested relief. The court found that the Negro schools were inferior to the white schools and ordered the defendants to begin immediately to equalize the facilities. But the court sustained the validity of the contested provisions and denied the plaintiffs admission to the white

schools during the equalization program. 98 F. Supp. 529. This Court vacated the District Court's judgment and remanded the case for the purpose of obtaining the court's views on a report filed by the defendants concerning the progress made in the equalization program. 342 U.S. 350. On remand, the District Court found that substantial equality had been achieved except for buildings and that the defendants were proceeding to rectify this inequality as well. 103 F. Supp. 920. The case is again here on direct appeal under 28 U.S.C. 1253. In the Virginia case, *Davis v. County School Board,* the plaintiffs are Negro children of high school age residing in Prince Edward county. They brought this action in the United States District Court for the Eastern District of Virginia to enjoin enforcement of provisions in the state constitution and statutory code which require the segregation of Negroes and whites in public schools. Va. Const., 140; Va. Code 22-221 (1950). The three-judge District Court, convened under 28 U.S.C. 2281 and 2284, denied the requested relief. The court found the Negro school inferior in physical plant, curricula, and transportation, and ordered the defendants forthwith to provide substantially equal curricula and transportation and to "proceed with all reasonable diligence and dispatch to remove" the inequality in physical plant. But, as in the South Carolina case, the court sustained the validity of the contested provisions and denied the plaintiffs admission to the white schools during the equalization program. 103 F. Supp. 337. The case is here on direct appeal under 28 U.S.C. 1253. In the Delaware case, *Gebhart v. Belton,* the plaintiffs are Negro children of both elementary and high school age residing in New Castle County. They brought this action in the Delaware Court of Chancery to enjoin enforcement of provisions in the state constitution and statutory code which require the segregation of Negroes and whites in public schools. Del. Const., Art. X, 2; Del. Rev. Code 2631 (1935). The Chancellor gave judgment for the plaintiffs and ordered their immediate admission to schools previously attended only by white children, on the ground that the Negro schools were inferior with respect to teacher training, pupil-teacher ratio, extracurricular activities, physical plant, and time and distance involved in travel. 87 A. 2d 862. The Chancellor also found that segregation itself results in an inferior education for Negro children (see note 10, infra), but did not rest his decision on that ground. Id., at 865. The Chancellor's decree was affirmed by the Supreme Court of Delaware, which intimated, however, that the defendants might be able to obtain a modification of the decree after equalization of the Negro and white schools had been accomplished. 91 A. 2d 137, 152. The defendants, contending only that the Delaware courts had erred in ordering the immediate admission of the Negro plaintiffs to the white schools, applied to this Court for certiorari. The writ was granted, 344 U.S. 891. The plaintiffs, who were successful below, did not submit a cross-petition.

[2] 344 U.S. 1, 141, 891.

[3] 345 U.S. 972. The Attorney General of the United States participated both Terms as amicus curiae.

[4] For a general study of the development of public education prior to the Amendment, see Butts and Cremin, *A History of Education in American Culture* (1953), Pts. I, II; Cubberley, *Public Education in the United States* (1934 ed.), cc. II-XII. School practices current at the time of the adoption of the Fourteenth Amendment are described in Butts and Cremin, supra, at 269-275; Cubberley, supra, at 288-339, 408-431; Knight, *Public Education in the South* (1922), cc. VIII, IX. See also H. Ex. Doc. No. 315, 41st Cong., 2d Sess. (1871). Although the demand for free public schools followed substantially the same pattern in both the North and the South, the development in the South did not begin to gain momentum until about 1850, some twenty years after that in the North. The reasons for the somewhat slower development in the South (e. g., the rural character of the South and the different regional attitudes toward state assistance) are well explained in Cubberley, supra, at 408-423. In the country as a whole, but particularly in the South, the War virtually stopped all progress in public education. Id., at 427-428. The low status of Negro education in all sections of the country,

both before and immediately after the War, is described in Beale, *A History of Freedom of Teaching in American Schools* (1941), 112-132, 175-195. Compulsory school attendance laws were not generally adopted until after the ratification of the Fourteenth Amendment, and it was not until 1918 that such laws were in force in all the states. Cubberley, supra, at 563-565.

[5] *Slaughter-House Cases,* 16 Wall. 36, 67-72 (1873); *Strauder v. West Virginia,* 100 U.S. 303, 307-308 (1880): "It ordains that no State shall deprive any person of life, liberty, or property, without due process of law, or deny to any person within its jurisdiction the equal protection of the laws. What is this but declaring that the law in the States shall be the same for the black as for the white; that all persons, whether colored or white, shall stand equal before the laws of the States, and, in regard to the colored race, for whose protection the amendment was primarily designed, that no discrimination shall be made against them by law because of their color? The words of the amendment, it is true, are prohibitory, but they contain a necessary implication of a positive immunity, or right, most valuable to the colored race, - the right to exemption from unfriendly legislation against them distinctively as colored, - exemption from legal discriminations, implying inferiority in civil society, lessening the security of their enjoyment of the rights which others enjoy, and discriminations which are steps towards reducing them to the condition of a subject race." See also *Virginia v. Rives,* 100 U.S. 313, 318 (1880); *Ex parte Virginia,* 100 U.S. 339, 344-345 (1880).

[6] The doctrine apparently originated in *Roberts v. City of Boston,* 59 Mass. 198, 206 (1850), upholding school segregation against attack as being violative of a state constitutional guarantee of equality. Segregation in Boston public schools was eliminated in 1855. Mass. Acts 1855, c. 256. But elsewhere in the North segregation in public education has persisted in some communities until recent years. It is apparent that such segregation has long been a nationwide problem, not merely one of sectional concern.

[7] See also *Berea College v. Kentucky,* 211 U.S. 45 (1908).

[8] In the *Cumming* case, Negro taxpayers sought an injunction requiring the defendant school board to discontinue the operation of a high school for white children until the board resumed operation of a high school for Negro children. Similarly, in the *Gong Lum* case, the plaintiff, a child of Chinese descent, contended only that state authorities had misapplied the doctrine by classifying him with Negro children and requiring him to attend a Negro school.

[9] In the Kansas case, the court below found substantial equality as to all such factors. 98 F. Supp. 797, 798. In the South Carolina case, the court below found that the defendants were proceeding "promptly and in good faith to comply with the court's decree." 103 F. Supp. 920, 921. In the Virginia case, the court below noted that the equalization program was already "afoot and progressing" (103 F. Supp. 337, 341); since then, we have been advised, in the Virginia Attorney General's brief on reargument, that the program has now been completed. In the Delaware case, the court below similarly noted that the state's equalization program was well under way. 91 A. 2d 137, 149.

[10] A similar finding was made in the Delaware case: "I conclude from the testimony that in our Delaware society, State-imposed segregation in education itself results in the Negro children, as a class, receiving educational opportunities which are substantially inferior to those available to white children otherwise similarly situated." 87 A. 2d 862, 865.

[11] K. B. Clark, *Effect of Prejudice and Discrimination on Personality Development* (Midcentury White House Conference on Children and Youth, 1950); Witmer and Kotinsky, *Personality in the Making* (1952), c. VI; Deutscher and Chein, *The Psychological Effects of Enforced Segregation: A Survey of Social Science Opinion,* 26 J. Psychol. 259 (1948); Chein, *What are the Psychological Effects of Segre-*

*gation Under Conditions of Equal Facilities?*, 3 *Int. J. Opinion and Attitude Res.* 229 (1949); Brameld, *Educational Costs, in Discrimination and National Welfare* (MacIver, ed., (1949), 44-48; Frazier, *The Negro in the United States* (1949), 674-681. And see generally Myrdal, *An American Dilemma* (1944).

[12] See *Bolling v. Sharpe,* post, p. 497, concerning the Due Process Clause of the Fifth Amendment.

[13] "4. Assuming it is decided that segregation in public schools violates the Fourteenth Amendment "(a) would a decree necessarily follow providing that, within the limits set by normal geographic school districting, Negro children should forthwith be admitted to schools of their choice, or "(b) may this Court, in the exercise of its equity powers, permit an effective gradual adjustment to be brought about from existing segregated systems to a system not based on color distinctions? "5. On the assumption on which questions 4 (a) and (b) are based, and assuming further that this Court will exercise its equity powers to the end described in question 4 (b), "(a) should this Court formulate detailed decrees in these cases; "(b) if so, what specific issues should the decrees reach; "(c) should this Court appoint a special master to hear evidence with a view to recommending specific terms for such decrees; "(d) should this Court remand to the courts of first instance with directions to frame decrees in these cases, and if so what general directions should the decrees of this Court include and what procedures should the courts of first instance follow in arriving at the specific terms of more detailed decrees?"

[14] See Rule 42, Revised Rules of this Court (effective July 1, 1954).

Source: *Brown v. Board of Education of Topeka* 347 U.S. 483, FedWorld.gov, "Supreme Court Decisions," http://www.fedworld.gov/supcourt/.

## "All God's Chillun," a *New York Times* Editorial

*The ruling in the* Brown *case was the focus of considerable nationwide attention, as onlookers around the country anticipated the Supreme Court's decision. While many in the South decried the Court's order to end school segregation, other Americans hailed the ruling as fulfilling the Declaration of Independence's promise that "all men are created equal." In its editorial of May 18, 1954, the* New York Times *reflected what was becoming an increasingly mainstream view: that a modern country touting itself as a leader of the free world must end segregation in order to move toward "a more perfect democracy." The title of the editorial is taken from American playwright Eugene O'Neill's controversial 1924 drama about a tragic interracial romance,* All God's Chillun Got Wings.

The Supreme Court took a long and careful time to arrive at the unanimous decision read yesterday by Chief Justice Warren that "segregation of children in the public schools solely on the basis of race, even though the physical facilities and other 'tangible' factors may be equal, deprives the children of the minority group of equal educational opportunities." But the decision reached was inevitable in the year 1954 regardless of what may have been the case in 1868, when the Fourteenth Amendment was adopted, or in 1896, when the "separate but equal" doctrine was laid down in the case of *Plessy v. Ferguson.*

In the cases under consideration the facilities offered to Negro children appeared to be equal, or were to be made equal, "with respect to buildings, curricula, qualifications and salaries of teachers and other 'tangible' factors," to those available to white children. The question, therefore, was more fundamental than in any previous case. It was whether Negro children segregated solely on the basis of race, even though offered equal facilities, were thereby deprived of equal educational opportunities. The court holds that such segregation does have "a detrimental effect upon the colored children," that it had "a tendency to retard [their] educational and mental development …and to deprive them of some of the benefits they would receive in a racially integrated school system."

The court, speaking through Chief Justice Warren, therefore concludes that "separate educational facilities are inherently unequal," that the plaintiffs and others similarly situated "are by reason of the segregation complained of deprived of the equal protection of the laws guaranteed by the Fourteenth Amendment." The due process clause is not involved. It is not needed.

What the court is saying, in its formal but not complicated style, is a part of what Eugene O'Neill said in a play called *All God's Chillun Got Wings*. It is true, of course, that the court is not talking of that sort of "equality" which produces interracial marriages. It is not talking of a social system at all. It is talking of a system of human rights which is foreshadowed in the second paragraph of the Declaration of Independence, which stated "that all men are created equal." Mr. Jefferson and the others who were responsible for the Declaration did not intend to say that all men are equally intelligent, equally good or equal in height or weight. They meant to say that men were, and ought to be, equal before the law. If men are equal, children are equal, too. There is an even greater necessity in the case of children, whose opportunities to advance themselves and to be useful to the community may be lost if they do not have the right to be educated.

No one can deny that the mingling of the races in the schools of the seventeen states which have required segregation and the three states which have permitted it will create problems. The folkways in southern communities will have to be adapted to new conditions if white and Negro children, together with white and Negro teachers, are to enjoy not only equal facilities but the same facilities in the same schools. The Constitution and the Bill of Rights are at times hard masters. The court has recognized these difficulties by withholding a decree and by inviting "the full assistance of the parties in formulating decrees." The cases are therefore restored to the docket and the Attorney General of the United States and the Attorneys General of the states requiring or permitting segregation in public education will be permitted to appear before the court next fall. There will be some delay before orders issue, and it may be that petitions for rehearing and modification will take up a good deal of time. These matters cannot be hurried.

A constitutional principle inherent in the Declaration of Independence and never entirely forgotten, even in the days of human slavery, has, however, been restated. This nation is often criticized for its treatment of racial minorities, and particularly of the Negro. There have been grounds for this criticism. Little by little, however, in the folk customs and in such decisions as the one rendered yesterday, we move toward a more perfect democracy. When some hostile propagandist rises in Moscow or Peiping [Beijing] to accuse us of being a class society we can if we wish recite the courageous words of yesterday's opinion. The highest court in the land, the guardian of our national conscience, has reaffirmed its faith—and the undying American faith—in the equality of all men and all children before the law.

# The U.S. Supreme Court's Decision in *Brown II*

*Although the Court had decided in its 1954* Brown v. Board of Education *decision that school segregation was unconstitutional, it left the question of relief—what remedies should be ordered in the cases—for a new argument. On May 31, 1955, the court made a second ruling in the case, commonly known as* Brown II. *In an effort to stave off Southern protests, the Court allowed for gradual desegregation in ordering the school districts in question to admit African American students "with all deliberate speed." This ambiguous directive ultimately inspired more resistance than cooperation in the South.*

349 U.S. 294

BROWN ET AL. V. BOARD OF EDUCATION OF TOPEKA ET AL.

Appeal from the United States District Court for the District of Kansas.

*No. 1. Reargued on the question of relief April 11-14, 1955. Opinion and judgments announced May 31, 1955.

**1.** Racial discrimination in public education is unconstitutional, 347 U.S. 483, 497, and all provisions of federal, state or local law requiring or permitting such discrimination must yield to this principle.

**2.** The judgments below (except that in the Delaware case) are reversed and the cases are remanded to the District Courts to take such proceedings and enter such orders and decrees consistent with this opinion as are necessary and proper to admit the parties to these cases to public schools on a racially nondiscriminatory basis with all deliberate speed.

> (a) School authorities have the primary responsibility for elucidating, assessing and solving the varied local school problems which may require solution in fully implementing the governing constitutional principles.
>
> (b) Courts will have to consider whether the action of school authorities constitutes good faith implementation of the governing constitutional principles.
>
> (c) Because of their proximity to local conditions and the possible need for further hearings, the courts which originally heard these cases can best perform this judicial appraisal.
>
> (d) In fashioning and effectuating the decrees, the courts will be guided by equitable principles—characterized by a

practical flexibility in shaping remedies and a facility for adjusting and reconciling public and private needs.

(e) At stake is the personal interest of the plaintiffs in admission to public schools as soon as practicable on a nondiscriminatory basis.

(f) Courts of equity may properly take into account the public interest in the elimination in a systematic and effective manner of a variety of obstacles in making the transition to school systems operated in accordance with the constitutional principles enunciated in 347 U.S. 483, 497; but the vitality of these constitutional principles cannot be allowed to yield simply because of disagreement with them.

(g) While giving weight to these public and private considerations, the courts will require that the defendants make a prompt and reasonable start toward full compliance with the ruling of this Court.

(h) Once such a start has been made, the courts may find that additional time is necessary to carry out the ruling in an effective manner.

(i) The burden rests on the defendants to establish that additional time is necessary in the public interest and is consistent with good faith compliance at the earliest practicable date.

(j) The courts may consider problems related to administration, arising from the physical condition of the school plant, the school transportation system, personnel, revision of school districts and attendance areas into compact units to achieve a system of determining admission to the public schools on a nonracial basis, and revision of local laws and regulations which may be necessary in solving the foregoing problems.

(k) The courts will also consider the adequacy of any plans the defendants may propose to meet these problems and to effectuate a transition to a racially nondiscriminatory school system.

(l) During the period of transition, the courts will retain jurisdiction of these cases.

3. The judgment in the Delaware case, ordering the immediate admission of
the plaintiffs to schools previously attended only by white children, is affirmed on
the basis of the principles stated by this Court in its opinion, 347 U.S. 483; but
the case is remanded to the Supreme Court of Delaware for such further proceedings as that Court may deem necessary in the light of this opinion.

MR. CHIEF JUSTICE WARREN delivered the opinion of the Court.

These cases were decided on May 17, 1954. The opinions of that date[1],
declaring the fundamental principle that racial discrimination in public education is unconstitutional, are incorporated herein by reference. All provisions of federal, state, or local law requiring or permitting such discrimination must yield to this principle. There remains for consideration the manner
in which relief is to be accorded.

Because these cases arose under different local conditions and their disposition will involve a variety of local problems, we requested further argument on the question of relief.[2] In view of the nationwide importance of the
decision, we invited the Attorney General of the United States and the Attorneys General of all states requiring or permitting racial discrimination in public education to present their views on that question. The parties, the United
States, and the States of Florida, North Carolina, Arkansas, Oklahoma, Maryland, and Texas filed briefs and participated in the oral argument.

These presentations were informative and helpful to the Court in its
consideration of the complexities arising from the transition to a system of
public education freed of racial discrimination. The presentations also
demonstrated that substantial steps to eliminate racial discrimination in public schools have already been taken, not only in some of the communities in
which these cases arose, but in some of the states appearing as amici curiae,
and in other states as well. Substantial progress has been made in the District
of Columbia and in the communities in Kansas and Delaware involved in this
litigation. The defendants in the cases coming to us from South Carolina and
Virginia are awaiting the decision of this Court concerning relief.

Full implementation of these constitutional principles may require solution
of varied local school problems. School authorities have the primary responsibility for elucidating, assessing, and solving these problems; courts will have to

consider whether the action of school authorities constitutes good faith implementation of the governing constitutional principles. Because of their proximity to local conditions and the possible need for further hearings, the courts which originally heard these cases can best perform this judicial appraisal. Accordingly, we believe it appropriate to remand the cases to those courts.[3]

In fashioning and effectuating the decrees, the courts will be guided by equitable principles. Traditionally, equity has been characterized by a practical flexibility in shaping its remedies[4] and by a facility for adjusting and reconciling public and private needs.[5] These cases call for the exercise of these traditional attributes of equity power. At stake is the personal interest of the plaintiffs in admission to public schools as soon as practicable on a nondiscriminatory basis. To effectuate this interest may call for elimination of a variety of obstacles in making the transition to school systems operated in accordance with the constitutional principles set forth in our May 17, 1954, decision. Courts of equity may properly take into account the public interest in the elimination of such obstacles in a systematic and effective manner. But it should go without saying that the vitality of these constitutional principles cannot be allowed to yield simply because of disagreement with them.

While giving weight to these public and private considerations, the courts will require that the defendants make a prompt and reasonable start toward full compliance with our May 17, 1954, ruling. Once such a start has been made, the courts may find that additional time is necessary to carry out the ruling in an effective manner. The burden rests upon the defendants to establish that such time is necessary in the public interest and is consistent with good faith compliance at the earliest practicable date. To that end, the courts may consider problems related to administration, arising from the physical condition of the school plant, the school transportation system, personnel, revision of school districts and attendance areas into compact units to achieve a system of determining admission to the public schools on a nonracial basis, and revision of local laws and regulations which may be necessary in solving the foregoing problems. They will also consider the adequacy of any plans the defendants may propose to meet these problems and to effectuate a transition to a racially nondiscriminatory school system. During this period of transition, the courts will retain jurisdiction of these cases.

The judgments below, except that in the Delaware case, are accordingly reversed and the cases are remanded to the District Courts to take such proceedings and enter such orders and decrees consistent with this opinion as are necessary and proper to admit to public schools on a racially nondiscriminatory basis with all deliberate speed the parties to these cases. The judgment in the Delaware case—ordering the immediate admission of the plaintiffs to schools previously attended only by white children—is affirmed on the basis of the principles stated in our May 17, 1954, opinion, but the case is remanded to the Supreme Court of Delaware for such further proceedings as that Court may deem necessary in light of this opinion.

It is so ordered.

---

* Together with No. 2, *Briggs et al. v. Elliott et al.,* on appeal from the United States District Court for the Eastern District of South Carolina; No. 3, *Davis et al. v. County School Board of Prince Edward County, Virginia, et al.,* on appeal from the United States District Court for the Eastern District of Virginia; No. 4, *Bolling et al. v. Sharpe et al.,* on certiorari to the United States Court of Appeals for the District of Columbia Circuit; and No. 5, *Gebhart et al. v. Belton et al.,* on certiorari to the Supreme Court of Delaware.

1 347 U.S. 483; 347 U.S. 497.

2 Further argument was requested on the following questions, 347 U.S. 483, 495-496, n. 13, previously propounded by the Court: "4. Assuming it is decided that segregation in public schools violates the Fourteenth Amendment "(a) would a decree necessarily follow providing that, within the limits set by normal geographic school districting, Negro children should forthwith be admitted to schools of their choice, or "(b) may this Court, in the exercise of its equity powers, permit an effective gradual adjustment to be brought about from existing segregated systems to a system not based on color distinctions? "5. On the assumption on which questions 4 (a) and (b) are based, and assuming further that this Court will exercise its equity powers to the end described in question 4 (b), "(a) should this Court formulate detailed decrees in these cases; "(b) if so, what specific issues should the decrees reach; "(c) should this Court appoint a special master to hear evidence with a view to recommending specific terms for such decrees; "(d) should this Court remand to the courts of first instance with directions to frame decrees in these cases, and if so what general directions should the decrees of this Court include and what procedures should the courts of first instance follow in arriving at the specific terms of more detailed decrees?"

3 The cases coming to us from Kansas, South Carolina, and Virginia were originally heard by three-judge District Courts convened under 28 U.S.C. 2281 and 2284. These cases will accordingly be remanded to those three-judge courts. See *Briggs v. Elliott,* 342 U.S. 350.

4 See *Alexander v. Hillman,* 296 U.S. 222, 239.

5 See *Hecht Co. v. Bowles,* 321 U.S. 321, 329-330.

---

Source: *Brown v. Board of Education of Topeka* 349 U.S. 294, FedWorld.gov, "Supreme Court Decisions," http://www.fedworld.gov/supcourt/.

# The Southern Manifesto

*The 1955* Brown II *decision mandated desegregation to be implemented with "all deliberate speed," a deliberately ambiguous phrase designed to appease the South by permitting a gradual transition to desegregated schools. Nevertheless, many politicians in the South refused to accept the validity of the Supreme Court's decision. They challenged the reasoning of the decision, as well as the Court's authority to "legislate" a change in accepted state practices. This defiance crystallized with the so-called "Southern Manifesto." Drafted by South Carolina Senator Strom Thurmond, who ran for president in 1948 on the segregationist "Dixiecrat" ticket, the Southern Manifesto was read into the Congressional Record and was signed by 96 senators and congressmen, almost every member from the South. It articulated the determination of Southern politicians to resist desegregation "by any lawful means." Although the Manifesto appealed to Southerners "to scrupulously refrain from disorder and lawless acts," its effect was to strengthen resistance to desegregation by all means, including violence.*

## DECLARATION OF CONSTITUTIONAL PRINCIPLES

The unwarranted decision of the Supreme Court in the public school cases is now bearing the fruit always produced when men substitute naked power for established law.

The Founding Fathers gave us a Constitution of checks and balances because they realized the inescapable lesson of history that no man or group of men can be safely entrusted with unlimited power. They framed this Constitution with its provisions for change by amendment in order to secure the fundamentals of government against the dangers of temporary popular passion or the personal predilections of public officeholders.

We regard the decisions of the Supreme Court in the school cases as a clear abuse of judicial power. It climaxes a trend in the Federal Judiciary undertaking to legislate, in derogation of the authority of Congress, and to encroach upon the reserved rights of the States and the people.

The original Constitution does not mention education. Neither does the 14th Amendment nor any other amendment. The debates preceding the submission of the 14th Amendment clearly show that there was no intent that it should affect the system of education maintained by the States.

The very Congress which proposed the amendment subsequently provided for segregated schools in the District of Columbia.

When the amendment was adopted in 1868, there were 37 States of the Union....

Every one of the 26 States that had any substantial racial differences among its people, either approved the operation of segregated schools already in existence or subsequently established such schools by action of the same law-making body which considered the 14th Amendment.

As admitted by the Supreme Court in the public school case (*Brown v. Board of Education*), the doctrine of separate but equal schools "apparently originated in *Roberts v. City of Boston* (1849), upholding school segregation against attack as being violative of a State constitutional guarantee of equality." This constitutional doctrine began in the North, not in the South, and it was followed not only in Massachusetts, but in Connecticut, New York, Illinois, Indiana, Michigan, Minnesota, New Jersey, Ohio, Pennsylvania and other northern states until they, exercising their rights as states through the constitutional processes of local self-government, changed their school systems.

In the case of *Plessy v. Ferguson* in 1896 the Supreme Court expressly declared that under the 14th Amendment no person was denied any of his rights if the States provided separate but equal facilities. This decision has been followed in many other cases. It is notable that the Supreme Court, speaking through Chief Justice Taft, a former President of the United States, unanimously declared in 1927 in *Lum v. Rice* that the "separate but equal" principle is "within the discretion of the State in regulating its public schools and does not conflict with the 14th Amendment."

This interpretation, restated time and again, became a part of the life of the people of many of the States and confirmed their habits, traditions, and way of life. It is founded on elemental humanity and commonsense, for parents should not be deprived by Government of the right to direct the lives and education of their own children.

Though there has been no constitutional amendment or act of Congress changing this established legal principle almost a century old, the Supreme Court of the United States, with no legal basis for such action, undertook to exercise their naked judicial power and substituted their personal political and social ideas for the established law of the land.

This unwarranted exercise of power by the Court, contrary to the Constitution, is creating chaos and confusion in the States principally affected. It is destroying the amicable relations between the white and Negro races that have been created through 90 years of patient effort by the good people of both races. It has planted hatred and suspicion where there has been heretofore friendship and understanding.

Without regard to the consent of the governed, outside mediators are threatening immediate and revolutionary changes in our public schools systems. If done, this is certain to destroy the system of public education in some of the States.

With the gravest concern for the explosive and dangerous condition created by this decision and inflamed by outside meddlers:

We reaffirm our reliance on the Constitution as the fundamental law of the land.

We decry the Supreme Court's encroachment on the rights reserved to the States and to the people, contrary to established law, and to the Constitution.

We commend the motives of those States which have declared the intention to resist forced integration by any lawful means.

We appeal to the States and people who are not directly affected by these decisions to consider the constitutional principles involved against the time when they too, on issues vital to them, may be the victims of judicial encroachment.

Even though we constitute a minority in the present Congress, we have full faith that a majority of the American people believe in the dual system of government which has enabled us to achieve our greatness and will in time demand that the reserved rights of the States and of the people be made secure against judicial usurpation.

We pledge ourselves to use all lawful means to bring about a reversal of this decision which is contrary to the Constitution and to prevent the use of force in its implementation.

In this trying period, as we all seek to right this wrong, we appeal to our people not to be provoked by the agitators and troublemakers invading our States and to scrupulously refrain from disorder and lawless acts.

**Signed by:**

**MEMBERS OF THE UNITED STATES SENATE**

Walter F. George, Richard B. Russell, John Stennis, Sam J. Ervin, Jr., Strom Thurmond, Harry F. Byrd, A. Willis Robertson, John L. McClellan, Allen J. Ellender, Russell B. Long, Lister Hill, James O. Eastland, W. Kerr Scott, John Sparkman, Olin D. Johnston, Price Daniel, J.W. Fulbright, George A. Smathers, Spessard L. Holland.

## MEMBERS OF THE UNITED STATES HOUSE OF REPRESENTATIVES

**Alabama:** Frank W. Boykin, George M. Grant, George W. Andrews, Kenneth A. Roberts, Albert Rains, Armistead I. Selden, Jr., Carl Elliott, Robert E. Jones, George Huddleston, Jr.

**Arkansas:** E.C. Gathings, Wilbur D. Mills, James W. Trimble, Oren Harris, Brooks Hays, W.F. Norrell.

**Florida:** Charles E. Bennett, Robert L.F. Sikes, A.S. Herlong, Jr., Paul G. Rogers, James A. Haley, D.R. Matthews.

**Georgia:** Prince H. Preston, John L. Pilcher, E.L. Forrester, John James Flynt, Jr., James C. Davis, Carl Vinson, Henderson Lanham, Iris F. Blitch, Phil M. Landrum, Paul Brown.

**Louisiana:** F. Edward Hebert, Hale Boggs, Edwin E. Willis, Overton Brooks, Otto E. Passman, James H. Morrison, T. Ashton Thompson, George S. Long.

**Mississippi:** Thomas G. Abernathy, Jamie L. Whitten, Frank E. Smith, John Bell Williams, Arthur Winstead, William M. Colmer.

**North Carolina:** Herbert C. Bonner, L.H. Fountain, Graham A. Barden, Carl T. Durham, F. Ertel Carlyle, Hugh Q. Alexander, Woodrow W. Jones, George A. Shuford.

**South Carolina:** L. Mendel Rivers, John J. Riley, W.J. Bryan Dorn, Robert T. Ashmore, James P. Richards, John L. McMillan.

**Tennessee:** James B. Frazier, Jr., Tom Murray, Jere Cooper, Clifford Davis.

Source: *Congressional Record,* 84th Congress Second Session. March 12, 1956. Washington, D.C.: Governmental Printing Office, 1956. Online at Strom Thurmond Institute, Clemson University, http://www.strom.clemson.edu/strom/manifesto.html.

# A Member of the Little Rock Nine Recalls the Effort to Integrate Central High School

*After the* Brown *decision, the school board of Little Rock, Arkansas, made plans to begin desegregating their school system over the course of three years, starting with the high schools. The local NAACP, led by Daisy Bates and J. C. Crenshaw, sued to accelerate the pace of desegregation; a court order approved the school board's plan and instructed them to begin in the fall of 1957. Of the seventeen African American students approved to transfer into Central High School, nine chose to begin classes. On the first day of school, a crowd of segregationists formed around the school. Governor Orval Faubus called up the Arkansas National Guard to "keep order"—but their instructions were to keep the Nine from entering. Nevertheless, on September 4 the Nine attempted to enter Central High for the first time. In this excerpt from her memoir* Warriors Don't Cry, *Melba Patillo Beals, one of the Nine, recounts her experiences on that morning.*

The [radio] announcer said it was 7:55 as Mama squeezed into a parking space, and we settled ourselves quietly for a moment, trying to identify the buzzing noise that seemed as if it were all around us. It resembled the sound of crowds at my high school football games. But how could that be? The announcer said there was a crowd, but surely it couldn't be that big.

Anxious to see the familiar faces of our friends or some of our own people, we hurried up the block lined with wood-frame houses and screened-in porches. I strained to see what lay ahead of us. In the distance, large crowds of white people were lining the curb directly across from the front of Central High. As we approached behind them, we could see only the clusters of white people that stretched for a distance of two blocks along the entire span of the school building. My mind could take in the sights and sounds only one by one: flashing cameras, voices shouting in my ears, men and women jostling each other, old people, young people, people running, uniformed police officers walking, men standing still, men and women waving their fists, and then the long line of uniformed soldiers carrying weapons just like in the war movies I had seen.

Everyone's attention seemed riveted on the center of the line of soldiers where a big commotion was taking place. At first we couldn't see what they were looking at. People were shouting and pointing, and the noise hurt my ears and muffled the words. We couldn't understand what they were saying. As we drew near, the angry outbursts became even more intense, and we began to hear their words more clearly. "Niggers, go home! Niggers, go back where you belong!"

I stood motionless, stunned by the hurtful words. I searched for something to hang on to, something familiar that would comfort me or make sense, but there was nothing.

"Two, four, six, eight, we ain't gonna integrate!" Over and over, the words rang out. The terrifying frenzy of the crowd was building like steam in an erupting volcano.

"We have to find the others," Mama yelled in my ear. "We'll be safer with the group." She grabbed my arm to pull me forward, out of my trance. The look on her face mirrored the terror I felt. Some of the white men and women standing around us seemed to be observing anxiously. Others with angry faces and wide-open mouths were screaming their rage. Their words were becoming increasingly vile, fueled by whatever was happening directly in front of the school.

The sun beat down on our heads as we made our way through the crowd, searching for our friends. Most people ignored us, jostling each other and craning their necks to see whatever was at the center of the furor. Finally, we got closer to the hub of activity. Standing on our toes, we stretched as tall as we could to see what everyone was watching.

"Oh, my Lord," Mother said.

It was my friend Elizabeth they were watching. The anger of that huge crowd was directed toward Elizabeth Eckford as she stood alone, in front of Central High, facing the long line of soldiers, with a huge crowd of white people screeching at her back. Barely five feet tall, Elizabeth cradled her books in her arms as she desperately searched for the right place to enter. Soldiers in uniforms and helmets, cradling their rifles, towered over her. Slowly she walked first to one and then another opening in their line. Each time she approached, the soldiers closed ranks, shutting her out. As she turned toward us, her eyes hidden by dark glasses, we could see how erect and proud she stood despite the fear she must have been feeling.

As Elizabeth walked along the line of guardsmen, they did nothing to protect her from her stalkers. When a crowd of fifty or more closed in like

214

diving vultures, the soldiers stared straight ahead, as if posing for a photograph. Once more Elizabeth stood still, stunned, not knowing what to do. The people surrounding us shouted, stomped, and whistled as though her awful predicament were a triumph for them.

I wanted to help her, but the human wall in front of us would not be moved. We could only wedge through partway. Finally, we realized our efforts were futile; we could only pray as we watched her struggle to survive. People began to applaud and shout, "Get her, get the nigger out of there. Hang her black ass!" Not one of those white adults attempted to rescue Elizabeth. The hulking soldiers continued to observe her peril like spectators enjoying a sport.

Under siege, Elizabeth slowly made her way toward the bench at the bus stop. Looking straight ahead as she walked, she did not acknowledge the people yelping at her heels, like mad dogs. Mother and I looked at each other, suddenly conscious that we, too, were trapped by a violent mob.

Ever so slowly, we eased our way backward through the crowd, being careful not to attract attention. But a white man clawed at me, grabbing my sleeve and yelling, "We got us a nigger right here!" Just then another man tugged at his arm distracting him. Somehow I managed to scramble away. As a commotion began building around us, Mother took my arm, and we moved fast, sometimes crouching to avoid attracting more attention.

We gained some distance from the center of the crowd and made our way down the block. But when I looked back, I saw a man following us, yelling, "They're getting away! Those niggers are getting away!" Pointing to us, he enlisted others to join him. Now we were being chased by four men, and their number was growing.

We scurried down the sidewalk, bumping into people. Most of the crowd was still preoccupied watching Elizabeth. Panic-stricken, I wanted to shout for help. But I knew it would do no good. Policemen stood by watching Elizabeth being accosted. Why would they help us?

"Melba, take these keys," Mother commanded as she tossed them at me. "Get to the car. Leave without me if you have to."

I plucked the car keys from the air. "No, Mama, I won't go without you." Suddenly I felt the sting of her hand as it struck the side of my face. She had never slapped me before. "Do what I say!" she shouted. Still, I knew I couldn't leave her there. I reached back to take her arm. Her pace was slowing, and I tried to pull her forward. The men were gaining on us. If we yelled for help or made any fuss, others might join our attackers. Running faster, I felt myself begin to wear out. I didn't have enough breath to keep moving so fast. My knees hurt, my calves were aching, but the car was just around the next corner.

The men chasing us were joined by another carrying a rope. At times, our pursuers were so close I could look back and see the anger in their eyes. Mama's pace slowed, and one man came close enough to touch her. He grabbed for her arm but instead tugged at her blouse. The fabric ripped, and he fell backward. Mama stepped out of her high-heeled shoes, leaving them behind, her pace quickening in stocking feet.

One of the men closest to me swung at me with a large tree branch but missed. I felt even more panic rise up in my throat. If he hit me hard enough to knock me over, I would be at his mercy. I could hear Grandma India's voice saying, God is always with you, even when things seem awful. I felt a surge of strength and a new wind. As I turned the corner, our car came into sight. I ran hard—faster than ever before—unlocked the door, and jumped in.

Mother was struggling, barely able to keep ahead of her attackers. I could see them turning the corner close on her heels, moving fast toward us. I swung open the passenger door for Mother and revved the engine. Barely waiting for her to shut the door, I shoved the gearshift into reverse and backed down the street with more speed than I'd ever driven forward. I slowed to back around the corner. One of the men caught up and pounded his fists on the hood of our car, while another threw a brick at the windshield.

Turning left, we gained speed as we drove through a hail of shouts and stones and glaring faces. But I knew I would make it because the car was moving fast and Mama was with me.

We sped away from Central High School's neighborhood and into more familiar streets where we should have felt safe. Mother directed me not to drive straight home but to circle around until we knew for certain that the men from the mob weren't chasing us. Even though I didn't have a license and had only practiced driving in the parking lot, she wouldn't allow me to stop so we could switch places. Her face was drained and her eyes haunted by a kind of fear I had not seen in her before.

As I drove, I couldn't help noticing that the streets were clogged with cars and people that did not belong in our neighborhood. There were dust-covered trucks full of tobacco-chewing white men, their naked arms and shoulders sporting tattoos. When we pulled into our backyard, Grandmother India was waiting for us with an anxious expression. "Thank God, you made it home," she gasped.

Source: Melba Patillo Beals. *Warriors Don't Cry: A Searing Memoir of the Battle to Integrate Little Rock's Central High,* abridged edition. New York: Archway Books, 1995.

## President Eisenhower Explains His Decision to Send Federal Troops to Little Rock

*Eisenhower had hoped to stay out of the growing desegregation crisis in Little Rock, Arkansas, where Governor Orval Faubus had called out the Arkansas National Guard on September 2, 1957. Eisenhower met with Faubus on September 14 in hopes of resolving the situation. Although Faubus withdrew the National Guard, he did nothing to prevent mobs from interfering with the desegregation of Central High. Disappointed and angered, Eisenhower accepted that it was his responsibility to ensure compliance with federal orders in the face of state and public opposition. On September 24, he addressed the nation to explain his decision to use federal troops to put an end to the crisis.*

M y Fellow Citizens:

For a few minutes I want to speak to you about the serious situation that has arisen in Little Rock. For this talk I have come to the President's office in the White House. I could have spoken from Rhode Island, but I felt that, in speaking from the house of Lincoln, of Jackson and of Wilson, my words would more clearly convey both the sadness I feel in the action I was compelled today to take and the firmness with which I intend to pursue this course until the orders of the Federal Court at Little Rock can be executed without unlawful interference.

In that city, under the leadership of demagogic extremists, disorderly mobs have deliberately prevented the carrying out of proper orders from a Federal Court. Local authorities have not eliminated that violent opposition and, under the law, I yesterday issued a Proclamation calling upon the mob to disperse.

This morning the mob again gathered in front of the Central High School of Little Rock, obviously for the purpose of again preventing the carrying out of the Court's order relating to the admission of Negro children to the school.

Whenever normal agencies prove inadequate to the task and it becomes necessary for the Executive Branch of the Federal Government to use its powers and authority to uphold Federal Courts, the President's responsibility is inescapable.

In accordance with that responsibility, I have today issued an Executive Order directing the use of troops under Federal authority to aid in the execution of Federal law at Little Rock, Arkansas. This became necessary when my Proclamation of yesterday was not observed, and the obstruction of justice still continues.

It is important that the reasons for my action be understood by all citizens.

As you know, the Supreme Court of the United States has decided that separate public educational facilities for the races are inherently unequal and therefore compulsory school segregation laws are unconstitutional.

Our personal opinions about the decision have no bearing on the matter of enforcement; the responsibility and authority of the Supreme Court to interpret the Constitution are clear. Local Federal Courts were instructed by the Supreme Court to issue such orders and decrees as might be necessary to achieve admission to public schools without regard to race—and with all deliberate speed.

During the past several years, many communities in our Southern States have instituted public school plans for gradual progress in the enrollment and attendance of school children of all races in order to bring themselves into compliance with the law of the land.

They thus demonstrated to the world that we are a nation in which laws, not men, are supreme.

I regret to say that this truth—this cornerstone of our liberties—was not observed in this instance.

It was my hope that this localized situation would be brought under control by city and State authorities. If the use of local police powers had been sufficient, our traditional method of leaving the problem in these hands would have been pursued. But when large gatherings of obstructionists made it impossible for the decrees of the Court to be carried out, both the law and the national interest demanded that the President take action.

Here is the sequence of events in the development of the Little Rock school case.

In May of 1955, the Little Rock School Board approved a moderate plan for the gradual desegregation of the public schools in that city. It provided that a start toward integration would be made at the present term in the high school, and that the plan would be in full operation by 1963. This plan was challenged in the courts by some who believed that the period of time as proposed was too long.

The United States Court at Little Rock, which has supervisory responsibility under the law for the plan of desegregation in the public schools, dismissed the challenge, thus approving a gradual rather than an abrupt change from the existing system. It found that the school board had acted in good faith in planning for a public school system free from racial discrimination.

Since that time, the court has on three separate occasions issued orders directing that the plan be carried out. All persons were instructed to refrain from interfering with the efforts of the school board to comply with the law.

Proper and sensible observance of the law then demanded the respectful obedience which the nation has a right to expect from all the people. This, unfortunately, has not been the case at Little Rock. Certain misguided persons, many of them imported into Little Rock by agitators, have insisted upon defying the law and have sought to bring it into disrepute. The orders of the court have thus been frustrated.

The very basis of our individual rights and freedoms is the certainty that the President and the Executive Branch of Government will support and insure the carrying out of the decisions of the Federal Courts, even, when necessary with all the means at the President's command.

Unless the President did so, anarchy would result.

There would be no security for any except that which each one of us could provide for himself.

The interest of the nation in the proper fulfillment of the law's requirements cannot yield to opposition and demonstrations by some few persons.

Mob rule cannot be allowed to override the decisions of the courts.

Let me make it very clear that Federal troops are not being used to relieve local and state authorities of their primary duty to preserve the peace and order of the community. Nor are the troops there for the purpose of taking over the responsibility of the School Board and the other responsible local officials in running Central High School. In the present case the troops are there, pursuant to law, solely for the purpose of preventing interference with the orders of the Court.

The proper use of the powers of the Executive Branch to enforce the orders of a Federal Court is limited to extraordinary and compelling circumstances. Manifestly, such an extreme situation has been created in Little Rock. This challenge must be met with such measures as will preserve to the people as a whole their lawfully-protected rights in a climate permitting their free and fair exercise.

The overwhelming majority of our people in every section of the country are united in their respect for observance of the law—even in those cases where they may disagree with that law.

They deplore the call of extremists to violence.

The decision of the Supreme Court concerning school integration affects the South more seriously than it does other sections of the country. In that region I have many warm friends, some of them in the city of Little Rock. I have deemed it a great personal privilege to spend in our Southland tours of duty while in the military service and enjoyable recreational periods since that time.

So from intimate personal knowledge, I know that the overwhelming majority of the people in the South—including those of Arkansas and of Little Rock—are of good will, united in their efforts to preserve and respect the law even when they disagree with it.

They do not sympathize with mob rule. They, like the rest of the nation, have proved in two great wars their readiness to sacrifice for America.

A foundation of our American way of life is our national respect for law.

In the South, as elsewhere, citizens are keenly aware of the tremendous disservice that has been done to the people of Arkansas in the eyes of the nation, and that has been done to the nation in the eyes of the world.

At a time when we face a grave situation abroad because of the hatred that Communism bears toward a system of government based on human rights, it would be difficult to exaggerate the harm that is being done to the prestige and influence, and indeed to the safety, of our nation and the world.

Our enemies are gloating over this incident and using it everywhere to misrepresent our nation. We are portrayed as a violator of those standards of conduct which the peoples of the world united to proclaim in the Charter of the United Nations. There they affirmed "faith in fundamental human rights and in the dignity of the human person" and did so "without distinction as to race, sex, language or religion."

And so, with confidence, I call upon citizens of the State of Arkansas to assist in bringing to an immediate end all interference with the law and its processes. If resistance to the Federal Court orders ceases at once, the further presence of Federal troops will be unnecessary and the City of Little Rock will return to its normal habits of peace and order and a blot upon the fair name and high honor of our nation in the world will be removed.

Thus will be restored the image of America and of all its parts as one nation, indivisible, with liberty and justice for all.

Source: The Dwight D. Eisenhower Library and Museum, http://www.eisenhower.archives. gov/dl/LittleRock/littlerockdocuments.html

# Reflecting on *Brown v. Board of Education,* Fifty Years Later

*The Supreme Court's 1954* Brown v. Board of Education *ruling is universally recognized as a landmark in American history. But the United States still falls short of its stated goal of providing equal social and educational opportunities for people of all races. In 2004 historian Ellis Cose offered his perspective on the* Brown *decision and its impact on American education and society in the fifty years since it became law.*

Sometimes history serves as a magnifying mirror—making momentous what actually was not. But *Brown v. Board of Topeka, Kansas,* is the real thing: a Supreme Court decision that fundamentally and forever changed America. It jump-started the modern civil rights movement and excised a cancer eating a hole in the heart of the U.S. Constitution. It forced America to accept the idea—totally foreign to its experience—that all God's children are fully human. The story of *Brown* is one with full-blown, self-sacrificing heroes who wrestled American apartheid to the mat.

So why is the celebration of its 50th anniversary so bittersweet? Why are we not all joyfully dancing, celebrating our collective release from the bondage of prejudice and inequality? Why as we raise our glasses are there tears in our eyes? The answer is simple: *Brown,* for all its glory, is something of a bust. Yes, it was a judicial coup and a textbook illustration of how to build a case. It was a shining triumph of idealism over tradition, of sense over Southern sanctimony, of good over bad. It was a moral and legal victory that resonated around the world and made its valiant and brilliant architects, quite deservedly, into giants....

Clearly *Brown* altered forever, and for the better, the political and social landscape of an insufficiently conscience-stricken nation. It succeeded ...in dramatically shaking things up and, in the process, of transforming a reluctant America. Yet, measured by its effects on the poor schoolchildren of color at its center, *Brown* is a disappointment—in many respects, a failure. Between past hopes and current results lies an abyss filled with forsaken dreams. So, this commemoration, this toasting of the heroes who slew Jim Crow, is muted by the realization that *Brown* was not nearly enough....

---

Source: Excerpted from *Beyond* Brown v. Board: *The Final Battle for Excellence in American Education: A Report by Ellis Cose to the Rockefeller Foundation.* Reprinted by permission of Don Congdon Associates Inc., on behalf of the author. © 2004 Ellis Cose.

Now, 50 years after the Supreme Court case that changed America, another battle is upon us—one whose scale and scope are only at this moment becoming clear. Like the barely discernible clouds of an approaching storm, this battle began quietly, somewhere along the margins of public awareness—and now threatens to become something unexpectedly grand, with the future of America's educationally disadvantaged dangling in the balance.

It began at the intersection of conflicting good intentions, where the demands of politicians and policymakers for high educational standards collided with the demands of educators and children's advocates for resources. Throw in a host of initiatives spawned, at least in part, by frustration at low student achievement—vouchers, charter schools, privatization, high-stakes testing—and you have the making of an educational upheaval that may rival *Brown* in its ramifications, that may in some ways be the second phase of *Brown:* a continuation, by other means, of the battle for access to a decent education by those whom fortune left behind.

But why is a second battle necessary? Why didn't *Brown* solve, for once and for all, the problem of race-based educational failure? To ask the question is to invite a lesson on why stirring pronouncements don't necessarily yield correspondingly grand outcomes, and of why simple answers to complex problems are almost always incomplete....

Something—actually a lot of somethings—went wrong. What seemed such a glorious victory back then appears, in retrospect, to have been merely a stage (albeit a momentous one) in a campaign much longer and more convoluted than any of the combatants conceivably could have imagined.

On that day in May when the walls of segregation fell there were actually two decisions, involving five separate cases—in South Carolina, Virginia, Delaware, Kansas, and Washington, D.C.—all of which came collectively to be known as "*Brown.*" Instead of abolishing segregation straight away, the justices sought advice on how—and when—desegregation was to come about. So *Brown* spawned what came to be known as *Brown II*—a decision in May 1955 that provided neither a timetable nor a plan. Instead, it ordered the South—a region filled with the most obstructionist politicians imaginable—to proceed with "all deliberate speed." And it advised the lower courts, which would oversee compliance, to show "a practical flexibility in shaping remedies and a facility for adjusting and reconciling public and private needs." All deliberate speed, as we now know, was seen by the South as an invitation to stall and gave opportunistic politicians a chance to mobilize against the very notion of integration. That mobilization, in some places, left black students worse off, at least initially, then they [had] been in the bad old days. But something more was wrong.

The decision rested on an assumption that simply wasn't true. That assumption, buried in the core of the decision, was that formal, state-mandated segregation was the root of all evil, or at least the root of all that ailed poor black schoolchildren (including their feelings of inferiority)—and that once it was ended "equal education opportunities" would be the result. Time, of course, has proven how elusive such opportunities can be—just as it has proven how difficult meaningful integration can be to achieve.

This is not to say things have gotten no better since 1954. For black school children, particularly in the South, there is no comparison between now and then. Still, Thurgood Marshall's hope—the hope of one America, the hope of educational parity, the hope, as Justice [Earl] Warren put it, that the opportunity for an education would be "made available to all on equal terms"—still awaits realization. And there is little possibility that realization will come soon.

A half century after Marshall made his bold prediction, school segregation is far from dead. Instead, according to political scientist Gary Orfield and his colleagues at Harvard University, it has experienced a resurgence. After the initial and lengthy period of determined and violent resistance, the country slowly, if grudgingly, accepted the ruling of the Supreme Court. Substantial progress was made in ending the state of racial apartheid in America's schools. But since the early 1990s, despite the continued growth of integration in other sectors of society, black and Latino children are increasingly likely to find themselves in classes with few, if any nonminority faces.[i]

The shift is due, at least in part, to Supreme Court decisions that essentially undermined *Brown*. In 1974 (*Milliken v. Bradley*), the Court ruled that white suburbs were not obliged to admit black kids from the inner city. And in 1992 (*Freeman v. Pitts*), the Court decided that local school boards should be released from court supervision as quickly as possible. Even if they were not in full compliance with desegregation orders, local authorities could begin to reassert control…. Desegregation efforts, inevitably, lost much of their steam….

For most black parents, of course, *Brown* was never just about integration for "its own sake"—though blacks strongly support integration.... Instead, it was about recognition of the fact that unless their children went to school with the children of the whites who controlled the purse strings, everything the school provided for their children would be lacking—including the education their children would receive....

Behind *Brown* was the hope that when the dust finally cleared, black students—and not just the occasional exception—would finally leave education's ghetto behind. "Most of us believed, or pretended to believe, that if children of all races and classes sat in the same classrooms or if schools in different communities and neighborhoods received equal financing ...the gaps in educational outcomes among children of different races, classes and cultures could be closed," observed Peter Schrag in *Final Test.*[ii]

Today, it's harder to believe any of that. Harder to believe that school integration will succeed. Harder to believe that the so-called achievement gap will close anytime soon. Indeed, when asked what will happen to the achievement gap between blacks and whites and between Hispanics and whites over the next 10 years, roughly half of respondents of all races told *Newsweek*'s pollsters [in a 2004 poll] that it will be about the same as it is now. If that prediction turns out to be accurate, it will be to America's eternal shame. But there is little hard evidence with which to argue against it....

Editors of a Brookings Institution publication entitled *Bridging the Achievement Gap* were blunter in their assessment. "The difference in educational achievement between white students, on the one hand, and African-American and Hispanic students, on the other, is large and persistent. In the last decade it has gotten worse. The average black or Hispanic student, in elementary, middle or high school currently achieves at about the same level as the average white student in the lower quartile of white achievement."[iii]

No one fully understands why that pattern persists. Clearly no single factor explains it. A range of things, from bad prenatal care to intellectually destructive neighborhood or home environments, have been implicated. But certainly one reason for the difference in achievement is that blacks (and Puerto Ricans and Mexican-Americans) do not, for the most part, go to the same schools, or even the same types of schools, as do the majority of non-Hispanic whites. They are more likely to go to schools such as those found in parts of rural South Carolina; schools that, were it not for the American flags proudly flying over the roofs, might have been plucked out of some impoverished country that sees education as a luxury it can barely afford....

How can we, as a society, give a child a decent education, even if he or she is born into the most indecent of circumstances? Ultimately, we must seriously face that question—if only because the fate of our great country will rest increasingly on the shoulders of its growing black and Latino populations. It is a question, in some sense, much bigger than *Brown*. But it really is what *Brown* was all about: equality of opportunity for those children of the children cursed by the country of their birth.

"Between me and the other world there is ever an unasked question: unasked by some through feelings of delicacy; by others through the difficulty of rightly framing it. All, nevertheless, flutter round it. They approach me in a half-hesitant sort of way, eye me curiously or compassionately, and then, instead of saying directly, How does it feel to be a problem? They say, I know an excellent colored man in my town; or I fought at Mechanicsville; or, Do not these Southern outrages make your blood boil? At these I smile, or am interested, or reduce the boiling to a simmer, as the occasion may require. To the real question, How does it feel to be a problem? I answer seldom a word."[iv]

W.E.B. Dubois wrote those words over a century ago. Yet, in too many ways, when it comes to children of color, we continue to ask the wrong question. We poke and probe and test those kids as we wrinkle our brow and ask, with requisite concern, "How does it feel to be a problem?" when we should be asking: "What can we do to allow you to thrive? What have we not given to you that we routinely give to upper middle-class white kids? What do they have that you don't?"

Part of the answer, of course, is money and the intellectually stimulating playthings money can buy; but it is really much more than that. They have a society that grants them the presumption of competence and the expectation of success; they have an environment that nurtures aspiration, peers who provide support, and guardians who provide direction. If we are serious about closing the achievement gap, about realizing the promise of *Brown*, about decently educating those who begin with the least, we will have to ponder deeply how to deliver those things where they are desperately needed. And we will not rest until we find the answers.

I suspect the answers will not be found in such things as rigid testing regimes, so-called choice programs, or in new and fashionable pedagogic techniques—useful as some of those things might be. They will be found, most likely, by a society collectively opening its heart to possibilities not normally seen in places and people perennially written off.

"I, too, sing America," wrote Langston Hughes, in a 1921 poem that voiced the yearning felt by America's "darker brother" to enjoy the bounty of America's main table—to be no longer shooed away into the kitchen to sit, undernourished, underdeveloped, unseen for what he was or could be. "I, too, am America," Hughes insisted.[v]

In the end, it may be that the true and lasting legacy of *Brown* has little to do with desegregation, as such. It may, instead, be that *Brown* put us on a path that will, ideally, let us see children of color—and therefore our entire country—in a wholly new and beautiful light.

---

[i] Gary Orfield and Chungmei Lee, *Brown at 50: King's Dream or Plessy's Nightmare?* Cambridge: The Civil Rights Project, Harvard University, January 2004, 4.

[ii] Peter Schrag, *Final Test.* New York: The New Press, 2003, 1

[iii] John L. Cubb and Tom Loveless, "Bridging the Achievement Gap," in *Bridging the Achievement Gap,* edited by John L. Cubb and Tom Loveless. Washington, DC: Brookings Institution Press, 2002, 1.

[iv] W.E.Burghardt Du Bois, "Strivings of the Negro People," *The Atlantic Monthly,* August 1897.

[v] Langston Hughes, "I, Too," in *Selected Poems.* New York: Vintage, 1990, 275.

Source: Cose, Ellis. *Beyond* Brown v. Board: *The Final Battle for Excellence in American Education.* New York: Rockefeller Foundation, 2004.

# SOURCES FOR FURTHER STUDY

*Argument: The Oral Argument before the Supreme Court in* Brown v. Board of Education, Topeka, *1952-55*. Edited by Leon Friedman. New York: Chelsea House, 1969. This volume reproduces all Brown oral arguments as heard before the Supreme Court in 1952, 1953, and 1954, and also reproduces the text of all five lower court decisions that made up the *Brown* case. A good source with helpful introductions for those interested in learning how argument before the Supreme Court actually works.

Bell, Derrick. *Silent Covenants:* Brown v. Board of Education *and the Unfulfilled Hopes for Racial Reform*. New York, Oxford University Press, 2004. This survey of school desegregation before and after *Brown* includes a provocative discussion of whether the decision was best for African Americans.

Cose, Ellis. *Beyond* Brown v. Board: *The Final Battle for Excellence in American Education*. New York: Rockefeller Foundation, 2004. An incisive analysis of the *Brown* decision and its impact on American education over the ensuing half-century. Includes fascinating updates on some of the school systems involved in the *Brown* case, as well as examinations of vouchers, testing, and other education initiatives being utilized today to improve struggling schools.

Greenberg, Jack. *Crusaders in the Courts: How a Dedicated Band of Lawyers Fought for the Civil Rights Revolution*. New York: Basic Books, 1994. In this first-person account, former NAACP Legal Defense and Education Fund Associate Counsel (and later Director-Counsel) Greenberg recounts what it was like to fight for civil rights from the front lines.

Kluger, Richard. *Simple Justice: The History of* Brown v. Board of Education *and Black America's Struggle for Equality*. New York, Knopf, 1975. The definitive history of the events leading up to the *Brown* decision, Kluger's history is a thorough, informative, and entertaining volume. An updated edition with a new chapter on *Brown's* legacy was published in 2004.

National Museum of American History, Smithsonian Institute. "Separate Is Not Equal: *Brown v. Board of Education.*" http://www.americanhistory.si.edu/brown/index.html. One of the best websites covering the history of school desegregation and the *Brown* decision. Includes a teacher's guide.

Tushnet, Mark. *Making Civil Rights Law: Thurgood Marshall and the Supreme Court, 1936-1961*. New York: Oxford University Press, 1994. This book recounts Marshall's career with the NAACP Legal Defense and Education Fund, focusing on the school desegregation cases but also exploring the immediate ramifications of *Brown.*

*The Unfinished Agenda of* Brown v. Board of Education. Editors of *Black Issues in Education.* Hoboken, NJ: John Wiley & Sons, 2004. A diverse collection of essays and oral histories focusing on school desegregation after *Brown.*

# BIBLIOGRAPHY

## Books and Periodicals

Alvarez, Robert R. Jr. "The Lemon Grove Incident: The Nation's First Successful Desegregation Court Case." *Journal of San Diego History,* Spring 1986.

*Argument: The Oral Argument before the Supreme Court in* Brown v. Board of Education, Topeka, *1952-55.* Edited by Leon Friedman. Introduction by Yale Kamisar. New York: Chelsea House, 1969.

Arriola, Christopher J. "A Landmark Little Noted—Until Today; Children of Mexican Heritage Were Segregated until a Federal Court Order Was Won against Orange County Schools." *Los Angeles Times,* April 14, 1997.

Austin, Regina. "Back to Basics: Returning to the Matter of Black Inferiority and White Supremacy in the Post-*Brown* Era." *Journal of Appellate Practice and Process,* Spring 2004.

Bates, Daisy. *The Long Shadow of Little Rock.* New York: David McKay, 1962.

Bell, Derrick. *Silent Covenants:* Brown v. Board of Education *and the Unfulfilled Hopes for Racial Reform.* New York: Oxford University Press, 2004.

Brown v. Board of Education: *A Brief History of Documents.* Edited with introduction by Waldo E. Martin, Jr. Boston: Bedford/St. Martin's, 1998.

Carter, Robert L. "The Long Road to Equality: The Product of Black Legal Skill and Strategy, *Brown* Has a Black Copyright." *Nation,* May 3, 2004.

Clark, Kenneth B. *Toward Humanity and Justice: The Writings of Kenneth B. Clark, Scholar of the* Brown v. Board of Education *Decision.* Edited by Woody Klein. Westport, CT: Praeger, 2004.

Clotfelter, Charles T. *After* Brown: *The Rise and Retreat of School Desegregation.* Princeton, NJ: Princeton University Press, 2004.

Cose, Ellis. *Beyond* Brown v. Board: *The Final Battle for Excellence in American Education.* New York: Rockefeller Foundation, 2004.

Cottrol, Robert J., Raymond T. Diamond, and Leland B. Ware. Brown v. Board of Education: *Caste, Culture, and the Constitution.* Lawrence, KS: University of Kansas Press, 2003.

Du Bois, W. E. B. "The Talented Tenth." In *The Negro Problem.* New York: James Pott and Co., 1903.

Du Bois, W. E. B. "Does the Negro Need Separate Schools?" *Journal of Negro Education,* July 1935.

Greenberg, Jack. *Crusaders in the Courts: How a Dedicated Band of Lawyers Fought for the Civil Rights Revolution.* New York: Basic Books, 1994.

Halberstam, David. *The Fifties.* New York: Villard, 1993.

Henderson, Cheryl Brown. "Reaffirming the Legacy," in *The Unfinished Agenda of* Brown v. Board of Education. Editors of *Black Issues in Education.* Hoboken, NJ: John Wiley & Sons, 2004.

Holst, Brad. "Resegregation's Aftermath." *Atlantic Monthly,* July-August 2004.

Huckaby, Elizabeth. *Crisis at Central High: Little Rock, 1957-58.* Baton Rouge: Louisiana State University Press, 1980.

Hughes, Langston. *Fight for Freedom: The Story of the NAACP.* New York: W.W. Norton, 1962.

Irons, Peter. *Jim Crow's Children: The Broken Promise of the* Brown *Decision.* New York: Viking, 2002.

Jacobway, Elizabeth, and C. Fred Williams, editors. *Understanding the Little Rock Crisis: An Exercise in Remembrance and Reconciliation.* Fayetteville, AR: The University of Arkansas Press, 1999.

Kee, Ed. "The *Brown* Decision and Milford, Delaware, 1954-1965." *Delaware History,* no. 27, 1997-98.

Klarman, Michael J. "It Could Have Gone the Other Way: At the Time, the Justices Had Doubts That *Brown* Was Rightly Decided." *Nation,* May 3, 2004.

Kluger, Richard. *Simple Justice: The History of* Brown v. Board of Education *and Black America's Struggle for Equality.* New York: Knopf, 1975.

McCord, John H., ed. *With All Deliberate Speed: Civil Rights Theory and Reality.* Urbana, IL: University of Illinois Press, 1969.

Mead, Andy. "Taking a Stand in Sturgis, Kentucky." *Lexington Herald-Leader,* May 17, 2004.

Orfield, Gary. "*Brown* Misunderstood," in *The Unfinished Agenda of* Brown v. Board of Education. Editors of *Black Issues in Education.* Hoboken, NJ: John Wiley & Sons, 2004.

Orfield, Gary, Susan E. Eaton, and the Harvard Project on School Desegregation. *Dismantling Desegregation: The Quiet Reversal of* Brown v. Board of Education. New York: The New Press, 2002.

Patterson, James T. Brown v. Board of Education: *A Civil Rights Milestone and Its Troubled Legacy.* New York: Oxford University Press, 2001.

Peltason, J. W. *Fifty-Eight Lonely Men: Southern Federal Judges and School Desegregation.* Urbana, IL: University of Illinois Press, 1971.

Portales, Marco. "A History of Latino Segregation Lawsuits," in *The Unfinished Agenda of* Brown v. Board of Education. Editors of *Black Issues in Education.* Hoboken, NJ: John Wiley & Sons, 2004.

"Reflections on the *Brown* Decision after Fifty Years." *Journal of Southern History,* May 2004.

*Remembering Jim Crow: African Americans Tell about Life in the Segregated South.* William H. Chafe, Raymond Gavins, and Robert Korstad, eds. New York: The New Press, 2001.

Roach, Ronald. "The Scholar-activist of *Brown.*" *Black Issues in Higher Education,* May 20, 2004.

Roy, Beth. *Bitters in the Honey: Tales of Hope and Disappointment across Divides of Race and Time.* Fayetteville, AR: University of Arkansas Press, 1999.

Shoemaker, Don, ed. *With All Deliberate Speed: Segregation-Desegregation in Southern Schools.* New York: Harper & Bros., 1957.

Tatum, Beverly Daniel. "The Road to Racial Equality." *Black Issues in Higher Education,* July 1, 2004.

Tushnet, Mark V. *Making Civil Rights Law: Thurgood Marshall and the Supreme Court, 1936-1961.* New York: Oxford University Press, 1994.

Tushnet, Mark V. *The NAACP's Legal Strategy against Segregation, 1925-1950.* Chapel Hill, NC: The University of North Carolina Press, 1987.

*The Unfinished Agenda of* Brown v. Board of Education. Editors of *Black Issues in Education.* Hoboken, NJ: John Wiley & Sons, 2004.

Wilson, Paul E. *A Time to Lose: Representing Kansas in* Brown v. Board of Education. Lawrence, KS: University of Kansas Press, 1995.

Winters, Rebecca. "No Longer Separate, but Not Yet Equal." *Time,* May 10, 2004.

Wolters, Raymond. "From *Brown* to *Green* and Back: The Changing Meaning of Desegregation." *Journal of Southern History,* May 2004.

## Online

Africana Online. "Civil Rights—Black American History." http://www.africanaonline.com/civil_rights.htm.

The American Experience. "The Presidents." http://www.pbs.org/wgbh/amex/presidents/index.html.

Brown Foundation. "In Pursuit of Freedom and Equality: *Brown v. Board of Education of Topeka.*" http://www.brownvboard.org.

Delaney, Bill. "On Boston, Busing, and Walking to School." CNN Interactive. http://www.cnn.com/SPECIALS/views/y/1999/03/delaney.busing.mar18.

Du Bois, W. E. B. "The Talented Tenth." Douglass Archives of American Public Address. http://www.douglassarchives.org/dubo_b05.htm

Dwight D. Eisenhower Presidential Library. "Little Rock School Integration Crisis." http://www.eisenhower.utexas.edu/Dl/LittleRock/littlerockdocuments.html.

FindLaw. "Supreme Court Opinions." http://www.findlaw.com/casecode/supreme.html.

"The History of Jim Crow." http://www.jimcrowhistory.org/home.htm.

Howard University School of Law. "Brown @ 50: Fulfilling the Promise." http://www.brownat50.org.

Linder, Douglas O. "Before *Brown:* Charles H. Houston and the *Gaines* Case." http://www.law.umkc.edu/faculty/projects/ftrials/trialheroes/charleshoustonessayF.html.

Little Rock Central High Fortieth Anniversary. "The Little Rock Nine." http://www.centralhigh57.org/The_Little_Rock_Nine.html#LR9

NAACP Legal Defense and Education Fund. "*Brown v. Board of Education:* Fifty Years." http://www.brownmatters.org.

National Museum of American History, Smithsonian Institute. "Separate Is Not Equal: *Brown v. Board of Education.*" http://www.americanhistory.si.edu/brown/index.html.

National Park Service. "*Brown v. Board of Education* National Historic Site, Kansas." http://www.nps.gov/brvb/home.htm.

Oyez, Supreme Court History Multimedia Site. http://www.oyez.org/oyez/frontpage.

PBS. "Beyond *Brown:* Pursuing the Promise." http://www.pbs.org/beyondbrown.

PBS. "The Rise and Fall of Jim Crow." http://www.pbs.org/wnet/jimcrow/index.html.

Truman Presidential Library and Museum. "Oral History Interview with Tom Clark." http://www.trumanlibrary.org/oralhist/clarktc.htm.

United States Courts. "Understanding the Federal Courts." http://www.uscourts.gov/understand02/index.html.

## DVD and VHS

*Beyond* Brown: *Pursuing the Promise.* DVD. PBS and Firelight Media, 2004.

# PHOTO CREDITS

# INDEX